A Look at My Life

Eileen Agar

A LOOK AT MY LIFE

in collaboration with Andrew Lambirth

Methuen · London

First published in Great Britain 1988
by Methuen London
Michelin House, 81 Fulham Road, London SW3 6RB

Photoset by Rowland Phototypesetting Ltd
Bury St Edmunds, Suffolk
Printed and bound in Great Britain
by
Butler and Tanner Ltd
Frome, Somerset

British Library Cataloguing in Publication Data

Agar, Eileen
A look at my life.
1. English paintings. Agar, Eileen
I. Title II. Lambirth, Andrew
759.2

ISBN 0-413-18180-4

For Joseph Bard

Contents

List of illustrations	*page*	ix
Acknowledgements		xi
Prologue		1
1 The Beginning		3
2 Stepping Forwards and Sideways		27
3 The Sewing Machine and the Umbrella		54
4 Through the Broken Glass		95
5 Am I a Surrealist?		114
6 'All the Gods are Dead except the God of War'		150
7 Colour Comes Back into My World		165
8 The New Studio		187
9 Looking Back		203
10 Looking Forward		218
Index		236

Illustrations

Black and White

between pages 52 and 53

1a My father
b Family group at Quinta la Lila
2a Joe Drysdale's boathouse, Argentina
b Three Red Devils, Argentina
3 Self with Mama and my sisters
4 Self by Cecil Beaton
5a Sinclair Lewis and Dorothy Thompson
b Joseph, self and Mita Sewell, France
6 With Evelyn Waugh and others in Kent
7a The seashore monster
b Solarized self in Swanage
8a Sheila Legge, the Surrealist phantom
b Exhibition at the International Surrealist Exhibition, 1936

between pages 116 and 117

9 Rocks at Ploumanach, Brittany
10a Self in Bramham Gardens studio
b Rodney Thomas's clock,
11a 'Angel of Anarchy', 1937
b Paul Nash
12a Dancing on a roof outside Mougins
b Joseph on Picasso's balcony
13a Man Ray
b Paul Eluard and Picasso
14a 'Eileen pregnant with a camera'
b Roland Penrose and Lee Miller
15a Picasso leaving Mougins
b Hotel Vaste Horizon
16a Hugh Mackintosh
b Surrealist party-piece

between pages 212 and 213

17 Just Married!
18a 'Ceremonial Hat for Eating Bouillabaisse'
b Another Ceremonial Hat
19a Joseph at Sitio Litre, Tenerife
b Sitio Litre
20a In the studio at West House, 1975
b Modelling Issey Miyake clothes, by Snowdon
21a 'Family Trio', 1931
b 'Movement in Space', 1931
22a 'The Modern Muse', 1931
b 'Quadriga', 1935
23a 'The Battle Cry' ('Bullet-proof painting'), 1938
b 'Fish Circus', *c.*1938
24a 'Marine Object', 1939
b 'David and Jonathan', 1939

Colour

between pages 180 and 181

1a 'Head of Dylan Thomas', 1960
b 'Self-portrait', 1927
c 'The Sleepwalkers', 1979–81
2 'Wandering Minstrel', 1932
3 'Marine Collage', 1939
4a 'Angel of Anarchy' (second version), 1940–3
b 'Egyptian Family', 1932

Acknowledgements and thanks for permission to reproduce photographs are due to the following for the black and white photographs: Cecil Beaton, courtesy Sothebys for plate 4; Veronica Keeling for plate 6; Helen Muspratt for plates 7b and 11b; the Lee Miller Archive for plate 14a; Ferdinando Carpanini for plate 20a; and Lord Snowdon and Issey Miyake for plate 20b. Colour: the Tate Gallery for plates 1a and 4a; the National Portrait Gallery for plate 1b; Orde Eliason for plate 1c; and Espresso Productions/ Cinewomen Productions for plates 2, 3 and 4b.

Plate 12a was taken by Joseph Bard. Plates 7a, 9, 11a, 12b, 13a, 13b, 14b, 15a, 15b, 19a and 19b were taken by Eileen Agar.

Acknowledgements

Thanks are due to the following for giving their permission to reproduce quoted material: the Trustees of the Ezra Pound Literary Property Trust, courtesy of Faber and Faber Limited, London, and New Directions Publishing Corporation Agents, New York; the Paul Nash Trust.

I wish to make special mention of the following for their generous help and advice in the early stages of this book: John Press, who first convinced me to continue the work my husband Joseph Bàrd had begun, Annette Armstrong, who would not allow me to give up, and particularly Barry Carman, a very dear friend who helped so much to shape the book but who sadly did not live to see the final version. My heartfelt thanks to them all.

I would also like to thank Andrew Lambirth, without whom this book might not have been published, who helped to consolidate and edit my original manuscript, and who has assisted me in every way with its preparation and completion. However, the story of my life, and the other lives which have touched me, ultimately springs from my memories and recollections. Any unintended error of fact is thus a result of the shifting, collaging processes of the mind; the narrative of this book is the reality I perceived at the time.

Prologue

Today I have started on a new series of paintings, based on photographs I took fifty years ago in Brittany. They are of massive convoluted rocks of immense age, images so strong that they printed themselves on my unconscious, to surface decades later as urgent themes for painting. On canvas I now try to interpret their ambivalent message.

Around me in this studio, I see interacting the different facets of my artistic personality. I see intellectual and emotional passions fusing with memories and hopes and technical strivings. Subjects become objects and vice versa. Dominating all is a large female figure with androgynous double-visage. Elsewhere birds swallow a landscape, magicians burst out of their frames and a plaster head, crested with feathers, blindfolded by Chinese cloths and hanging bead-curtains of hair, becomes an angel of anarchy.

I lay down my brushes and catch sight of myself in the mirror. What else do I see besides this small slightly lop-sided figure in her eighties? Perhaps a sort of metaphysical serpent who regularly sloughs her painter's skin to reveal a new one. I look and try to find what others saw in me many years ago and, seen through the eyes of my friends, I immediately become younger. 'As a young woman you had a beautiful face in which humour and a sharp eye overlay the sensuous,' said Meredith Luyten, an American friend. 'A face like a Babylonian whore,' said Boris Anrep, thinking of models for his National Gallery mosaics. 'Among other things, you are endless,' said Paul Nash. 'Ma brillante amie quie donne la couleur du rêve a tout ce qu'elle regarde par delà les murs maudits' ('My sparkling friend who brings the colour of dreams to all she sees beyond the cursed walls'), wrote the French poet Paul Eluard. And from that most perceptive of critics, my husband Joseph Bard: 'Eileen's special trend is trying to do something in a way that cannot be done, such as making love standing up in a hammock.'

Why do I now write my life story? Perhaps I do it for myself. Joseph used to warn me against living too single-mindedly in the present. I still live in the present, but I have come to believe with Proust that people who have no memories of the past, or do not reflect upon it, are like undeveloped negatives.

2 January 1985

CHAPTER ONE

The Beginning

Head first I tumbled out of my mother in December 1899, born not in the purple but (playing the game of hide-and-seek with words) in the soft web of lilac, flowers and good air, in the land of silver. To be more prosaic, this is the tale of a painter who was born and brought up between two sisters in a fashionable suburb called Flores, in Buenos Aires, Argentina.

My life is a collage, with time cutting and arranging the materials and laying them down, overlapping and contrasting, sometimes with the fresh shock of a surrealist painting. I wonder if traditional perspective is a necessary discipline for the art student, for over the years my life has taken on its own pattern and formed its own rules, adapting events and chronology in the sifting process of memory. As a mature artist, I can take liberties with perspective. We are not made of straight lines. As Picabia said: 'Our heads are round so that thoughts can change direction.'

And so I was born again, as the newly-converted often claim, into the world of art, when I drew a ship for a sea-captain and began my career in the magic of appearances. If painting has been one aspect of my reality, the other has been Joseph Bard. I was born for the third time when he came into my life in 1926. My physical birth in 1899, my artistic one five or six years later, and my emotional nativity at the age of twenty-seven: a painter's trinity. These things have made me and continue to re-make me, alongside or between the straight lines of accepted history, in an artistic transformation which is daily repeated. The mystery can be approached but not explained, we must keep our wits as well as our distance. Perhaps it is wiser to turn to the relative safety of remembered facts, even if truth is at the mercy of interpretation. For I was born in December, yet it was the beginning of summer: the Argentine has differed with England over more than the Falkland Islands . . .

My family was part of the large British community in Buenos Aires, at that time famous for its affluence and its elegance. BA is a handsome chequer-board tree-planted city with fine French Renaissance architecture, a cosmopolitan city, sited at the bottom of the world, singing its way to fame with a distinguished Opera House in which sophisticated ladies in Paris gowns had been known to boo Caruso. For men, the race-course with polo and golf was a must for everyone of British nationality, whilst gauchos on the pampas ranged over miles of flat land, tending their herds of cattle and their horses in a sea of space.

Enormous estancias, wealthy Argentines, huge meals of outsized beefsteaks, dusty roads, mosquitoes, vast blue skies and a sizzling sun; from the Andes to the pampas it was a country of extremes and juxtapositions, with a mixed population of Spanish, Italians and Germans. Not surprisingly, as an artist, contrasts have been important to me.

My father James Agar was an agate – that is, one who is small in stature (the word is derived from the figures cut in seals). He was a cautious saint with a large head and the sea in his eyes, a direct look and a sunny nature, but rather silent. His most emphatic expressions of surprise or dismay were 'Holy Smokes!' or 'I'll be jiggered!' He was also a very successful businessman. As a youth he sailed from Scotland to the Argentine to join an uncle and three brothers in an exporting business established in 1884, connected with agricultural machinery. Initially the firm dealt mostly in ploughs and windmills, which I find attractive symbols. Particularly windmills – they move physically as well as emotionally, besides being well-implanted in the life of literature. Memory and the relish of today give me my own wings: I am more than happy to be a kind of metaphysical hang-glider.

It was the windmills which made Agar Cross, the family firm, so successful. The country needed water, and my father saw to it that spare parts for the windmills were available in all the small shops. His plan worked and the windmills are still to be seen here and there. This means that the whirling blades, with the name of the firm emblazoned on them, have been a landmark for up to a hundred years in that flat windy country.

I know little about my father's parents, except that he was one of a family of fourteen children. Some died, but I knew four brothers and four sisters as uncles and aunts, of whom two were twins, all being married and producing children in their turn, one of the twins again producing twins. My father was not given to revealing much, and what happened to the others remains a mystery, for we never enquired, perhaps thinking that with my mother's relations also married and being fertile, we had been endowed with enough relatives to keep us happy. And for myself, well, I have never been a tribal person.

My mother's father was born at Bagley in Maine, New England. He later came to Devon, married, produced five children – four girls and a boy – and then also went out to the Argentine, the promised land in those days, where my future mother Mamie later met and married James Agar. The American grandfather owned a biscuit factory in Buenos Aires which did well, and when my mother produced three girls, the name of a noted brand of their biscuits Tres Cosas Buenas (Three Good Things) became the delighted cry of the parents. Although I suppose we lived like the idle rich, my father worked very hard at the business of making money and, with the help of his brothers, expanded Agar Cross from a small exporting London-based firm of agricultural machinery to a seven-acre factory in Buenos Aires selling everything from loos to pianos. Entire trains were taken over to deliver the goods. A sort of Harrods for the country. All the Agars would have been millionaries if it had not been for a villain of a Scot, who was a trustee and member of the board of Agar Cross. He embezzled an enormous sum and then shot himself in 1919 when he was found out.

The British presence in the Argentine at that time was one of the more bizarre manifestations of the national energy.

Britons placed more long-term investment in South America during the nineteenth century than in any other geographic region. Although many British in the Argentine kept to themselves, it was their energy which opened up the country and helped to build the railways and tram network. Soon families with names like MacDonald or MacIver could speak less English than Spanish, as it was their grandparents who had first arrived in the country and learnt to adapt. But on the other hand, if a verbal promise was made, the native to seal the contract simply said 'palabra de ingles' ('the word of an Englishman') and that was enough.

I have a touching letter from my father dated 1896 proposing marriage to Mamie Bagley. In some ways it sounds impulsive, and although impetuosity was characteristic of my mother, my father did not usually share it. I can only assume that he was too smitten by my mother's famous charm to abide any longer a state of bachelorhood.

Defensa 124 Buenos Aires

June 26th 1896

Dear Miss Bagley,

I am afraid I am showing great weakness in saying so, but the fact remains that unable to bear the suspense nor restrain my feelings longer I have decided to declare them and acknowledge the great regard and affection with which you have inspired me, and if you think you can reciprocate these feelings sufficiently to place your future happiness in my hands you will make me the very happiest man in the world. I admit you have never given me any encouragement to warrant me in supposing you entertained other feelings than friendship, but I can assure you that if you feel you can place your future in my care, I will devote my life to making you happy.

In asking you to become my wife I hesitate at the enormity of my presumption, as I realise how much too good you are for me, but I would beg of you to believe that the present is not the outcome of a sudden fancy and that my love for you has grown steadily to such an intensity that I realise now my happiness in life is centred in you, and I pray your answer may be a favourable one.

If you require it, take time to decide, but do not keep me longer in suspense than you can help, and believe me,

Yours very sincerely,

James S. Agar

P.S. Should you decide right away and the answer be favourable may I beg you to telephone me at the office here and I will call and see Mrs Bagley.

I also have the letter my father wrote humbly acknowledging Mamie Bagley's refusal of his offer. My future mother seems to have taken exception to the fact that James Agar proposed by letter instead of speaking to her first. Perhaps his characteristic reticence, no doubt a product of shyness, prevented him from approaching Mamie more directly. However, it was the accepted thing in Victorian times first to refuse a man before accepting him. So I wonder whether Mamie was following a custom or whether she was gently persuaded by her own family to change her mind. For there is no doubt that she was a worldly woman who loved the good things in life, and James Agar was a hard-working Scot with good prospects who adored her.

The letter which my triumphant father-to-be subsequently wrote to his own mother is also of interest:

per 'Danube'

Defensa 124
Buenos Aires
7th August

My dear Mother,

I am writing this to let you know that something new has come into my life. On Tuesday last I became engaged to Mamie Bagley and I need hardly tell you it has made me quite the happiest man in the world.

I sincerely trust in God my choice will meet with your

approval. I think you will realise how much my happiness will be intensified if we feel that your blessing and best wishes go with us.

I know you have not had many opportunities of forming an opinion of Mamie and I do not attempt to tell you all I think of her. I need only say that I love her dearly and that beneath her bright and lively manner there is a depth of character unknown to those who love her less than I do.

Mamie has fears, realising the place in your heart your sons occupy (and not the least this one) that our engagement might not be the source of happiness to you which I fondly hope it will, and I have endeavoured to calm her doubts by explaining how little she knew of you who always put your children's happiness before your own. I pray that you will realise that you are not losing a son but gaining a daughter, more than worthy of all the love that I can bestow on her, and her mother's trust in me.

I feel quite impatient to see you all back again and wish the time were closer at hand. I hope you have been enjoying yourself in good health and strength. With best love to one and all as if named, accept the same for yourself.

Ever your affectionate son,
James

The tone of the letter is a little anxious, suggesting a doubt in my father's mind that his good news would be received as joyfully as he would hope. But there again, his mother was far away in Scotland, and parental approval was much more important to that generation than is now the case. Whatever the emotional undercurrents actually were, Mamie and James were married and seemed, to me at least, to enjoy a happy and fulfilling life together. But as I shall relate, my knowledge of their true relationship must remain largely speculative, for as children our lives were centred around the nursery. And that world was equally as far removed from our parents' glamorous social life as it was from their private existence.

My mother was very good-looking in her youth, with large expressive eyes. She was well-built but not tall in stature, with the commanding presence that comes from always having had money at one's disposal. Money gave her the confidence that American women often have, but many English women lack. She had belief in herself as a woman, she never hesitated, she was aware (in spite of an endearing innocence), she flirted, danced, dressed with distinction, loved entertaining, but kept to the rules and expected to be obeyed. Convention was something she never questioned, saying of a breach of it, 'supposing everybody did that?' She would be horrified to find that nowadays everybody does do that. She belonged completely to her Edwardian age and class, believing that the poor did not work hard enough, and that was why they were poor. She even thought it was wrong to read novels in the mornings (she herself was very fond of books by Phyllis Bottome), because it was not work. Undoubtedly she was a bit of an actress, who enjoyed playing to her audience. She grew easily animated in conversation, and I remember her often crying 'Oh la-la!' and 'Ha-ha, said the duck laughing!' when somebody told her a tall story. I even have a photograph of her standing in a barrel holding a glass of champagne. I wonder what my father thought.

She did not love my father as much as he loved her. For him she could do no wrong, and although she never strayed from the straight and narrow, it must have been a great temptation, for she had many devoted admirers and was a gay and amusing person with no particular religious background. Towards the end of her life when she became more and more addicted to the whisky bottle, I believe she regretted her caution, for she felt that the Tres Cosas Buenas had let her down, and it was for them that she had led such a circumspect existence. Is it more selfish to refrain from having children because of the demands they make, or to have them and expect them to be an insurance against boredom and loneliness? (Human motive is rarely simple.) First Dorothy, then two years later me, and finally Winifred were born to Mamie and James. We were not a close family, but we rubbed along together.

In fact, much more of my early life was spent with servants than with my parents. I know that we took with us back to England from the Argentine our nurse, known to us simply as Nursey, of whom we all became very fond. Nursey must have been about thirty-five or forty as I remember her, a comfortable reassuring woman who slept in the nursery or with the youngest child. I think my mother got annoyed when Nursey wanted to take me into her own bed to comfort me. I must have been two or three years old at the time, and my mother would certainly have been a greater stranger to me than Nursey. Often the children were only brought down to say goodnight to their parents: our one contact with our mother and father during a whole day.

As I write about it, my childhood begins at last to interest me. Previously I have been too concerned with the present to pay the past much attention, but now I am forced to look back. Perhaps misleadingly I see in those early years the seeds of later adventures; memory adopts a capricious system of highlights, and masses together events which may not have been related. But it is not such a bad spectacle, and I try to make the most of the insight it offers.

I had a violent temper as a child, while my two sisters were quieter, though Winifred also showed signs of temperament. I would refuse to eat or anyhow finish my food and would burst into a rage when told to get on with it; probably I wanted to go out to play in the garden, or perhaps just get on with my life, not waste precious time eating. Periodically we used to be put through our paces as entertainers. The three of us would have to appear before friends at the appointed time and sing. Either we did 'Three Little Maids from School are We' (from the Gilbert & Sullivan opera *The Mikado*), or 'The Moon and I, We are not Shy', in which I had to step forward and sing alone. At other times we dressed up in clogs and many-coloured Dutch skirts, and had to sing and dance. The only words I remember from that particular song were 'One pink and yellow from some other fellow, and one that I haven't got on'. This was always followed by uproarious applause from the audience! As far as I remember I rather enjoyed it, for children love dressing up and showing off, however shy.

We had jig-saw puzzles to keep us quiet in the nursery and then hectic games of Demon Patience, a card game full of shrieks and exclamations, to compensate. I remember that we kept tortoises as pets, but I do not know if we raced them. There were skipping ropes and other games. I was particularly fond of my hoop. I used to run away with it – or it used to run away with me – and Nursey would have to go looking for me. Now I realise that I had simply strayed into the world of magic and illusion and must have resembled de Chirico's painting 'Child with Hoop'.

I was more like my mother in temperament than my father. She was very emotional, direct and passionate, and only her sense of social propriety kept her from being as spontaneous in speech as she was in gesture. I think she had something Spanish in her make-up and she spoke the language with ease, though so did my quiet and reasonable father. Somehow he managed to keep this rather unruly quartet under control – probably by his calm attitude to everything. He was the one who would insist: 'Mamie, don't get upset,' when things seemed to go wrong.

I remember that when I was two or three I refused to apologise for some misdemeanour and my mother slapped me with the back-end of a hairbrush. At the time I was quiet, but afterwards I spluttered with rage and indignation. There are a number of events during the first twenty-five years of my life which share this feeling of resentment. That was the only occasion I can remember being really naughty as a child, but I am sure I was often sullen and obstinate. Is it so fanciful to suppose that the foundations were being laid for my later rebellion?

The house where I was born was called Quinta la Lila – The Villa of the Lilacs – a creeper-clad double-fronted house reminiscent of those comfortable Victorian residences in

Wimbledon or Sunningdale. I can recall a polar bear skin in front of the fireplace in the hall, and an outsize St Bernard dog who used to knock us down every time he wagged his tail. The dog was in fact very well-trained and we used to ride on his back; he must have been well-behaved because he was even allowed in the nursery.

The pace of life was much more leisurely in those days, people did not develop as quickly as they do now, children especially were slower, kept in so that their parents could show them off. Nowadays the aeroplane has supplanted the motor car, just as the cinema has supplanted the theatre, for the world is shrinking, and we are engaged in trapping time. Time and space have become the two great question marks of the twentieth century.

Despite isolated incidents of confrontation, I had a happy childhood, making mud-pies by a running stream in the garden, and selling them to the grown-ups for a penny a time. (Mud-pies gratify one of our first and best instincts: so long as we are dirty we are happy. The very physical activity of painting is not so different.) I certainly had a happier nature than my younger sister Winifred, who was more rational than I was yet always seemed to be crying. Perhaps the real world (whatever it may be) does not respond very well to the arguments of reason.

Winifred took strong likes and dislikes to people, and was more secretive than I was. I would describe her as opaque, whereas I was more transparent, for I would show my feelings, whether of joy or despair. But she had great inner resources and a natural talent for drawing and writing. Alas she was lazy, saying 'I can't be bothered', when I urged her to do more. Her observations on people and her descriptions of landscape were full of colour, thoughtful and to the point. Eventually, with the encouragement of her friend Alec Waugh, she had two novels published, *Living Aloud*, really a novel about our mother, and *Mermaids Sleep Alone*. I think *Living Aloud* is her best, well worth re-reading despite its sharpness.

Dorothy, my elder sister, was even more conventional and

law-abiding than Winifred, and, as such, she remains a distant figure of my childhood. Winifred was considered to be the cleverest of the children, a little green-eyed sprite, but she always thought Dorothy and I outdid her in looks. Dorothy was very good looking, with masses of dark hair and large blue eyes, supposed to be an Irish inheritance. She was badly ill with scarlet fever which left her with a weakened back. Often she stayed in bed and did not join in our games.

Fragments of visual memory of the time are stained glass on the staircase: gold and amethyst and patches of dark crimson bleeding on to the carpet. The family motto spelt out 'Via trita via tuta' – 'the frequented path is the prudent path' (though perhaps not for me). The dazzle of sunlight against the shadowy mahogany inside the house. Carved Japanese chairs in the drawing room, scrolled hideous with high-relief dragons and waves. Whitewashed buildings and lumpy cobblestones with tufts of grass between them. A cabinet of netsuke which intrigued me. The open green carriage drawn by a pair of dark horses with glinting bridles (the ride would have been a rare treat had I not been miserable and afraid – I was going to have my tonsils seen to), the busy streets crammed with colourful people, the bright flower stalls, the long avenues and tall trees of Buenos Aires. And back in the sombre house, large Japanese screens embellished with mother-of-pearl, one depicting a heron improbably hunched amidst cherry blossom . . .

I must explain our living arrangements in those far-off days. Half of the year was spent in our villa in Flores, while the summer months were passed on the river. A distant relation and admirer of my mother was Joseph Drysdale, a close friend of my parents. He was a robust ebullient man with a roaring laugh, a millionaire who smoked stinking cigars, and was head of a rival firm called, I believe, Drysdale and Dunn. He had interests in estancias and paid enormous sums for handsome bulls.

He also owned a villa on the river Tigré, where large

luncheon or dinner parties took place. We used to live there throughout the summer, in fact I always thought (until a year or two ago) that the house belonged to my parents, as I knew that 'Old Joe', as we children used to call him, had a house in town. My mother ran the Tigré house for him, ordered the meals, flirted and danced with him. He obviously adored her, and constantly thought of ways to please her. In fact, when my parents and he went off together on a world trip, he engaged an orchestra to play on board the liner because he knew she delighted in dancing. Everybody thought she was his mistress, but it was not true. Her upbringing, her fear for her children, plus, I suspect, a puritan streak, kept her strictly within the bounds of matrimony. So my father had no concrete cause for jealousy, and, reserved and reticent as he was, enjoyed seeing her happiness in being admired.

Every two years or so, the whole family would travel back by ship to England for a brief holiday in the old country. The trip would take some three weeks, and there would be constant entertainment with fancy-dress balls and quoits or egg-and-spoon races for the children. There must have been between three and four hundred people on board each of those ships of the Royal Mail, and they seemed huge to a child. I remember one small boy shouting at his mother, 'Mummy, mummy where's the boat?' when he was already standing in the middle of the deck. The journey included several stops en route: at Montevideo, Rio, Olinda in Brazil and then Lisbon, before docking in England.

On our way across the great Atlantic, the ship also used to stop at the island of Madeira, and we children looked forward enormously to sliding down the cobbled street of the mountainside in basket chairs which held two or even three grown-ups. In Rio lived an uncle and aunt with whom we sometimes stayed. I have seen Rio on other voyages to and from England, and remember it always as a romantic Chinese landscape dropped on the coast of South America. Entering the bay at dawn by ship is an unforgettable experience as mysterious shapes become landscape, the earth seems to breathe through the mist like a prehistoric monster, the living land separates itself from the water, and the sky, that excellent canopy, reveals itself. A magical place, but I believe that it is not so pleasant to live there, as clothes put in a cupboard come out mildewed in a matter of months – like some marriages.

It was on my first voyage that the captain of the liner became a friend of the family, and came to tea in the nursery when we returned to Buenos Aires, where I entertained him by drawing his large ship on the blackboard. My second birth was as natural as breathing.

It might seem from all this that we had something of a rootless existence as children. I do remember my life being full of excitement, but I do not remember feeling threatened or insecure. A degree of stability is perhaps more necessary for children than it is for adults, and although we seemed to be often on the move, a sense of security was maintained by the style of travel. In those days it was still possible to travel with everything you needed. It was not a question of one suitcase and an umbrella for my mother, she had entire baggage trains to follow her about. And my father would not so much as think of crossing the English Channel without engaging a courier to arrange everything for us. There is something stately about this leisurely progress through foreign countries, but undoubtedly it cushioned us from the harsher realities of travel. We were like the tortoises in the garden at home with our own built-in protection: travel for my parents meant maintaining their own environment rather than adapting to a new one.

By way of a change to the return trips to England, my parents decided to go off round the world in 1909, with Joe Drysdale. They took about nine months over this excursion and this time did not take the children. We were transported to Joe Drysdale's house in Bournemouth, where we would apparently be safer. But it was there that I first saw death, in the shape of a young bird lying dead on the drive-way. Yet our time there for the most part was enjoyable, and I remember excursions to Corfe Castle and Swanage, and how even then I was struck by the engraved stone globe resting on the Dorset cliffs.

The country which made the greatest impression on me when my parents returned, and perhaps on them also judging by the shipload of treasures they brought back with them, was Japan. There was a rickshaw in which the children were allowed to ride around the garden, and besides the horrible lacquered furniture, I remember lots of those delightful paper flowers which open in water. There were also a number of rather bloodthirsty battle scenes done on parchment scrolls which my mother proceeded to hang in her bedroom.

Those summers spent by the river Tigré at the villa San José, named after Old Joe, were happy ones. I can vividly picture my mother doing her pokerwork on the verandah, overdressed in the latest cream embroidered Edwardian fashion, while the French chef came to receive the day's orders. Humming birds darted around the garden, peaches and apricots hung from the trees, and there were innumerable tennis parties in spite of the heat. I was too young to play, but watched while English, Scottish, Welsh and Irishmen battled fiercely on the tennis court.

A certain high wind was an ominous sign anywhere in the Argentine, except in the Andes, and people would shut their doors and windows against what they knew was coming, verily a plague of locusts. It could have been a biblical plague for they descended like evil spirits at the villa San José, on the trees, rose bushes and other vegetation. It was dramatic and frightening as the sky darkened with the hordes of dry rasping insects. The women would go indoors with the children, while all the available men would be called upon to fight the invasion as best they could, beating the insects against the bushes with spades, large fly-whisks or anything else to hand, while old laundry baskets crammed with corpses would be carried away. The strange thing was that a few miles down the road, lucky people would have no locusts, for it all depended on the way the wind blew!

But when the wind favoured us, the games were plentiful at Old Joe's house. The most popular was the aptly-named Giant's Stride. A strong pole was inserted into a hole in a spacious lawn, with six or eight strong ropes ending in handles attached to the pole. Each child and one or two grown-ups would catch hold of the handles and with one foot on the ground would start swinging or pushing round the vast circle till we were all flying round and round the pole, gradually getting higher and higher till the exhilaration and excitement grew too much, and slowly we would descend to the green earth again.

Looking back, I can see that there was a fairly glittering social life amongst the prosperous British colony in the Argentine. My parents mixed with the diplomatic set and entertained distinguished visitors. When a passing prince came to dinner my little sister was curious to know whether he would be coming in his crown, and when a travelling duke arrived to meet my parents at Mar del Plata (the well-known Argentine seaside resort), at the age of four I was introduced to the Duke of Richmond and Gordon and immediately asked him if he had any shells in his pocket. When he said no, I exclaimed, 'What a silly man!' Among the people who came out to the Argentine and were entertained at the villa San José by my parents and Joe Drysdale were Lord Hawke and the visiting MCC cricket team. I remember particularly Bosanquet the inventor of googly-bowling, showing us how he held and delivered the ball.

Joe Drysdale discovered that the children had never read or heard of Kipling's *Just So Stories*. Perhaps my parents were shamed by this hole in our education, for the nurse was dispatched to buy a copy at the English bookshop in Buenos Aires, only to find that the last copy had been sold two hours before. She got back to find it on the nursery table: Old Joe had stepped in before her, and bought the last copy himself. We listened with wonder and amazement as the stories unfolded, of how the elephant got his trunk (a favourite of mine), and also the cat that walked alone, one that I particularly identified with at that early age. I find that I still wave my tail.

Another time at the villa San José I was promised by Nursey that if I got up early I should see a bun dance. In great excitement I did so, but to my disappointment found nothing extraordinary going on at the breakfast table. And when I complained bitterly, she pointed out that there was abundance on the table. I suppose I had been expecting an early version of Charlie Chaplin's Bun Dance; evidently I was too young to appreciate her pun.

I rode a lot as a child since it was almost obligatory to ride in the Argentine, and my pony Strawberry Cream and I learnt to jump and not be afraid. There were early morning rides along dusty roads, with the smell of eucalyptus trees and the vista of endless plains, space and open sky and the occasional *bottega* (or general store-cum-bar) on the way, where horses were tied up, flicking their tails at the flies. The wide pampas, shorn of people in my parents' time, lay bare and flat, and in the emptiness of space there is an absence of all boundaries, and time is freed from the one-way stream which flows through inhabited towns. In the country you could smell the newness of nature, and feel the nothingness of the almost invisible landscape, until you came to the foothills of the Andes, those gigantic outcrops of rock, with scrubby turf to ride or lie on, and the great high sky above you, not the low wet blanket that England knows so well.

We travelled happily back to the Villa of the Lilacs for the winter after my parents' return from their world trip. There was a splendid party with the house hung with wisteria and Japanese lanterns in the spacious grounds, turning the place into a veritable fairyland for a child. The gardens of Quinta la Lila were already exotic, full of palms and ombu as well as other unidentified trees to climb or hide in. There was even a miniature jungle attached to the house: a conservatory full of beautifully laid-out tropical plants and small birds. But on this particular occasion, the night of the party, there was a fly in the ointment of delight, since I had to dress in a kimono and recite a welcome in Japanese to the assembled guests. I was told to stand in the centre of the room while the guests sat around at small tables under a canopy of wisteria. Inevitably, I got stage fright. I remember being deeply ashamed of myself for I forgot what I was supposed to say and was embarrassed and stuttered. I find that I still get angry with myself – as if the spirit wants to leap ahead of the body.

On the trips back to England we used to stay at the Hyde Park Hotel in London, and our English nurse told us that it was opposite two of the best shops in London – Harvey Nichols and Woollands. This was obviously agreeable to my mother, whose wardrobe was extensive. She had a chinchilla fur coat, full-length to the ground, long before chinchillas were bred in captivity. And her hats were myriad. In fact she would not dream of going to stay at the seaside (Felixstowe or Brighton in England, Mar del Plata in the Argentine) without some forty hats. And what hats! Enormous constructions of straw, velvet or fur like frigates under sail or birds on the wing, embellished with vast bows, ribbons or ostrich feathers. I have a particular fondness for making hat-shaped surrealistic objects, and I have sometimes thought that, for instance, my 'Ceremonial Hat for Eating Bouillabaisse', composed of a curved slab of cork, shells and fishbones, might have been inspired by my mother's spectacular headgear.

My father retired early in order to come back once and for all to England with his wife and family, and so in 1911 we left the Argentine. However, James Agar was a sufficiently dedicated businessman to want to keep an eye on his firm, so he had to be in easy reach of the London office. My parents decided to take the lease on a sumptuous corner house in Belgrave Square, No. 25, now the Norwegian Embassy, which had a lovely ballroom. What I enjoyed was being able to keep a rabbit on the low outside roof of my father's study. The rabbit was called 'Catastrophe' for some obscure reason. We lived in those 'upstairs-downstairs' days, with a butler, a couple of footmen and innumerable maids, some twelve servants in all. Incidentally my mother's maid always put on her stockings for her, and applied the correct amount of toothpaste to the brush. We were called to meals by an immense barrel-shaped gong, which when struck gave out a deep-throated reverberation, that once had echoed slowly through a Japanese temple.

In this house, my mother came into her own, even more than in the Argentine. As my father had written of her: 'Beneath her bright and lively manner there is a depth of character unknown to those who love her less than I.' He almost echoes Chesterton's words about women: 'Variability and versatility are the virtues of a woman. If you have one good wife, you are sure of a spiritual harem.' Certainly, in spite of her commanding personality, she appeared to me romantic and beautiful and I loved her very much. But she had her quirks. For instance, she had a particular dislike of ruins, however picturesque, and was likely to say of them, and even of the Parthenon: 'Couldn't they do something about it?' Similarly, she disliked antique pieces of furniture, speculating whether they might have bugs in them or whether dogs might have slept on them. So everything in our London house was a copy, except the immense gong and a few original Chinese or Japanese lacquer cabinets.

As in the Argentine, my mother had in London various platonic beaux around her. One was a youngish man, known as Buddha because of his handsome profile, who was an expert on eighteenth-century furniture, as well as possessing the full compliment of social graces. He helped my mother choose furniture for our London homes, and also engaged the butler and footmen for her. Years later she discovered he was a homosexual. I think she was not so much shocked by this as by a suspicion that the butler had been his lover. Another admirer was Arthur le Rossignol, universally known as 'The Bird', a dashing man-about-town in London, Paris and Buenos Aires. Born in Jersey to a well-known family, he had gone out as a young man to the Argentine to enter some business or other, but was really a playboy, devoted to sport, girls and fast cars. Although a good driver, he was reputed to be a dangerous one, for he always had his eye on the pavement parade rather than on the road.

25 Belgrave Square was the scene of much gaiety and good feeling, and the ballroom was often in use. For big parties there was a small orchestra (with our own piano), for small ones a gramophone. The children were only allowed a quick glimpse of the shining dresses and the white ties and tails through the ballroom door before being whisked to bed. My parents were also fond of the theatre and the opera, and

sometimes they would take a dozen or so guests with them. Afterwards, they would come back to a chafing-dish supper laid out in the dining room. The footman who had not gone with the chauffeur in the Rolls, was on duty to take the overcoats at the door, and see that there was enough champagne, for 'Pink Pop' as they called it, was the favourite for supper. Eggs and anchovies and smoked salmon were laid out before the footman was dismissed, after which the guests scrambled their own eggs. In such gatherings, my mother was in her element as a society hostess.

My father was a more shadowy figure to me when I was young, for he was immersed in business, and I think he was a difficult man to know – quiet, reserved, more a spectator than a contributor. He could be very amusing at parties, but he would always retire from them at about ten o'clock. I looked up to him and liked him, and used to bring him a buttonhole from the garden every morning. But you could not open your heart to him; he was too composed and reasonable. He had the rigid ideas of his generation about morality, and when we were in the Argentine he refused to allow a Dutch friend of my mother to enter the house because she was divorced. (They could only exchange greetings in public, as on the beach at Mar del Plata.) Yet I suppose that in his own way he was somewhat unconventional, for although a Tory he had a sneaking sympathy for Socialism. And when he was offered a knighthood shortly after the First World War, to my mother's disappointment he declined it – on two grounds: he objected to being expected to contribute to Tory Party funds, and he believed in hereditary titles only.

As well as our London home, we had an autumn residence – Alton House at Nairn in Scotland. It was a rather grim, forbidding-looking manse, but near the golf-links, which was the main attraction for my parents, who divided their leisure between golf and bridge. However, when the guests played tennis on a Sunday, the villagers came up the drive and threw stones at them for daring to play on the Sabbath.

I realise now that my parents had moved effortlessly into English society, largely because of the Argentine connection.

Many of their friends from Buenos Aires were already established in London. For instance, Hilda Krabbe (who married Ivon Moore-Brabazon, or Lord Brabazon of Tara as he later became) was one of my mother's bridesmaids, as was Gracie Duggan who later became Lord Curzon's wife.

My mother was asked if we three children would be bridesmaids at the wedding of Lily Elsie, the reigning theatrical beauty of her day, who was a friend of my godmother Mita Sewell. Mita herself was something of a character, a great friend of my mother but no family relation. She loved telling ribald smoking-room stories and I can still hear my father interrupting them with, 'Not in front of the children, Mita'. Dorothy and Winifred and I used to be seen at all the big children's parties so popular in those days. Apparently we were considered a beautiful trio and were much admired. But Mama declined the chance of letting us appear at Lily Elsie's wedding, as though it would not be proper to be so connected with the theatrical world. Only in appearance was my mother a Gertie Miller type; not in morals. Mama was very glamorous, and always wore beautiful clothes, often in subtle hydrangea colours, by Poiret, Lanvin or Lucille, many with embroidery on them which enthralled me.

I loved outspoken Mita for her disregard of convention, her gorgeous laugh and because she spoiled me when she was allowed to. (Her nickname for me was moon-face.) She was a fascinating character, always falling in love or having nightmares. When she laughed, her whole body shook with pleasure. She was a 'natural' in the mould of Mrs Patrick Campbell, just as my mother was an 'original'. I do not believe they make them like that anymore.

Mita and my mother would have looked well together in a novel. Although they were both quick-tempered, they rubbed along despite occasional flare-ups. Mita was a good companion and helped Mama at parties and picnics. I know men liked Mita, but they took her for granted and she never succeeded in marrying until she was in her seventies. Joseph and I met her in Nice, in the late twenties, with an Irishman from Buenos Aires we had always known as Baby Green. I had never noticed before that the Babe and Mita were together much, but they had been married for six months when we ran into them. The doctors had told Baby Green (an immense fellow, hence his nickname) that he had only about a year to live, so he and Mita had decided to get married. She was distraught when her husband died. It was a great pity that she married so late, for she adored children and told me once that a baby crying was the most beautiful sound in the world.

I was now accumulating important visual experiences. My parents had brought back a great many colour photographs of Japan. We used to view them through a stereoscopic box with enormous delight as the walls of the nursery melted away and were replaced by the snowy peak of Mount Fuji, or waterfalls and sand gardens, or the roofs of Kyoto, or a storm-tossed sea bearing boats with curious sails. At about the same time I was fascinated by Edmund Dulac's exotic illustrations to fairy stories. I loved them and tried to draw myself, sometimes succeeding, sometimes not. Arthur Rackham's illustrations also gave me my first taste of the strange and grotesque.

Before the family had settled in London I was left with my elder sister Dorothy in the tender care of a prep school in Canford Cliffs, Dorset. Winifred was thought to be too young to be left, so she travelled back to Buenos Aires with my parents while they organised the move to England. I was very shy but not particularly alarmed at being abandoned in Dorset. As a family we were not very close, and brought up as we were mostly by servants, to go to school at seven or eight years of age was really to exchange one distant authority for another. I do not remember relying on Dorothy very much, for I was too caught up in the excitement of this new adventure. I remember long hot summers and picnics among the sand-dunes, and at last learning to play tennis.

Shyness did get the better of me sometimes in class. On one occasion I got absolutely furious with myself because I was too shy to answer the simple question: 'What is irrigation?' What was so infuriating was that it seemed that I was the only one who knew, because of my experience in the Argentine.

It was during this period that we visited Engelberg in Switzerland for a winter holiday, two years in succession. One day while we were lunching in the hotel, a small rather swarthy man with gig-lamp spectacles and an air of being somebody entered the dining room, and greeted my mother. She told me that this was Rudyard Kipling who had written the *Just So Stories*. I was so excited I leapt at him, and he picked me up and kissed me. Thereafter for the rest of our stay, and as a special mark of our friendship, he always let me light his cigar. It appeared that my mother knew him through her friendship with Cherry Poynter, the wife of Sir Edward Poynter, RA, who was a cousin of Kipling.

Quite soon, Dorothy and I were sent to another school – Heathfield, near Ascot. Miss Wyatt was the headmistress, and what an overbubbling superfluous person she was. She would arrive in a swirl of adjectives and well-filled black lace, cooing: 'Dear children, charming children,' looking like a false copy of Queen Victoria. There was a private chapel adjoining the buildings, and she, being very High Church, always had a good-looking curate in tow. We were encouraged to keep inoffensive animals, and most of the girls had guinea-pigs, but I plumped for a grass snake, which was an undulating dream. I remember one occasion when the bell for chapel was going, and as I did not have time to put away my snake, I stuffed him into my pocket and settled demurely in the pew with the others, only to watch with dismay as my slinky grass snake slithered down the aisle between two facing rows of giggling school girls.

We were a very mixed batch at Heathfield. I adored Angela Leyland, the tall blonde daughter of the founder of a famous firm. There were several assorted Cadogans, and an Armenian millionaire's daughter, the scruffiest girl I have ever seen. Rita Gulbenkian got pneumonia badly and there was a great to-do in the school when her father Calouste came to see his sick daughter; but she recovered, and he gave a large sum to the school as thanksgiving. My particular china was Elizabeth de Kay, who was small and blue-eyed like me, and a relation of the Mrs de Kay Bronson who had a place in Venice and was the model for the all-knowing Mrs Prest in Henry James' novel *The Aspern Papers.* She and I used to shin up a high pine tree in the grounds at Heathfield and sit among the branches at the top, thus escaping the wearisome round of church-going on Sundays. We could hear them looking for us down below, but they never discovered our nest in the sky.

At Heathfield, the girls all had small single bedrooms named after a flower (mine was Veronica), and were allowed to put up pictures of their choice. My print was of a painting by Greuze called 'La Cruche Cassée', or The Broken Jug, an oddly prophetic choice, since it was meant to refer to a young girl's erotic dream. I also remember the hip-baths at Heathfield, for if you did not get out of bed in time the water was cold.

For nearly as long as I can remember I had wished to be some kind of artist, and from the time I was nine or ten years old I was continually drawing. My inclination was reinforced at Heathfield by the painting mistress, Lucy Kemp-Welch, a Royal Academician who specialised in painting heavy cart-horses ploughing. Even then, that sort of painting was not at all my thing, but she was a sympathetic personality who reassured me that I should always have something to do with Art. I used to look after her small garden for her, in addition to the tiny plot I cultivated for myself (it was the Heathfield custom for everyone to have a little garden), and I remember she was generous enough to forgive me easily when I pulled up what I thought were weeds but turned out to be her new plants.

The racing at Ascot was a great event when we were at Heathfield, as parents were allowed to take their children out, and we had many happy hours devouring Fuller's walnut cake on picnics and visiting Lord Athlumney, a friend and beau of my mama's. He had a small house on the river at Bray near Maidenhead, a house in Charles Street in London and a lovely castle in Ireland. He used to instruct us in all sorts of devious ways of playing truant, and getting out of school and into matinées and other forbidden territory. He was an immense fellow, in the Irish guards, with a stride like a tiger; a *bon viveur* with a wicked wit and a love of ladies still in their prams, who said he was always ready to wait till they grew into their primes. During the First World War he was Lord Provost Marshall and Keeper of the Tower of London and was responsible for hanging traitors, which horrified me, for he kept a bit of the rope which hanged them in his dining room in Charles Street. After the war, he would call at our London house and leave not one but one hundred of his visiting cards if he found we were out.

'Papa Lordy' as my mother's French maid used to call him, first met my parents and my young sister on the boat returning to England from South America, when Dorothy and myself were at school in Canford Cliffs. Winifred must have been five or six years old at the time and Lord Athlumney in his thirties, but nothing daunted he gave her a minute gold ring set with tiny diamonds, and announced to all and sundry that they were engaged. When we met them at Southampton he immediately jilted my little sister and plumped for me as his bride-to-be. He indicated that it would be more fitting as I was older than Winifred, but of course he did not have another ring on him! But I believe he seriously had his eye on me when I was about eighteen, for apart from introducing me to Pink Pop and other sophisticated things, he gave me the lovely triple mirror of rosewood and ivory that I still have, saying that it was a frame for a picture which he hoped to possess.

The outbreak of war in 1914 brought many changes. Dorothy and I remained at Heathfield until 1915, but then for the sake of economy we were sent to a different school, Tudor Hall in Chislehurst, Kent. The world seemed to be changing almost as quickly as we were.

CHAPTER TWO

Stepping Forwards and Sideways

I was with my mother in Somerset staying with a friend or relation when the First World War burst like a time-bomb on the tranquil world of August 1914. We had arranged to visit the picturesque little village of Clovelly in Devon, and I remember walking up the steep cobbled streets, the grown-ups talking in hushed tones about the gravity of the situation, whilst I wondered whether one could dig up those splendid cobblestones and throw them at the Germans if they appeared round the corner.

Next day we returned to London, for my mother was anxious to confer with my father who had stayed with my sisters in Belgrave Square. Our way of life was fundamentally altered by the hostilities, though at this distance only the small details stand out. As children we did not experience the full horror and tragedy of the war, for we did not suffer directly. The significance of the details I remember lies in the changed emphasis of our existence; like the rest of the nation, we became aware of a new seriousness of intent, combining with an atmosphere of worry and grief. Money was less readily available even for my parents, and Heathfield proved to be too expensive. There was no more going to the theatre with a footman on the box of the Rolls, and my father relinquished the idea of buying the house in Belgrave Square and gave up the lease; in fact, the Rolls was handed over to the Red Cross.

My father, braving submarines and tin fish in the Atlantic, went out to the Argentine again to see if he could bring order to the chaos caused to the firm by the war. Unusually – considering it was a business matter – he asked my mother's advice, and she agreed with him that he should go; he returned safely within six months. My mother retired to the Berkeley Hotel in Wilton Place, and tried to comfort her weeping relations, who all lost either sons or fathers in the conflict. Says an English proverb: 'There's no seeing one's way through tears'. A German: 'Nothing dries faster than a tear'. Before we left Heathfield, I remember a telegram from my mother saying that under no circumstances should the children learn German.

At school, life maintained its secure rhythms. I had a good drawing master at Tudor Hall, who also said that I should always have something to do with Art. We used to fill a book with quick sketches of this, that and the other, always of people moving or playing games but never standing still for a moment. But it was Horace Kesteven, the music master, who remained my friend for many years. Slight in stature, with an impish expression and an underhung jaw, he looked as Paganini must have looked; indeed some years later he came with us to the Chelsea Arts Ball, dressed as Paganini. He was the first intellectual I had ever met, and though sometimes mischievous, displaying a mixture of meanness and generosity coupled with a horror of doing what was socially unacceptable, he was an important influence as I grew up and my mind became hungry for ideas. He used to throw out suggestions like: 'Why don't you go to see Ibsen's *Ghosts*?' or, 'Why don't you read Stendhal's *Chartreuse de Parme*?' His house in Sloane Gardens had a painting of his wife by Henry Lamb, and pale landscapes by Paul Nash (the first I had ever seen), and his small daughter, red-haired Mary, had been painted by Spencer Watson. At last I found myself in a milieu where art was a valued part of daily life.

At Tudor Hall I got a first taste of independence and responsibility. At home, we children lived a supervised, escorted existence. I did not ride on a bus until my teens were over, and there was no such thing as unadministered pocket money. At school there was, paradoxically, slightly more freedom. I was good at games and became Captain of Lacrosse, though I did not much like the cricket we had to play. I loved tennis and played that as often as possible. Besides art,

I was good at history and not at all bad at French. We had a French governess who took Nursey's place, since to be able to speak French was a social grace which my mother considered important. Music was another accomplishment we were expected to possess. Horace Kesteven said that I played the piano with more expression than my sister Winifred, although she was supposed to be the more musical. I continued to have piano lessons until I went to the Slade, when art seriously took over my life to the exclusion of all hobbies.

A middle-aged American millionairess called Princess Hatzfeldt was a portly friend of my mother. Loud-voiced with an authoritative manner, I thought she was dreadful; to me she looked like a boxer swathed in velvet and pearls, with a mauve hair-do and little to recommend her except her money. However, we spent a sumptuous weekend at her large house in the country. Lionel Tennyson (the nephew of the Poet – what poet?) was there with his mistress Claire, a very pretty cousin of his whose surname I forget, and there were other guests. The Princess believed in luxury, and although there was a war on, I have never seen such laden tables.

Our stay was not entirely harmonious for Mama disapproved strongly of Lionel calling to his mistress to run his bath-water for him! She was shocked that they should have been invited at all. Perhaps she thought it would give me ideas. Although gay and flirtatious, my mother was very proper, and when that ugly little word 'sex' raised its beautiful head, she could only condemn. She never knew the intoxicating and creative pleasures of having a lover.

But I must hand it to the American for she paid no attention to the silly social attitudes of the time. She was the widow of a German nobleman who traced his ancestry back to the fifteenth century. As she hated being alone in a big house, she used to stay with us at Stoke Poges when the family migrated to the golf-club there as another wartime economy. I remember Princess Hatzfeldt's disgust when war broke out, and her loud complaints that she could not cash any money. Some friend offered her £50. 'As much use as a dirty pocket handkerchief,' she said. I believe she went over to America to try to influence Woodrow Wilson to come into the fight against the Kaiser; it must have been an odd situation for the widow of a German.

At the age of sixteen or seventeen I was given my first camera, an old-fashioned box contraption that took surprisingly good photographs. In an album I have some of these early snaps, mostly holiday pictures and family gatherings. One photo taken by someone else is of a picnic at Burnham Beeches which must have occurred before I left Heathfield. The huge trunks of the trees, split and weathered and gnarled into curious shapes are like the images so beloved of Paul Nash. At that age I was struck by the elements of landscape, but I was also becoming more aware of painting and sculpture. About the same time, I began to collect small ivory statues, which I thought was a very sophisticated thing to do. Surreptitiously I spent some of my dress allowance on a sixteenth-century English warrior in ivory, which became the pride of my collection. Not so many years later, I sold them all, judging my taste to have been crude and undeveloped.

As well as music, theatre was of growing interest to me. I remember pleading with my mother when I was about seventeen to let me go to see a play called *Romance* which was taking London by storm. I think Owen Nares played the clergyman who fell in love with a well-known actress, and of course all the clergymen of England wrote to *The Times* and criticised the ambiguity of the production, saying that it must have been the minx who seduced him. The box office was kept humming for months or even years. I was longing to see the play but my mother was adamant and would not relent, so however Romantic I felt I never saw it.

I left Tudor Hall when I was eighteen, and was sent on to what was known as a finishing school, where you were polished and finished in French. The school was run by three unmarried French sisters named Ozanne, the daughters of a protestant clergyman from Calais, who had made friends with many English visitors. The family knew the headmistress of Heathfield, Miss Wyatt, and it was on her advice that the Ozanne sisters started their own establishment in

Paris, and later in London. It was to become one of the best known places of its kind, especially to parents anxious to give their children the flavour of France. One of the earliest pupils was Nancy Cunard who was slim and undulating and reminded me of my slinky grass snake. She was a favourite of Marie Ozanne, who was to be in future years much troubled by Nancy's growing reputation as a wild young woman who slept with negroes and quarrelled with her mother – both reprehensible activities.

I was a good friend of Peggy Tennant at the Ozannes. She was Sir Charles Tennant's daughter, and when he died her mother had married Geoffrey Lubbock. There was such a complicated family structure with the Lubbocks, Asquiths and Tennants all mixed up, that I never tried to sort them out. All I remember is that the young were sometimes aunts of the old.

While I was at the Ozannes at their second establishment in London, I went to the Byam Shaw School of Art off Church Street, Kensington, where I had my first smell of turpentine and oil paint. I only went once a week to the Byam Shaw, but the teaching was quite good if rather academic. Rex Vicat Cole taught there and set the students various copying tasks. We were allowed to paint as well as draw, but rather than work out our own compositions, we had to copy an old master landscape or reproduce a carefully-contrived still life.

Towards the end of the war mother and father took a long lease on a large house in Balfour Place, on the corner of Mount Street, just behind Park Lane. We also rented a house for the autumn at North Berwick in Scotland, where our guests included the former Prime Minister Herbert ('Wait and See') Asquith and his wife Margot. She was a friend of my mother, and came to play bridge with her, which resulted in much high-pitched disagreement, as she maintained her reputation as a 'witty menace'. Margot was reputed to have an acid and spiteful tongue, while my mother said she was too volatile to make a good bridge player. Yet they were good friends, for Margot had a kind heart and was often smitten with remorse after her spontaneous outbursts. When I think about her now, I am surprised how much she changed with her marriage. Apparently she had always thought of herself as a liberated woman untrammelled by the conventions of society, but when she married Herbert Asquith, she never criticised his views and even agreed with him that women should not be given the vote or allowed to sit in parliament.

Herbert Asquith – whom Margot always called Henry, thinking that Herbert was common – apparently disliked bridge; at all events, he preferred to play Musical Chairs with the younger guests. We were told always to let him win (one of the privileges of an ex-prime Minister?), by making sure that he could grab an empty chair when the music stopped. Our social standing must have leapt up, for when we returned to London from this holiday, the *Illustrated London News* wanted to take photographs of the three Agar girls for its society pages. Although the editor, Bruce Ingram, was a family friend, my mother refused to allow these photographs to be taken, on the somewhat obscure grounds that the footmen might use them as pin-ups.

The house in Balfour Place was not the most stimulating of cultural surroundings. There were paintings on the walls but probably only because empty spaces would have been more noticeable. But I do remember one big, spirited painting by an Italian I think, of a dancing woman, executed with bravura and dash. That was a lot better than the safest Academy pictures which my parents generally chose; works by Benjamin Leader for instance, and the dullest oils imaginable by Sir Edward Poynter. Art has many roles, but it should never be used simply to break up the monotony of wallpaper.

In his study, my father had hung a number of topographical scenes, which included rather a nice work by David Cox. This masculine abode was a study rather than a library, for there were never many books in the house. My father did read a little – Emerson and some Kipling, Galsworthy perhaps – but magazines were much more likely to be found. There were quantities of these, a great array of titles including *Country Life*, the *Tatler*, the *Sketch* and something called

Truth, which was not as religious as it sounds. There were also copies of *Strand Magazine*, in which I first met Sherlock Holmes and Doctor Watson. My mother read the occasional romantic novel but would always prefer to go to a musical comedy. Ours was not a literary household.

My mother used to complain that we spent all our dress allowance (a substantial sum, £300 a year) on books, and even on paintings. Dorothy, Winifred and I were expected to dress for dinner and to maintain certain standards of presentation. Our clothes were mostly chosen by Mama and made by her dressmaker. I can remember more than one occasion when I had dressed for dinner and my choice did not correspond to my mother's standards; humiliated, I was sent back upstairs to change. I grew daily more mutinous at this kind of treatment, for my mother was high-handed and strong-willed, and at the same time I was discovering my own self, a self which I felt my mother deliberately ignored. A serious confrontation of some sort became more and more of a probability.

The country-house-party whirlygig was still in full swing. At one party I found that my tennis partner, a lithe dark-haired Russian, was Prince Youssopov, the executioner of Rasputin. I tried to forget it by keeping my eye on the ball. At another, our host was Ernest Coats (of cotton-reel fame), a lively little man who called me 'the Countess of Rio' (after my tales of voyages to the Argentine) and who danced all night singing, 'Yes, we have no bananas!' at the top of his voice. This was whilst staying at Sundrum Castle in 1918 and 1919, where the principal occupation was grouse-shooting over the moors. I used to sit with the Coats children and tell them stories (the adults were too busy entertaining each other), and relish the castles and towers of my imagination.

We were all extremely fond of dancing, and besides the usual run-of-the-mill London dances, where one was partnered by effete young men who had not succeeded in getting into the war and had nothing to say for themselves, there were madcap *thés dansants*. I remember one dance at a house my parents rented near Pangbourne, when we pushed back the furniture and rolled up the carpet and danced all afternoon and evening to the gramophone with a houseful of guests, though it was a gorgeous day outside. Another time we gave an impromptu concert: I played the piano, Winifred the violin, and Dorothy sang.

When I danced, I was a creature transformed, possessed, I loved it so much. I even won a prize with a personable young man called Henry Martineau at the Palace Hotel in St Moritz one winter. A year or two later, my mother allowed Henry to take Winifred to a May Ball in Oxford one evening, on condition that he bring her back safe and sound. To her horror and dismay, they did not return until the next day. They had had to spend the night at an hotel on the way home after a motor accident. There were tantrums, scenes and explanations, but no more May Balls!

On the surface, everything seemed much as it had been when we lived in Belgrave Square before the First World War; but not quite. Although the butler or footmen still answered the door, maids scurried about, and we still went to musical comedies, dressed for dinner and arranged flowers, the war had left a scar. I had a great feeling of unease, and wanted to do something that I considered more worthwhile than the usual repetitive routine of marrying and having a brood of children, who would probably be slaughtered in the next war. I knew that if I stayed at home for long, my mother would want to make the decisions; in the meantime, I read a lot and pondered how I could strike out on my own to become a painter.

I had heard of Malthus or read about his ideas on the population explosion, and I remember thinking with a sigh of relief, 'that lets me out'. Yet it was almost unheard of in those days for young girls not to do what was expected of them and produce children. I read even more to support my newly-enlightened opinions: Samuel Butler, Oscar Wilde and Dostoyevski were favourites. Dickens and George Moore I disliked. One was too excessive, the other too chilly. *Amiel's Journal* I read with fascination, particularly admiring the inner life it showed with such sensitivity and poetic feeling.

I did not discuss such intellectual excursions with my parents, who no doubt had other aims for me. Sometimes I used to hear The Bird and my mother discussing my marriage prospects. Since the war had decimated the young men of the time, they seemed to think it was a matter of some urgency. The Bird insisted that I should meet a son of the Marquis of Exeter, Lord Burleigh, a marvellous dancer, good tennis player and sportsman and, according to The Bird, altogether a delightful chap. So I met this paragon among men at a dinner party, but felt no fascination, and soon afterwards, his engagement to another was announced. So, bang went one of my Phantom Suitors, as I called them. Next on The Bird's list was a Belgian Prince who was visiting London. The Bird was shepherding him around the social scene. The mere thought of meeting a Belgian, prince or no prince (I disliked Brussels sprouts) put me on my mettle. I thought I would be damned if I was going to have a dozen children to help uphold the Belgian aristocracy.

On my own account I had had far more interesting encounters. Once at a large house party in Scotland, there was among the guests an airforce officer who had a great dote on me. He had been a flying officer in the Ghastly War (as it should have been called), and one morning he landed his dual control bi-plane in the field opposite the house, in order to take me for a trip in the air, something most rare in those days. I accepted the invitation to fly, but not the proposal of marriage that went with it. I remember thinking when I saw the plane, that the whole thing was put together with string. But I got a few lessons in pulling the joy-stick in between the proposals, and before long I was looping the loop on my own. He of course was in the back of the plane ready to come to my rescue should I do anything disastrous. However, we got down safely, for I did not attempt the landing. It was a smashing morning.

Also in Scotland there was a dream of a dance given on board the warship *Revenge* on the Firth of the Forth, to which I was taken by the Flag-Lieutenant, who was an ardent admirer. The ship was decked out with coloured flags and glittered with lights, draped with enormous awnings; the naval officers resplendent in their uniforms and the beautiful dresses of the women in such unfamiliar surroundings added to the sinister charm and poignancy of the setting after such a terrible war. I was taken below decks and offered Nelson's Blood. This was almost mother's milk to me – after all, one of Nelson's middle names was Agar. I have always had a soft spot for the navy and almost succumbed to my Flag-Lieutenant.

A year or two later I accompanied my mother to Brides Les Bains, where she took the cure and I learned some of Shakespeare's sonnets by heart, which I used to recite aloud whilst bathing in the medicinal mud. I also amused myself by flirting with Comte Guy de Bourg de Borsas, who was staying in the same hotel. A nice young man with a blond moustache, he told me quite frankly that he was looking for a wife, and I told him equally frankly that I would not do as I was determined to be a painter. Without a doubt, this had become the most important impulse in my life.

My understanding of what it meant to be an artist was gradually coming together. Horace Kesteven gave me a definitive shove towards the painter's life. He had often talked to me about the artist Charles Sims, whom he knew well, and when I told Kesteven that I admired a painting by Sims in the Royal Academy, he promised to take me to see the artist. It was in 1920, when I was nearly twenty-one, that we went to see him; Sims was at that time Keeper at the Royal Academy. The excitement of the occasion remains in my mind, for it was the first time I had been in a professional artist's studio. I ate it up with my eyes, my nostrils snuffed the heady odour of wet paint, my fingers itched to turn the canvasses lined up against the wall, and find out what surprises lurked there. As I was to discover, bodies were lurking there, diaphanous and seductive and delicately erotic, depicted on the beaches, in the woods, or simply strolling in the open air. I was struck with wonder at what could be achieved by making marks on a blank canvas: a stick of bristles plus a vision and a gift – this was the initiation into a larger mystery.

I told Sims how much I liked his painting of two young

girls holding a child between them on the seashore. Now I would think it sentimental, but this was before I went to the Slade, and the Academy at that time was the only place where I could view painting. It was supposed to be a showcase for the nation's art, and however bad the work on display, the exhibitions as a whole fired my enthusiasm and confirmed me in my determination to be a painter. The work by Sims that I admired seemed to be full of light and grace and I bought it for £80.

The same year a watershed occurred in my life. I was staying in the South of France with my mother at the hotel Cap d'Antibes when she acquired a teacher of watercolour for me, a Monsieur William Thornley, an old bearded man who had known Rodin. We travelled to Paris and he took me to see the paintings by Puvis de Chavannes in the Pantheon. I still have a vivid recollection of their serene repose and muted colours. I also went with him to Rodin's studio at Meudon. The sculptor was dead by this time, and most things were covered up with dust sheets. Painting was definitely more interesting to me at that age than sculpture. I felt slightly flat after that visit, not at all inspired by the few things I had seen.

Thornley taught me to do watercolours so like his own that you could hardly tell the difference; strangely enough I still was not satisfied with the result. However, one day after our return to London, Lady Clerk, the wife of Sir George Clerk, the dandified worldly Ambassador to Turkey and later to Paris, came to stay with us in Balfour Place and saw some of the drawings I had done. 'You should go to the Slade,' she said, 'and take it up seriously.' She had been a friend of Renoir, Bonnard and Monet and exhibited with them. Her opinion even carried weight with my parents, though my mother was horrified at the thought that I might become a real artist. Other plans had been made for me, and the social whirl continued. I enjoyed parts of it, but I was growing increasingly rebellious. I had my own ideas about the future.

I was in a much stronger position now with Lady Clerk's backing, and so my parents consented to let me go to the Slade School of Fine Art, a part of London University, for an interview. All these momentous developments occurred in 1920, a kind of *annus mirabilis* for me, when events seemed to be collaborating marvellously with my own ambitions. When I went to see Professor Tonks, a tall lean figure with an autocratic look, it was the middle of term, and after gazing at my Agar-cum-Thornley watercolours and calling Wilson Steer over to have a look, he told me they would take me on as a student when I was a little older. In the meantime I was recommended to go to Leon Underwood's studio in Brook Green, since he gave excellent life classes. That is how I first sat on a donkey in Brook Green.

A donkey is a narrow wooden plank with four legs and an outward sloping side for the student to rest his or her drawing board on. Among the students at Leon Underwood's were Barbara Weekley, daughter of Frieda Lawrence by her first husband Professor Weekley; Rodney Thomas, who later built my monumental wardrobe, mirror and studio fittings which I kept for over fifty years; Gertrude Hermes, Blair Hughes-Stanton and Warren Vinton, the American who a few years later introduced me to my future husband Joseph Bard. At last, amongst this group of friends, I felt that I was taking my first steps into the real life of being an artist.

Leon Underwood had the air of a self-made man who was not prepared to forget his working-class origins. He was a strong personality who believed in the primacy of life drawing, and indeed he taught little else at the Brook Green school. I was very impressed by him as a draughtsman and later by his abilities as a sculptor, but his painting never had the same power to move or convince me. Underwood used his students as models, and I appeared in a walk-on part, so to speak, in his large painting 'Venus in Kensington Gardens' of 1922. Underwood also made at least one etching of me at work, which splendidly shows the freshness and clarity of line I admired so much.

New ideas and forms came rushing at me from all directions. It was a wonderfully exhilarating time, when every discovery had the shock of revelation. My mother came into my room on one occasion and found me absorbed in a book of photographs of Indian sculpture, a temple of erotic figures, an extraordinary mixture of the sacred and the profane. I was given a two-step lecture on what I was looking at, which my mother concluded with the exclamation: 'I don't want you to get like that'. Obviously, the 'terroristic god of Victorianism' was still strong in her. It was only too clear that my mother was scared that I would harbour lustful thoughts or have delicious black masses of the imagination before I was truly wed.

This kind of incident irked me, for I felt I was old enough to read or look at whatever I liked. At about the same time, I bought a small painting by Clement Cowles, a friend of Underwood. Although it was a nude, my mother let it pass without comment, for it was a very prim and proper nude, with its back to the world. My mind was still a disordered cavern of possibilities, but I was groping towards a larger understanding of life than shown by my mother. I knew I had to be myself and resist being drawn into the vortex of family or social life where I risked losing my identity.

My parents decided that they ought to return to the Argentine for a short while after the war, to see how the family firm, Agar Cross, had survived without shipments of goods from England or America. The trip was arranged for the autumn of 1920 to coincide with my twenty-first birthday, the Hurlingham Club outside Buenos Aires was booked for three hundred people and there was to be dancing through the night. I remember little about the party except that I wore a white dress made by Lucille in London with a large red poppy at the waist, and that we ate bacon and eggs at seven o'clock the next morning.

My mind was more and more in need of stimulation. Winifred was devouring almost as many books as I was, and in a rented house in Buenos Aires we discovered the novels of Arnold Bennett, left behind by a previous tenant. No one had ever told us about Bennett or Wells, not even Horace Kesteven, who perhaps thought we already knew of them. The shock and delight of personal discovery made these finds all the more important, but without a guide, it was easy to be over-ambitious. *War and Peace* proved to be a mistake, but usually the successes outweighed the failures.

My parents gave me a discreet pearl necklace for my birthday; Joe Drysdale, lavish as ever, gave me £500. Another unexpectedly extravagant present came from The Bird, Arthur le Rossignol, who gave me a Cartier diamond watch with a black moiré strap. He had taken to calling me a six-cylinder kid, in allusion to the new motor cars beginning to crowd the roads, meaning that I was lively rather than 'fast'! All this made my mother sit up and look at The Bird with different eyes, for she had always flirted with him herself; but I was allowed to keep my beautiful gift, and only lost it many years later.

That birthday visit was the last time I saw the Argentine, and I hold in my mind's eye the silken seashore at Mar del Plata – now, I believe, a sort of Blackpool – where the swirling foam made white calligraphic whisperings as it withdrew; and I see again Cordoba, where I rode on horseback through fantastic outcrops of rock, and lay on the grass watching the clouds in their distant and dreamlike context above.

Daydreaming: stepping into myself, stepping forwards and sideways, stepping into daydream. 'You're not listening, Eileen!' But which is more important, the outer or the inner life? I was St George and the damsel in distress, as I came to rescue myself from the dragon of necessity. I had to fight for my poetic fantasies, unclear images, future hopes and determined plans. Fortitude came from somewhere: 'What willpower the girl has, usually so gentle and dreamy a child!'

I was a little in love with myself as defender of the imagination and the good life. Beauty, colour, surprise, enjoyment, talk which mattered, not idle conversation which did not, warmth and real life-enhancing friendships – my ideals, my ambitions – besides good books and art which are beyond time, glimpses of eternity. This was what I wanted, what I needed.

John Houseman (later to become a film producer and actor) was a friend in those days, and came to one of our many fancy-dress balls perfectly disguised as a Japanese sandman. He was a trainee grain merchant at the time and used to escort us to dances or come to tea at Balfour Place and eat enormous quantities of fig jam. My first journey on a London bus (at an advanced age in those super-supervised days) was with John Houseman. I remember how we hared all over London till we tracked down *The Cabinet of Dr Caligari* playing in some cinema in Streatham. It was an extraordinary experience. It remains the most exciting and emotionally disturbing film I have ever seen, with image and content perfectly matched.

I was more prepared to go out of my way to avoid direct conflict with my parents in these years because they were obviously reconciled to allowing me to train as an artist. Perhaps they thought that if I was humoured, this disturbing passion would wear off, I would pass through this phase and settle down with a husband of their choice. But if they humoured my whim in this way, I also humoured theirs, and held back my retorts when my domineering mother tried to impose her will on the household, or on me in particular. But the irritation and rebellion which I was suppressing could not be contained forever; I was fortunate to have new friends who helped to relieve the pressure from time to time.

I got on particularly well with Rodney Thomas, whom I first met at Underwood's school. He was born in Camberwell, the son of an architect, but his parents died when he was young, and he was adopted by an architect uncle, Sir Brummel Thomas, who lived in Albany and was a traditionalist by nature, believing in Greek Pillars. He sent Rodney to Eton to cure him of his Cockney accent and turn him into a little gentleman. It was a mistake, for Rodney was a born nonconformist who became something of a George Orwell character, very tall and lean with a stone-age El Greco look about him. He and Eton did not get on well together, and like Samson he decided to do what he could to bring down the Greek Pillars.

I was very interested in what Rodney had to say about modern architecture; he particularly admired Le Corbusier, and the vision was rationalisation, liberation from a welter of ornament, emphasis on structural functions, and concentration on concise and economic solutions. He was also interested in furniture, and I determined that if ever I had the chance I would commission him to design some for me.

Gertrude Hermes was also a valued friend. 'Gerts' as she was known to all her friends, and she had many, was a delightful person full of humour and fun, and a marvellous mimic. She trained at Underwood's in wood engraving, and became a highly respected artist. She married Blair Hughes-Stanton, the son of a Royal Academician. He did not want to follow in his father's footsteps and eventually became well-known as a wood-engraver instead. He was a good-looking boy, about 5 feet 9 inches tall and very popular with the girls. The marriage did not last long (though they had two children) before Blair met a strapping blonde with outsize breasts and an inordinate love of babies. He left Gerts to fend for herself and the children, and for a time she was heart-broken, but then taking to the more aggressive art of sculpture she consoled herself by remarking: 'If he prefers a milk pudding to me, he can have her.'

I remember Blair bringing his strapping blonde to my studio one afternoon some years later. She practically undressed and breast-fed her baby in front of friends, while Blair looked on with pride at nature's way of feeding the hungry. He was fighting his puritanical upbringing I suppose and delighting in someone who had no inhibitions.

Underwood taught me a great deal – as well as providing me with a circle of friends – though he was not the easiest person to get on with. He had a complicated vocabulary in which he tried to explain his ideas on form – the way light fell on three-dimensional form and so revealed it. It was because of this interest that he believed in teaching etching and wood engraving; for him, the simple black and white without the complication of colour was the ABC of art, which was something that I do not think the Slade taught at that time.

I first met Robin Bartlett through a friend of the family, and then discovered that he was already at the Slade. He was a short, stocky, adventurous fellow with a beak nose, short legs and a rather large head. The son of yet another architect, he had been in the Merchant Navy, but decided that he wanted to be an artist on terra firma instead of knocking around the world at sea. We got on well together, for I liked his easy devil-may-care approach to things – such a contrast to the way I had been brought up. I had a real need of someone who had experience of the world and who could talk about it. I had lived such a sheltered life at home, and by contrast Robin had taken all sorts of jobs before settling down to be an artist.

In 1921 I was admitted to the Slade to study Fine Art on a part-time basis, with the qualified approval of my parents, who would only allow me to attend classes if the family Rolls took me to the door and picked me up. Rather than make an issue out of this, I made an arrangement with the chauffeur to drop me round the corner. So finally I found myself in the buildings off Gower Street, sitting on another donkey in an even bigger room, with the formidable Tonks peering over my shoulder. He had the reputation of making girls weep with his caustic remarks, but he drew no tears from me. He could be scathing, but he was not a destructive teacher – in fact the reverse – and certainly he was not rough with me. However he sometimes gave the impression that he was bored with the effort of drumming sense into the senseless young.

I went to the Slade at the same time as Jessie Aliston Smith, with whom I had studied at Underwood's; this at least was some moral support. We were set to work drawing male or female models as well as copying classical busts. I remember one monochrome painting I did from a classical head which particularly pleased Tonks. He even called over the visiting Royal Academician, Walter Russell, to have a look. Some students gathered round and congratulated me, but as far as I remember I never won a prize.

Wilson Steer was another teacher at the Slade, and I remember him telling me that I saw the world in heightened colours, and that Cappah Brown was a colour I should never be without. Luckily I was never seduced by the apparent delights of Cappah Brown. . . . Steer was a benevolent man, loose and large like a bear, who used to amble into the life class two or three times a week, say a few words and amble out again. He was inarticulate, incurious and easy-going, but a surprisingly enlivening presence.

While I was still at home in Balfour Place, I was asked one day to go to lunch with Sir George and Lady Marjoriebanks. They wanted me to meet Oliver Messell, since he was going next term to the Slade and I was already there. I was asked to keep an eye on the young man, show him around and introduce him to my friends. At lunch I soon realised that here was someone well-capable of looking after himself. Delightfully witty and good-looking and obviously talented, he was keen to meet Rex Whistler whom he admired, and who was the star turn of the Slade at the time.

I discovered that Oliver was also a marvellous mimic and caricaturist, taking off Tonks (when he was not in the room) and miming other people in an inimitable way. He was immediately successful in his career, so that I lost sight of him gradually, and then completely when he retired to the West Indies and built himself a house in Antigua. Until then we often met at dances, for like Cecil Beaton, he was a beautiful dancer. I think my parents hoped that I would fall for Oliver, but I quickly realised that he was more interested in boys than girls.

I saw a lot of Robin Bartlett at the Slade, and continued to enjoy his company. Men and women were no longer segregated in life classes as they had been in Augustus John's time, so we could compare notes and ideas about drawing and painting. I liked Robin, but I was not in love with him – though I may well have been in love with the idea of being in love. We used to play truant some sunny afternoons, and I especially remember one glorious autumn day in Arundel Park, when Robin read John Stuart Mill to me. We discussed Mill's *Essay On Liberty*, for I was fretting under my parents' authority and had a great desire to be more independent. Robin assured me that I need not follow in my parents' footsteps, and that I could and should strike out on my own.

In short, he opened the door of freedom a crack, and helped me to walk through it when the time came.

Romance for me was still the strange and untried, but I was now determined to try everything, including the delights of forbidden fruit, for sex and its master the phallus loomed large on my horizon. Although I was a well-brought up virgin I did not believe in chastity (a condition as selfish as it is dull), so that I had no hesitation in jumping the queue and solving the mystery when Robin started making advances to me.

I lost my virginity to Robin not in Sherwood Forest but in a leafy glade on the Isle of Wight. (We were there with my family on holiday.) There were enough leaves to make a deep ample bed, and they clung to me when I returned breathless to the house. My mother eyed me with suspicion, and demanded: 'Where have you been? You look flushed.' Meanwhile my satyr had gone for a swim in the English Channel which flowed past the bottom of the garden.

One day I announced that I was going with Robin to a concert, and my mother flew into a rage and forbade me to go. I was obdurate; after all, it was an afternoon concert, nothing so daring as an evening one. Suddenly she slapped my face. I was outraged, and a furious quarrel followed. My father tried to intervene ('Holy Smokes!'), but to no avail. My mother was used to being obeyed, but I was determined to disobey. That night, still shaking with emotion, I packed my bag in case I should falter in the morning, and resolved to leave home and set up somewhere on my own.

It was a leap in the dark, a reckless act for someone who had hardly ever seen the inside of a kitchen, and did not even know how to boil an egg. A quote from an anonymous letter I read in a magazine, whilst waiting to see the dentist years later, puts it quite well: 'A step in the dark, but the right step, is a discovery, a new expression, the sudden unpredictable departure from the imagined straight line of invariable necessity; the deviation is the creative principle and our evidence of freedom.'

The first steps to independence are always the most difficult, and require the most courage. It was a luxurious and comfortable life that I was leaving, but as Braque observed: 'Liberty is always taken, never given.' And so the spirit moved me, as the Quakers say, to catch a train next morning down to Truro in Cornwall, where I stayed the night, and then moved on to St Mawes. The proprietor looked at me in surprise when I asked for a room at The Ship, and said: 'This is a pub. No rooms here.' Now, of course, it is a comfortable hotel, so as usual I was a bit premature. I knew the de Kays were in St Mawes, and at last I found them and wrote to my parents telling them where I was, and not to worry because I was all right. My father immediately came down to Cornwall, and I met him in one of those large and lifeless hotels in Falmouth.

I was a bit scared of meeting my father. I had come over from St Mawes by ferry-boat and I was full of trepidation, my heart in my mouth, feeling slightly sea-sick and wondering what to expect. He had stayed the night in a large hotel which I knew was rather empty; this added to my apprehension. If it had been full of cheerful holiday-makers, with an orchestra going, I felt I could have coped better with what might turn out to be an angry father. But I need not have worried, for I had forgotten that he rarely showed much emotion, even if he felt it. I had never seen him really angry with any of us.

He was kind and considerate, and all he did was to remind me of the anxiety I had caused to both him and my mother by bolting so suddenly into the blue. He reasoned with me and tried to talk me into not doing anything too rash. He suggested that he and my mother would consider letting me go to Paris (all expenses paid) to study painting. They did not want me to live in London on my own, but in Paris I knew that I would either have to live with their friends, or be watched over by them. I was more emotional than my father was, and argued to the best of my ability that I was ready to accept whatever the future held for me, and that it would be my own responsibility and not theirs if I came to grief. (I was evidently a budding existentialist!)

I pointed out to him that as a young man he had also left his family and sailed to the Argentine to seek his fortune and start a new life, and all I was doing was really to follow in my father's footsteps. This point did not occur to me until the heat of the moment; but I was a determined young woman and quite convinced of the rightness of my decision to leave home. I felt sorry for him having come all the way to Falmouth, and a little sad that he had not won the battle. He warned me that the future seldom turns out as expected, and told me never to be a pioneer as I would not get any thanks for it. I did not take his advice, and thinking it over I wondered why he had said that, since the Argentine had richly rewarded him. My own future did not seem so rosy: I was making a statue out of nothing but hopes, and trying to catch desire by the tail and turn it into a solid object. I stayed at St Mawes for a few weeks and then decided I had better return to London to find somewhere to live.

The family had by this time gone to North Berwick for the autumn, so I slipped back to Balfour Place and collected a few of my things, including the triple mirror of rosewood and ivory given me by Lord Athlumney. I found two rooms in Royal Hospital Road in Chelsea, practically adjoining the gardens of the Pensioners, for which I paid £1 a week. There was a gas ring for boiling water or rudimentary cooking. I think I paid 10s. a week for one meal a day at the Blue Cockatoo nearby. Although my parents had cut off my dress allowance, I still had £300 left me by an uncle, so I felt that I could manage for the time being. The next thing was to find a studio. I did not have to look far, for there was one going in Royal Avenue – small, but with a good light and its own entrance. All I had to do now was to produce masterpieces, and for some reason that was more difficult.

I was still going part-time to the Slade and had not yet found my feet, hands or head, and so I started off by painting the nearest things I liked the look of – an empty milk bottle and a pot of flowers. I stepped back to consider the result, and crashed straight into a long standing mirror leaning against the wall, losing my balance completely. Disaster struck as the mirror fell loudly to pieces on the floor, broken glass everywhere. Bad luck, was my first thought, my second that I would have to pay for it, but then my thoughts changed direction. I realised that it was only the old image of myself that I had smashed, and that I could exorcise the bad luck by creating a new image of a more liberated and imaginative being. I was suddenly transposed, this time through broken glass (rather than Cocteau's mercury-bath mirror) into the real illusory world of art.

One of the first things I did to celebrate my new freedom and to demonstrate my unflinching resolution was to shave the hair back from my forehead. This gave me an altogether more intellectual look, and I did a drawing of my new self which I still have.

In 1923, Robin Bartlett and I visited a nightclub called The Cave of Harmony. The show was a revamped Victorian form of entertainment founded by Elsa Lanchester and Harold Scott which became very popular in the twenties. Cabaret of this kind was then an innovation, and with the added spice of music-hall, the taste for it grew and later infiltrated other London theatres. In my memory it was indeed a cave, filled with a smokey atmosphere, mirrors and flashing light, while anthropomorphic cornucopias decorated the walls. Sandwiches, beer, foxtrotting and couples kissing competed with a one-act play by Aldous Huxley called *The Flower in the Mouth*.

In the twenties, in the visual arts as elsewhere, it was of course the day of the Bright Young Things. A generation starved of superfluity did not relish stark Cubist paintings or the 'Purism' of Ozenfant. They wanted colour, fizz and bubble. It was the cocktail age of Evelyn Waugh, for the universal relief that the war was over at last brought with it the necessity of having a good time.

It was not until 1924 that I gave up studying at the Slade, feeling that I had swallowed by then as much of its old-fashioned but valuable teaching that I could stomach. Robin and I decided to clear our heads with a trip abroad. We went off to Paris, for what we thought would be a few days, then ran into a young American sculptor friend of Robin sitting at a café. This was Dud Talcott, accompanied by his wife; after some high-spirited discussion, we all decided on the spur of the moment to go off to Spain to see the Goyas in the Prado. Next day, we set off by train for Madrid. The following morning we arrived so early at the Prado that the museum was still shut, but at last we got in, and wandered round that universe of painting, drinking in some of the vast collection, and looking at the Goyas in particular.

'We Poets in our youth begin in gladness; but thereof come in the end despondency and madness', wrote Wordsworth in 'Resolution and Independence'. I hoped this would be no reflection on my own resolution and independence (though I was to discover that marriage offered little enough of that), but the quotation was certainly relevant to Goya. The gladness was to be seen in the delightful gay-coloured lyricism of his designs for tapestry. But then he chose the follies of civilised society and the horrors of war to exercise his imagination. Saturn devouring his children is a nightmare, but also the 'Family of Charles IV' made an impression on me – the painting Gautier described as a representation of a grocer's family who have won the big lottery prize. But what a painter! A picture in a museum perhaps hears more silly remarks than anything else in the world, so we should comport ourselves with the masterpieces of art as with exalted personages – stand quietly before them and wait for them to speak to us.

From Madrid we moved on to Toledo, visited El Greco's house, saw the 'Burial of Count Orgaz', supreme orgasm of the soul, and walked through dramatic and fantastic dreamscapes, not quite sure whether we were part of a waking dream or part of reality. We travelled on down to Ronda, that great chasm in the earth's surface, that metaphorical abyss that every painter has to leap. Later on I remember Seville with its tower and walks by the Guadalquivir, and the cool and mathematical beauty of Granada, with the white pillars echoing the snow-white mountains in the distance – and so we came home via the monkeys of Gibraltar.

Of course during this period I went to see my parents, and was a bridesmaid at my sister Winifred's wedding in July 1925. My parents may have been troubled by my independent spirit, but mostly they strongly disapproved of my continued friendship with Robin Bartlett. I think they suspected that I had lost my virginity on some Cornish beach. (Well, they were not far wrong.) My mother used to make scathing remarks (Tonks was mild in comparison) about Titania and Bottom and the spell that some Puck at the Slade had cast over me. She had learned that Robin's parents let part of their house to tenants. 'They are nothing but boarding-house keepers,' she declared.

Back in my box in Royal Avenue, I worked hard and destroyed a lot of paintings. Nothing was going very well. Robin was still living with his parents in Prince of Wales Terrace, and although friends from Balfour Place came to visit me, I am sure they all thought I was crazy. Then one day Robin announced that he had found an enchanting cottage in the middle of an orchard in Varengeville near Dieppe in Normandy, for £9 a year, and also a studio and living quarters off the Fulham Road. He was convinced that we should get married in order to placate my parents and be able to move abroad more easily.

I do not know why I agreed, I think perhaps I was getting slightly bored in those two small bins and that box of a studio. I was still working in a tentative and unsatisfactory manner, and was displeased with everything I did. In those days, I was never satisfied with things as they were, and was always ready for a change. So I took the plunge, and we were married at St Luke's in Chelsea at the beginning of November 1925. Like Robin, I thought that going abroad and living together without being married would distress my parents. None of my family came to the church. I later realised that my reasoning had been faulty. They would have much preferred my continuing to live 'in sin' with Robin, rather than formalising what they saw as a *mésalliance*. I had, in fact, underestimated their Edwardian sophistication.

By December, there were other family matters to concern me. My father, despite a major operation, was dying of cancer. I went home to Balfour Place to find him lying quite peacefully in his room. He knew I was there but his attention was fixed elsewhere. 'Look Eileen,' he said, 'do you see those figures climbing up the curtains?' I could see no figures but I did not want to upset him, so my response was non-committal although I knew he was hallucinating. He assured me that the figures were moving and that they were really there, but he did not or could not describe them; he was very weak. Was it a Jacob's Ladder reaching to Heaven that he saw? I went out of the room and called my mother and the nurse before going into the street to stop an organ-grinder from making a horrible din beneath his window. My mother and myself were the only ones in his room when he died soon after. The hole he made in my life was filled with his ghost, for one cannot easily forget one's father.

My feelings may also have been touched with guilt, for I knew I had been a disappointment to him for causing his beloved wife so much anguish. But I think he also respected me, perhaps for being a little like him, and he tried to re-establish communications after I had left home. I remember that he asked me to the theatre, but either I mistook the day or the time of the performance – at any rate, I did not turn up when expected. My father was put out by this accident, for he thought my behaviour deliberate.

Prudent and circumspect in life, discreet in death, my father left me £1,000 a year, which in those days was quite a sum. I had never wanted to be rich – enough to live on, yes, but to be weighed down with possessions before you have time to think who you are in life, I was sure this was not healthy for a young artist. I really did not trust anything except my own ability, remembering how we had been transplanted from Heathfield to Tudor Hall. And taking a long view, I was right; by 1949 the family fortune had begun to crumble.

Robin and I did go to the thatched cottage he had found in Varengeville, feeling that we were escaping from the gloom of London. The cottage had a mud floor which was eventually covered with rugs; no sanitation except a hut or earth closet at the end of a field full of cows; no electric light or proper cooking facilities; and friends used to point out that the thatched roof was certainly a fire hazard with only one tap in the field. However, Robin and I thought it most romantic, for we were in a back-to-nature mood. You had to walk through a field full of cows and apple blossom to collect the morning milk and the occasional egg from the farm opposite. The sight of the trees laden with blossom, the black-and-white cows and the squabbling rooks in the woods nearby, needed an Impressionist's palette to do it justice.

Robin's parents were very keen to visit the young married couple, and so we decided to invite them for a long weekend. His mother looked around on arrival and assured me that she would not like to live in such surroundings, however picturesque. She was on her high horse because she had somehow heard of my mother's exclamation about the boarding house.

However, the social amenities did not satisfy Robin's parents, for to cap everything I did not even play bridge! But they made the best of a bad job, and we sat for hours talking banalities. I realised that I had merely swapped another family for my own, not so lively or so interesting – in short, a bad idea! I decided then that one should never be swallowed up or overwhelmed by one's relations, which was why I was truly happy when I met Joseph Bard and learnt that he had no family in England, only some relatives in America and Australia.

My marriage to Robin was an exploration, but being young I had cast a romantic glamour over it. At the time I may even have supposed myself to be in love, but later I realised Robin was the escape-hatch which freed me from the clutches of my family. I will always be grateful to him for helping me to leap into a new life, but at the time I had become very disillusioned with the whole situation. An incident after a large party given by Winifred and her new husband Hugh Mackintosh made me realise that the escapade was over. Hugh was a persuasive host who liked his guests to drink, and Robin was a quiet man unused to alcohol. On the tube home, Robin was violently sick, and this disgusted and appalled me. The tide had turned: that tube ride cured me of thinking I had found my mate.

There was something slow and rather heavy about Robin.

1a My father, James Agar. My mother persuaded him to sit; he was reluctant.

1b Family group outside Quinta la Lila, Buenos Aires, in about 1900. I am on the extreme left, sitting on my mother's lap. My sister Dorothy is standing next to us; the rest are uncles, aunts, cousins and a grandmother. Notice the hats.

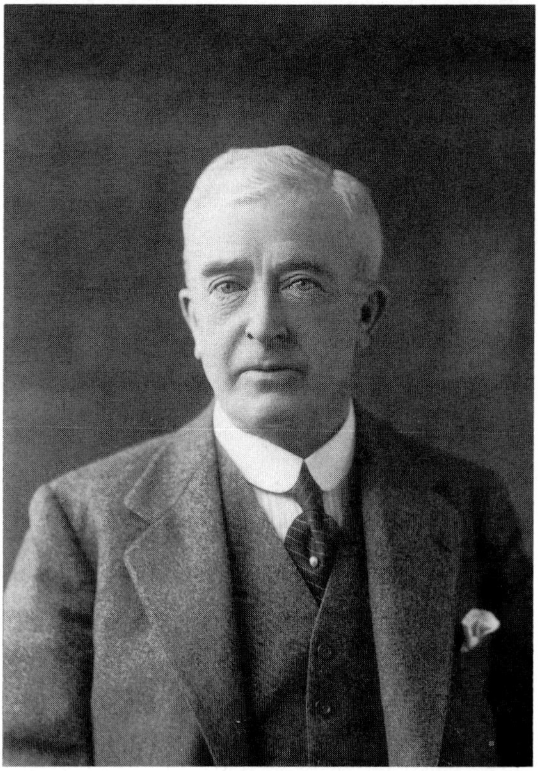

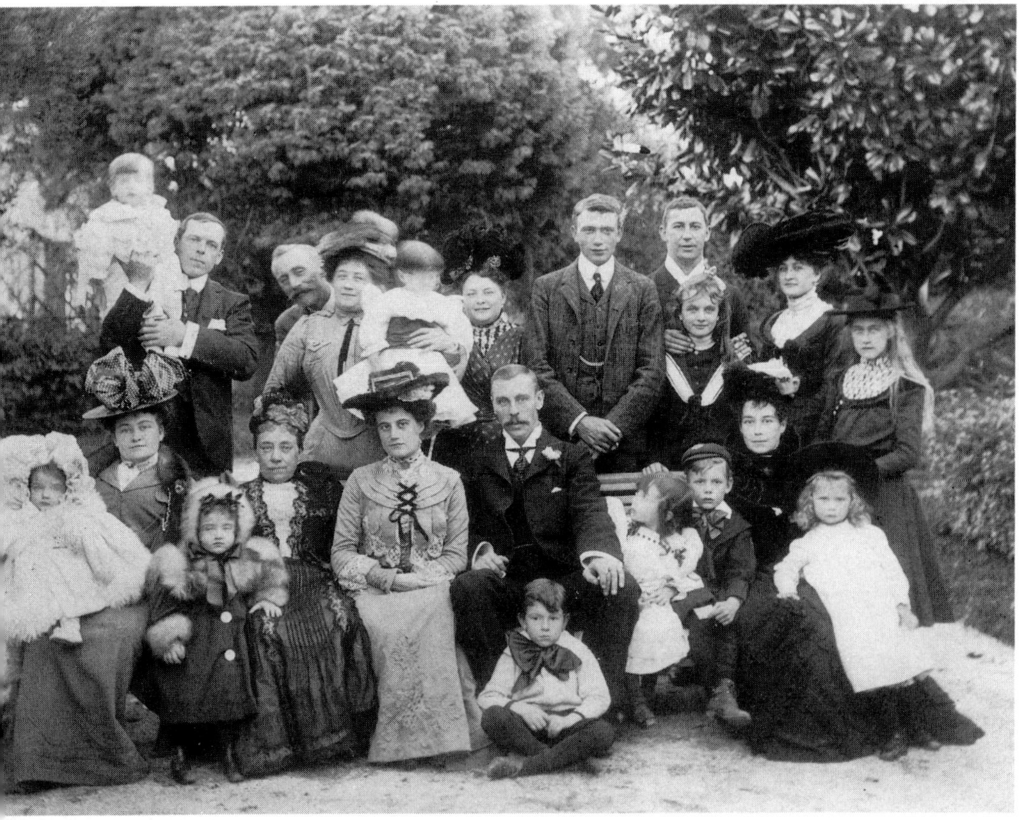

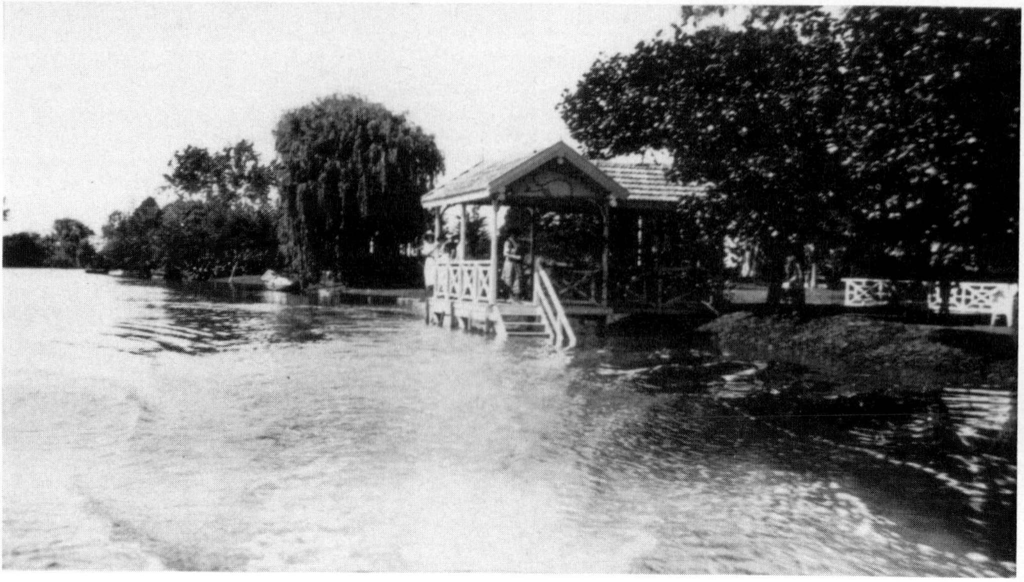

2a Joe Drysdale's boathouse on the Tigré river, Argentina, 1920.

2b Three Red Devils and Three Family Friends, 1905. Self, Dorothy and Winifred, dressed in red, with some admirers at Mar del Plata, Argentina.

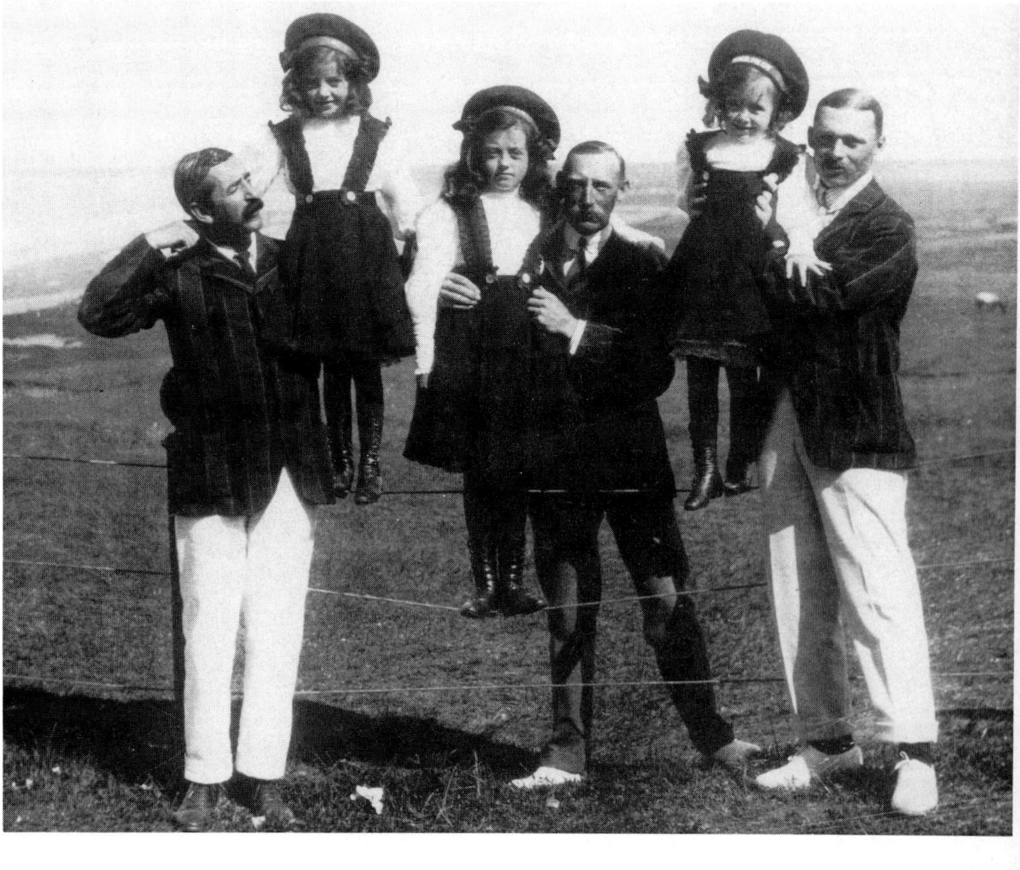

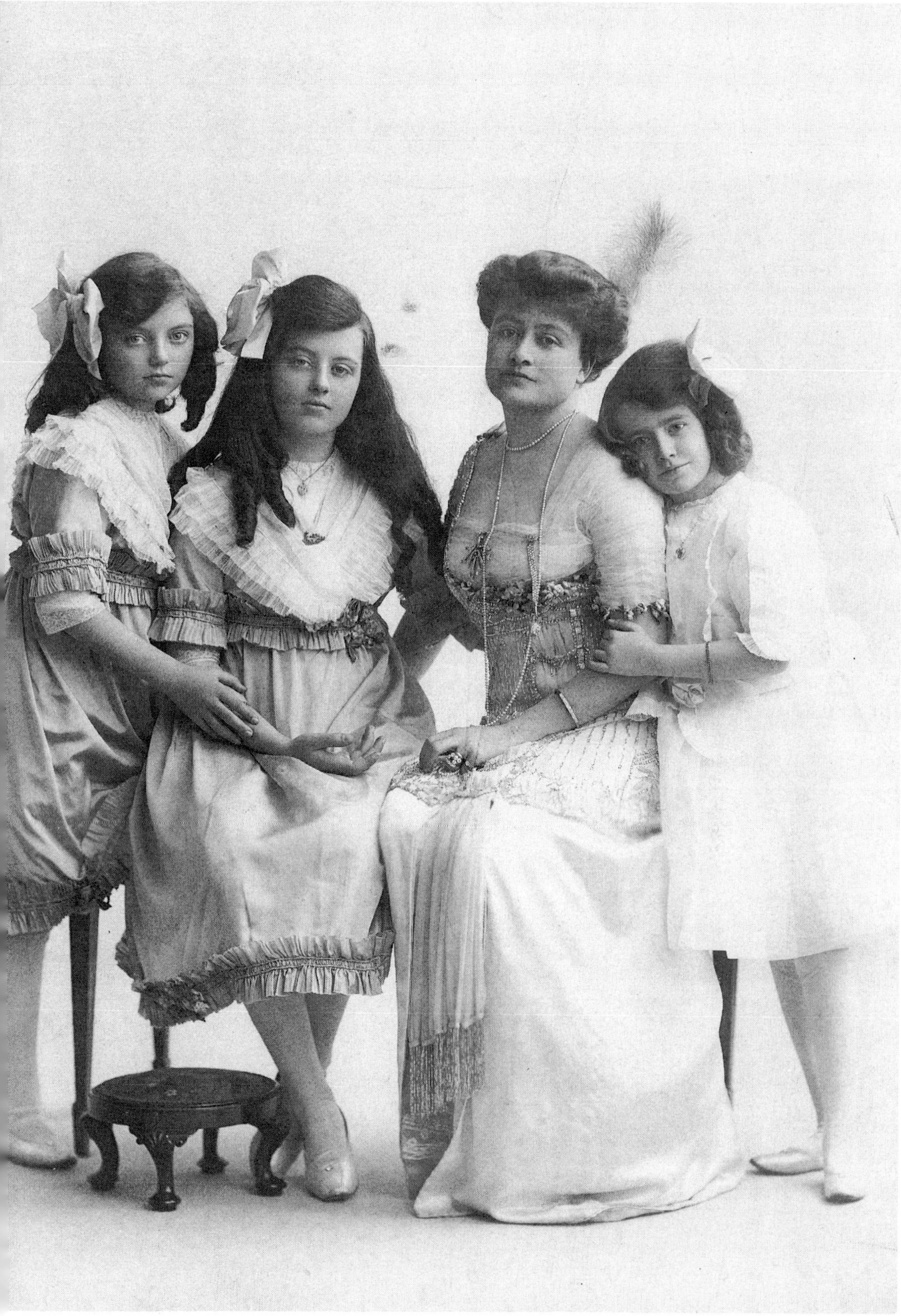

3 Self, Dorothy, Mama and Winifred in London *c.* 1912.

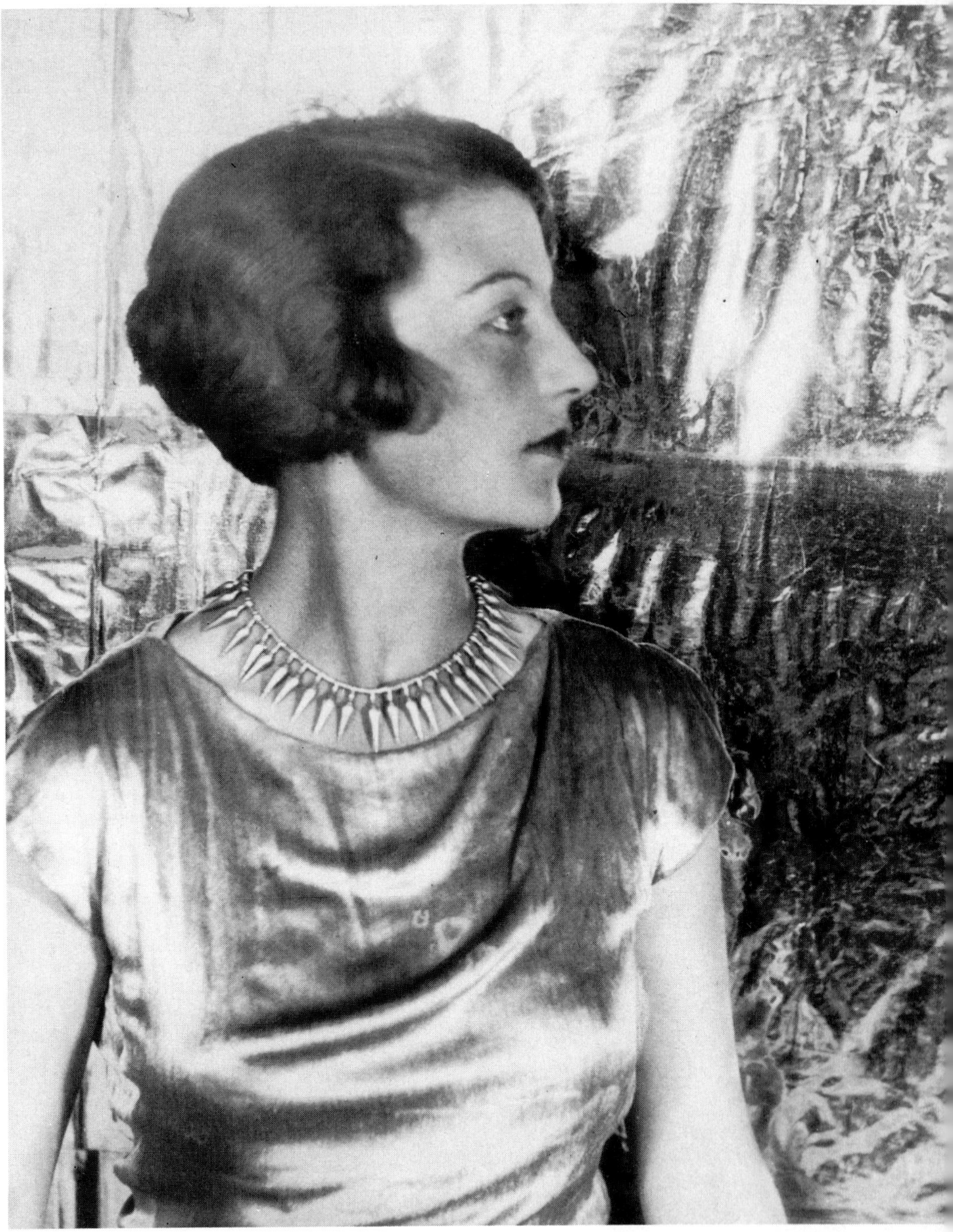

4 Self wearing a beautiful grey velvet dress
and an Egyptian necklace, photographed by Cecil Beaton in 1927.

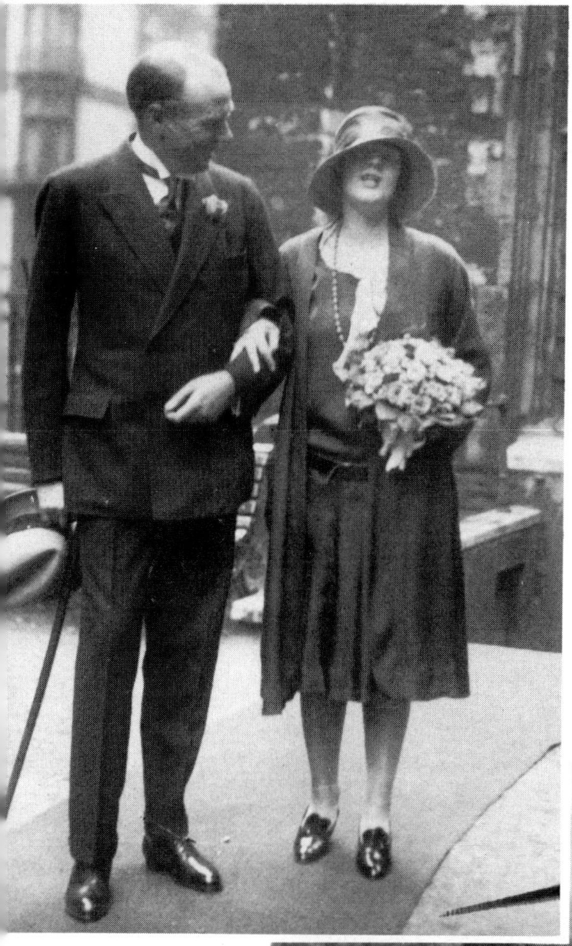

5a Sinclair Lewis and Dorothy Thompson on their wedding day in London in May 1928.

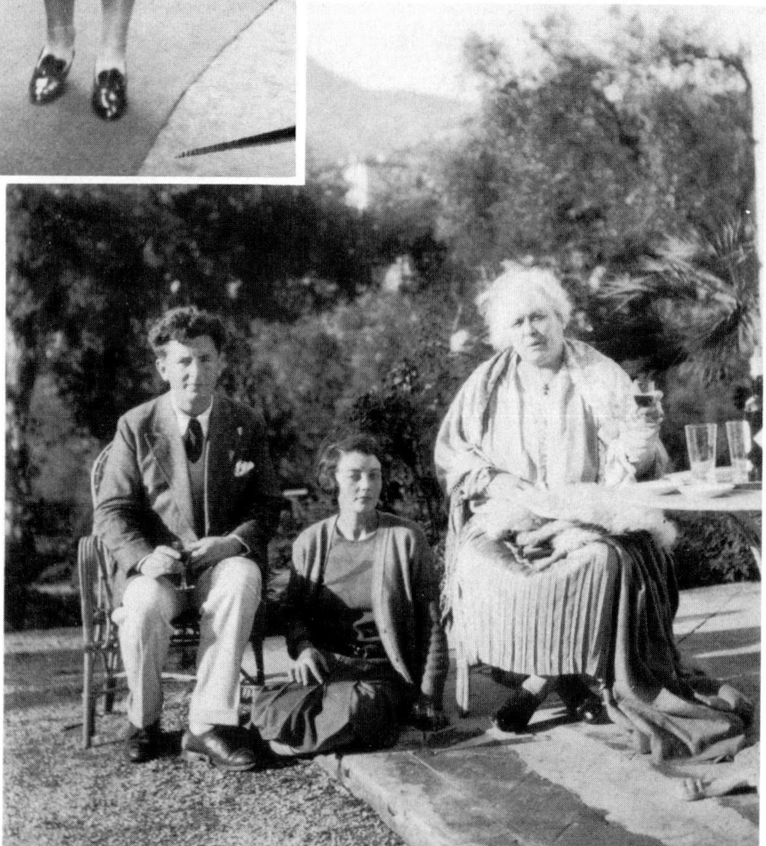

5b Joseph, self and my godmother Mita Sewell outside Villa Allegra, Cap Martin, South of France, in 1929. Wine to the fore.

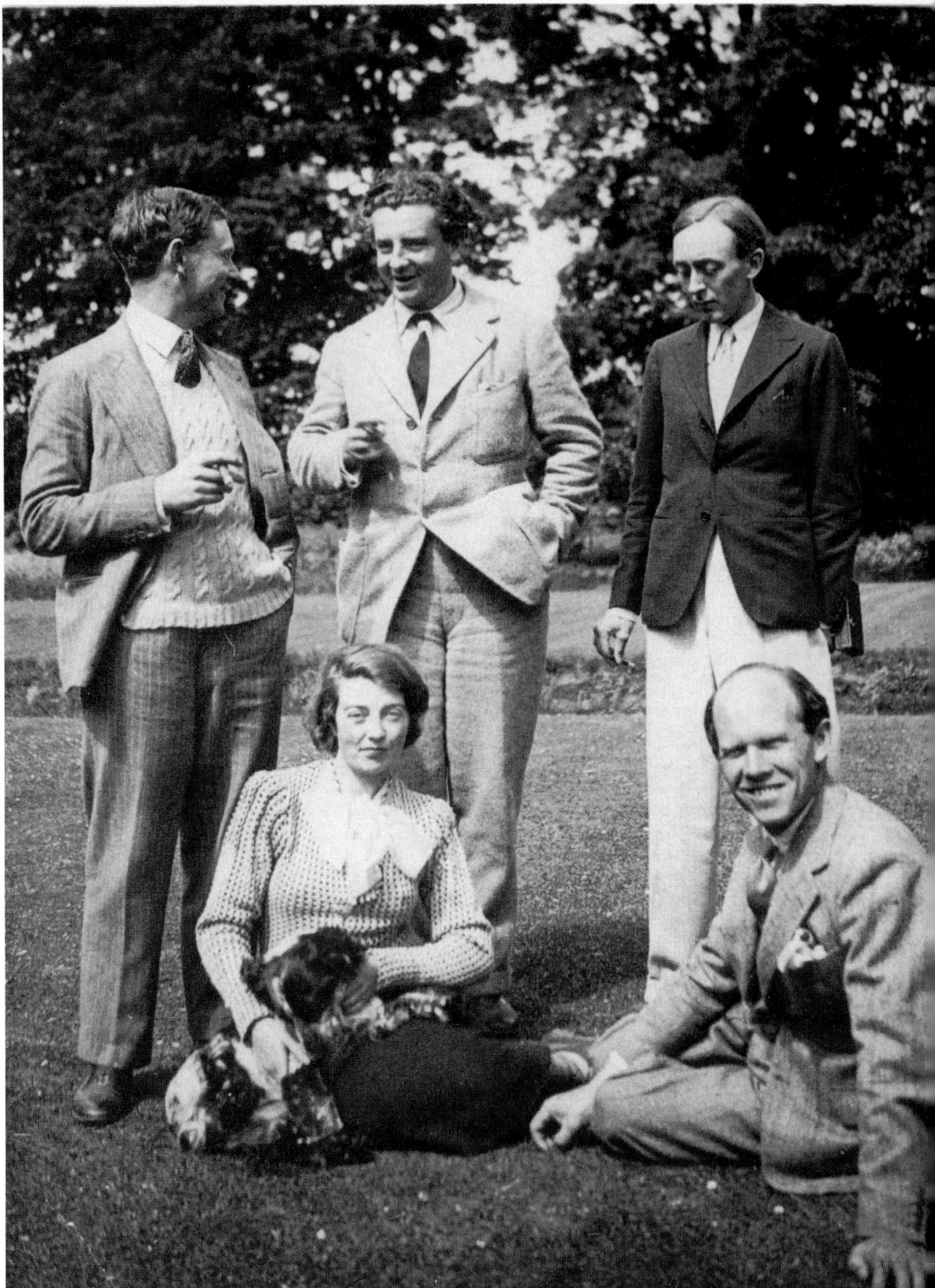

6 Joan Waugh's photograph of Evelyn Waugh, Joseph, Eddie Sackville-West, self and Alec Waugh at Oswalds, Bishopsbourne, Kent, during a stimulating weekend in 1933.

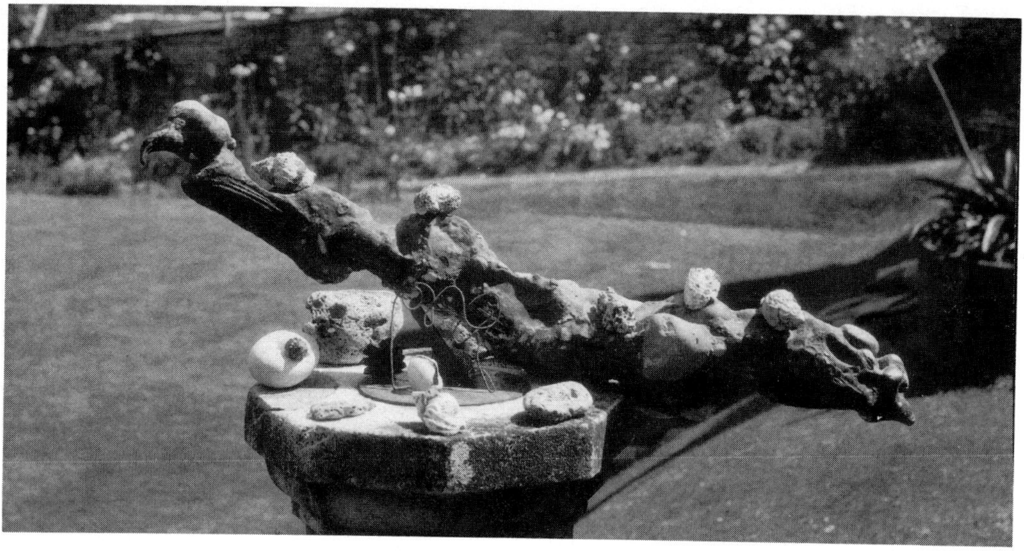

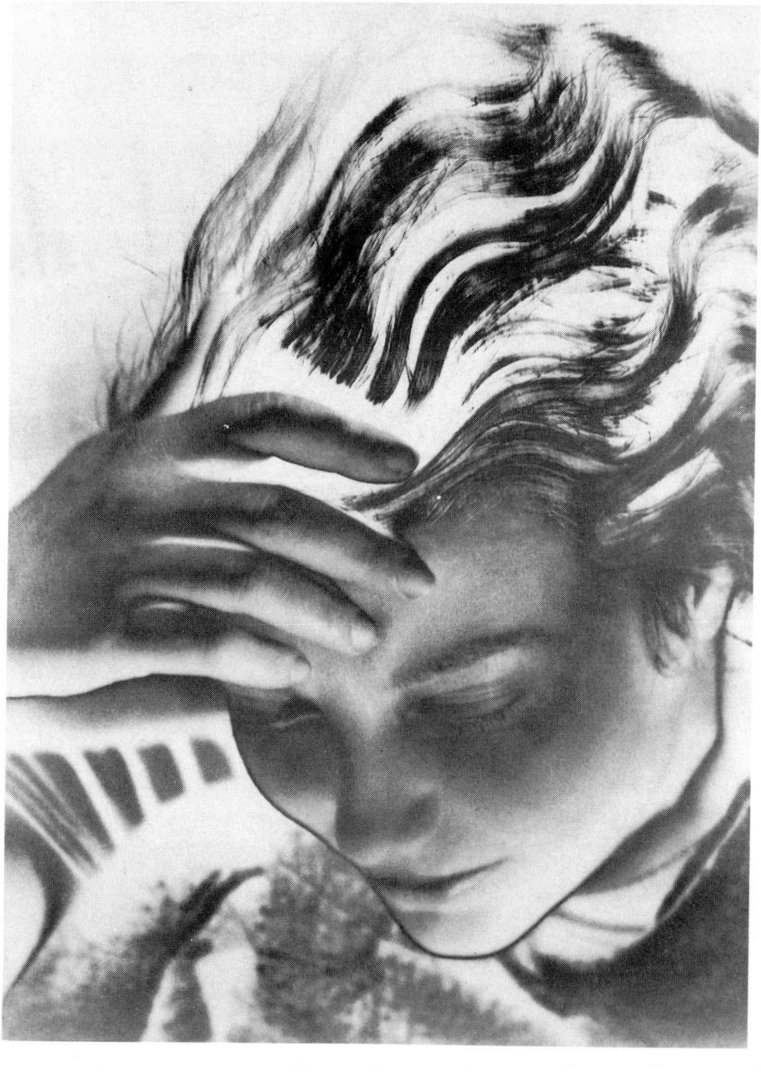

7a The seashore monster, on the sundial at Clarence Cottage in 1935.

7b Helen Muspratt's solarized photograph of myself in Swanage, 1935.

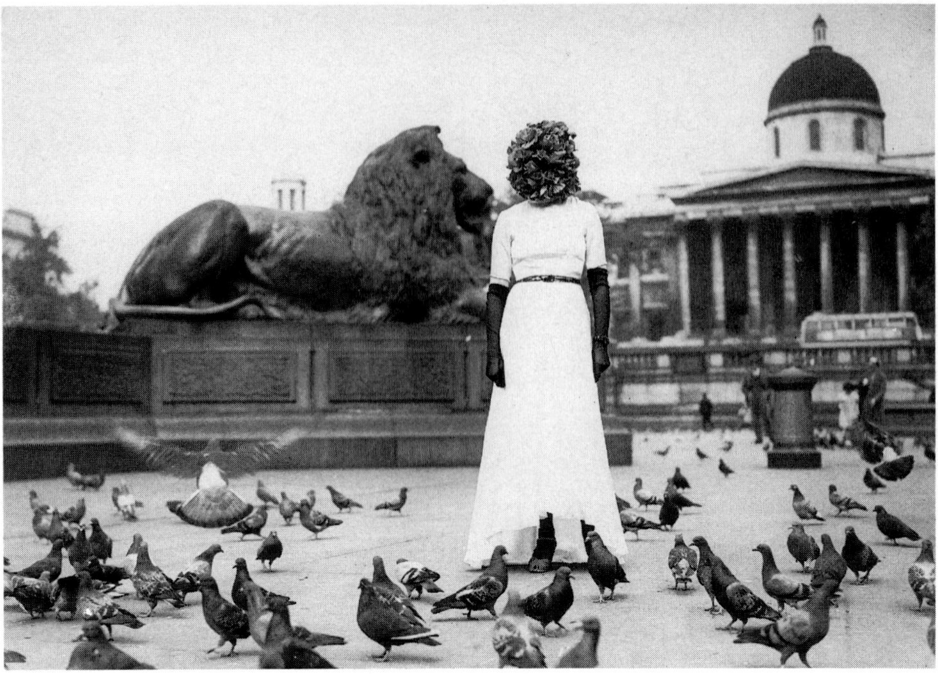

8a Sheila Legge, the Surrealist phantom, in Trafalgar Square, 1936.

8b Some of the exhibitors at the International Surrealist Exhibition at the New Burlington Galleries, London, in 1936. Standing (left to right): Rupert Lee, Ruthven Todd, Salvador Dali, Paul Eluard, Roland Penrose, Herbert Read, E. L. T. Mesens, George Reavey and George Sykes Davies. Sitting: Diana Brinton Lee, Nusch Eluard, self, Sheila Legge and a friend of Dali.

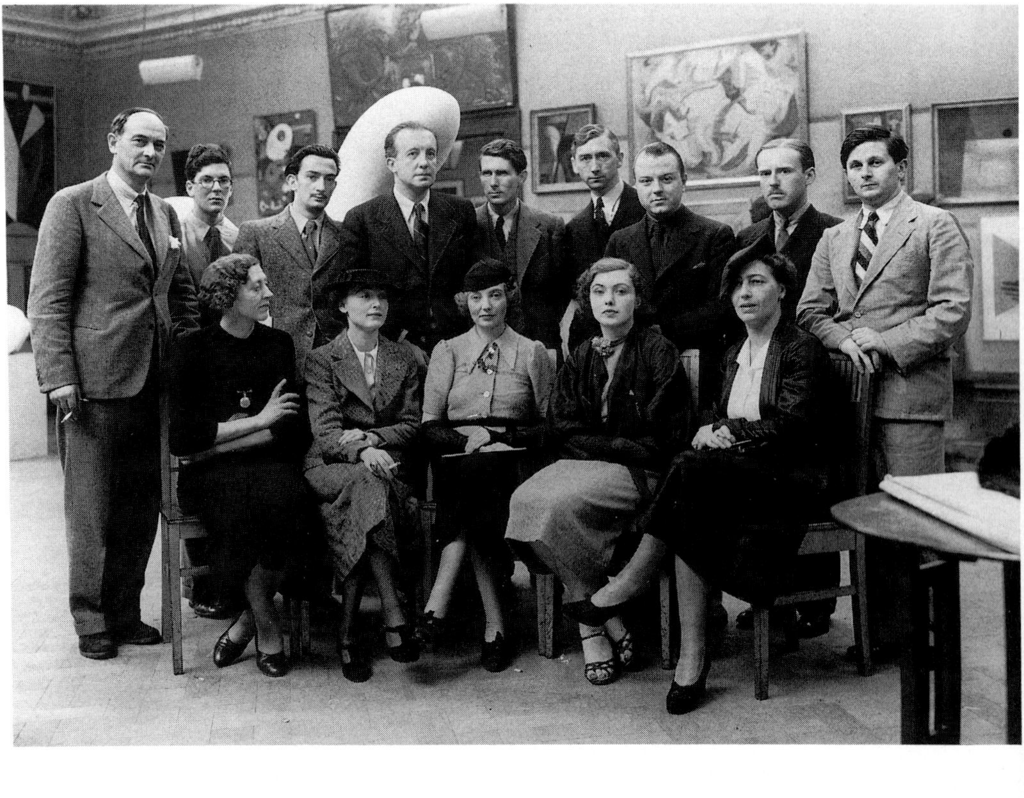

In a year of marriage I felt I had outgrown him, and so I left him for Joseph, who was a quick-witted, sophisticated man of the world. He had all the qualities that I felt Robin lacked, as well as being a good linguist, extremely handsome and erudite in philosophical matters. This time I really fell in love, and we got together soon after we met.

My poor mother did not approve at all of my way of life and refused to be associated with it. Most parents at that time wanted their children to develop along the lines of a plan fixed in advance. They shrank from a sequence of events which was open-ended to the future, because the specific outcome would be unknown to them. But whenever a pattern of order is changed, an entirely new set of harmonies is brought about, creating something which has not previously existed. That was precisely what happened when I met Joseph Bard.

CHAPTER THREE

The Sewing Machine and the Umbrella

As soon as I had married Robin in November 1925, we had moved into a flat in Fernshaw Road, Chelsea. Our new home consisted of basement living quarters and a ground floor studio which was supposed to be a shared working area. Robin was quite a good painter, certainly as far as academic technique is concerned, and he had an amusing gift for caricature. While we were at Fernshaw Road he painted a portrait of me (I wonder where it is now?), which Horace Kesteven said made me look as if I was wearing the trousers. Our living and working arrangements were far from ideal for we were thrown too much together, but then this flat was never intended to be a permanent home. The thought of living abroad was still immensely attractive.

Some time in the spring of 1926, I arrived with Robin at the Gate Theatre in Charing Cross. (The Gate Theatre was a club whose members were only interested in what they would otherwise be denied by the Lord Chamberlain.) Ridiculously, we had turned up on the wrong night and the theatre was closed. Robin suggested that we visit Warren Vinton instead, an American given to wearing loose brightly-coloured shirts without a tie, who had come to Europe to study culture. I had first met Warren at Leon Underwood's school where he had been busy doing a crash course in drawing and painting. He lived in Adelphi Terrace and entertained a great deal, so I accepted Robin's suggestion with alacrity.

When we arrived at the flat it was to discover that Warren had a guest in the shape of a handsome young Hungarian named Joseph Bard. Joseph had lately arrived from Berlin for a stay in London, while Warren's wife Helen Auger (a journalist), moved over to Berlin to stay with Dorothy Thompson, Joseph's masterful wife. I had heard about Joseph previously from Warren – how he was unhappy with a very brainy but dominating woman. Dorothy was just beginning to be a superstar journalist, and she had landed a plum job in Berlin, a city which Joseph hated. It was Dorothy's habit to lay out a programme for Joseph's daily behaviour – when he should take the dog Rolfe for a walk, how long he should take to dress in the morning, and so on. As Joseph said later with some asperity: 'Like all intellectual women, she thinks you can starch your prick at the nearest man's laundry.'

So I looked at this man from the faraway and to me mythical land of Hungary with a certain amount of interest: over six foot tall, well-built and with abundant wavy brown hair. Strangely enough he was wearing plus fours, country dress more suitable for golf than parties. I only discovered later that Joseph regarded this clothing as England's national costume, and wore it in tribute to a culture he much admired. I looked again at this man with the humorous eyes and the sensitive expressive oval face. Joseph had a sculptural head which turned into a splendid profile, completed by a Roman rudder of a nose. Cheek to cheek (or as near as our different heights would allow) we moved to a gramophone record; he had not got the faintest idea how to dance, but we circled the room slowly. There were three or four others present besides Warren, and after a time, when the rest had gone in search of snacks, Joseph went down on his knees (an old Hungarian custom?) and implored me to see him again. For a minute or two I was completely taken aback. But he intrigued me – he seemed sad and a bit lost. Warren had told me that Joseph was a quiet and studious person, witty and fond of women, though hating both publicity and journalism, which partly accounted for his present unhappiness. I decided that I would see him again.

From this moment of romantic attachment to a remarkable man developed a deeply loving friendship which was to ripen over forty years.

The truly imaginative person is permanently displaced in this materialistic world, yet Joseph's knack of sympathising with and understanding human nature gave him the necessary self-confidence to survive. He was a great teacher – not in the classical or mathematical sense (though he was later to examine for Oxford and Cambridge in Modern Languages) – but rather as somebody who could talk philosophically and yet with real feeling about human existence, someone who could cast a new and revealing light on the most mundane or difficult questions.

Joseph had the ability to awaken women to their full potential, if he was really interested in them, yet it was done in an oblique way without either being aware of what was happening. For instance, his first wife, Dorothy Thompson, worked as a publicist for the Red Cross when she came over from America to Europe. It was only when she met Joseph that she discovered that she was a born journalist, for he released a spark in her that led to her fame and success, besides teaching her the tricks of the trade, for he was working as a journalist himself at the time. His mother, I believe, used to tell him that he was some kind of Svengali.

Joseph was born in Budapest on 18 May 1892, the youngest son of middle-class parents who soon removed their family to a clap-board farmhouse in the tiny village of Elizabethville. He remembered going with his mother and the cook into the farmyard and hiding behind his mother's skirt while the chosen hen or duck had its throat cut for lunch. Joseph's father was a government inspector of farms whose job was to check procedures and the cleanliness of outhouses. Joseph sometimes accompanied his father on these visits, and once burst out: 'I don't want to see another pig in my life.'

Going to school, he used to pass a solitary building in the middle of a field. His parents were non-committal when he asked who lived there; only some time later did Joseph discover it was a brothel. His grandfather was the only member of the family who was an orthodox Jew. He wore a beard and the little black skull cap of those who observe the ritual ceremonies of the Jewish religion. Joseph's mother was a Protestant and his father believed that all religious ceremonies were unnecessary.

One of Joseph's most lasting memories was of finding a salamander in a running stream. This gave him immense delight, and he also used to keep silkworms as a child. When he was twelve years old, his mother took him to visit a sultan she knew who lived on an island in the Danube, and since he was only twelve, he was allowed into the harem to play with the slightly older children, some of them sons and daughters of the sultan. Joseph used to tell how he boasted to his schoolmates later that he had been in a harem as a visitor, and how he scandalised his friends.

Joseph remembered calling at the chemist in Kesthely on Lake Balaton in western Hungary, some time in 1906. His mother sent him for some medicine, and on the way he admired a poster for the circus that was going to perform next Sunday in the town. The image was of the leading artiste – a thing of tights, embroidered bodice and loose hair floating from an exalted cranium, leaping over a pair of white horses and about to land on another pair trotting in front. Joseph thought her beautiful, mysterious and desirable, and the suggestive lines in tights and bodice made his heart beat faster.

When he arrived at the chemist's shop, he peered through the window and saw that the shop was full. About half-a-dozen town notables were fingering a loose poster of the circus and laughing at the top of their lungs. There was a sudden silence when the boy entered, and he asked for something in a hushed voice. While taking the money, the pharmacist resumed his conversation with a solid figure who turned out to be the sheriff. But then he addressed the entire gathering saying: 'I suppose you will go and see her, and stay with her, and a week later, you will all be here again for medicines.'

There was a new outburst of laughter while the boy hurried out of the shop with burning ears. He had understood what had been meant, and the vicious connecting line between a thing of light and beauty and the chemist's jibe, seemed to him a blasphemy.

In Kesthely, the Bard family would stay at the pension of a sunny-faced Hungarian called Mr Talaber. The meals could be excellent, but if they were not, Joseph's quick-tempered mother would simply throw the food at the host or at least on to the floor. Nor did she hesitate to speak her mind. On a train once, mother and son were treated to the sight of a no-longer-young-lady constantly embracing and kissing her giant Alsatian dog. She kept saying that her husband was frequently abroad. Joseph's mother responded icily: 'Oh yes, a young dog can be more fun than an old husband.' Whereupon the lady and her pet promptly vacated the compartment.

His family returned to live in the capital, and Joseph always remembered with nostalgia the image of a civilised, quiet and happy Europe before the fists and bullets, when he was educated at a Latin-teaching public shool and at the Pazmany University in Budapest. In fact, his youth was spent in the midst of that old-fashioned and quintessentially European culture for which Henry James, Edna St Vincent Millay, Ezra Pound and so many other Americans were searching.

Budapest was a fascinating and attractive city, divided by the not-so-blue Danube. Buda was crowned by the old fortress and ancient Baroque palaces, while beyond were the marvellous gardens and courtyard restaurants filled with plaintive gypsy music. Great bridges spanned the Danube, some of them built by the British, and one a copy of the Albert Bridge in London. On the other side of the river was Pest, the modern town, the seat of Parliament. Here were the banks, and the centre of art as well as manufacture and politics. Along the broad avenues were political cabarets side by side with elegant and beautiful shops. All around were the coffee houses, and Joseph often remarked to me on the ironic wit, the sharpness of jokes and depth of dispute which took place during the constant conversations in these stimulating meeting places. The brilliance of intellect is well-attested by the number of Hungarian scientists, writers and musicians who have made their homes all over the world. As Kafka wrote: 'There are some things one can only achieve by a deliberate leap in the opposite direction.'

Joseph used to go to Vienna and Italy during the four-month summer break and often stayed in Reggio nell'Emilia, with a farmer's family. There was a huge old farmhouse, and an even bigger crop of sons and daughters who ran the farm and foregathered for meals around a long table, presided over by La Mama. No male was allowed to speak to another's wife, in case trouble ensued, though how that rule was kept with the amount of red wine consumed, I cannot imagine. Joseph certainly learnt to speak Italian fluently during these travels. I remember him telling me how in the train one day when he was fourteen or fifteen, he sat opposite an attractive woman, and, thinking to test his manhood, asked boldly (after they had conversed a little) if she would come out to tea with him. She looked him over and replied briefly: 'Meglior stare con la Mama.' ('Better stay with your mother'). He was very subdued for the rest of the journey.

In 1913 Joseph went to Paris where at the Sorbonne he heard Bergson lecture on intuition and Anatole France on the Classics. Already in some bookshops one could see copies of *Du côté de chez Swann* the first volume of Proust's *A la recherche du temps perdu*. Joseph lived in a little hotel in the Luxembourg quarter near the Senate and the Jardin. Here he met his student friends, as well as artists and their girlfriends. They were sorry for him being *seul* and one young sculptor who had two girls (he was working on a group of mermaids) handed over the prettier girl to Joseph to show that French *amitié* had no limit.

The Jardin du Luxembourg idyll ended with his return to Hungary, where aged twenty-two as a student of the Philosophy of Law, he lectured to the Hungarian Law Society on that little-known luminary, Augustus Pulszky. His audience consisted of eleven bald grey-bearded professors and judges, whose age, when added up, reached almost a thousand. At the time, Joseph worked in the office of a lawyer named Teller, and he used to play Mowgli (acting scenes from *The Jungle Book*) and other games with Teller's small son. This boy grew up to be the inventor of the Hydrogen Bomb. As Joseph often said, years later: 'If only I had strangled him. . . .'

The fertile decay of the Austro-Hungarian Empire led to Vienna becoming the most exciting intellectual centre in Europe before the First World War. In music there were Mahler and Schoenberg, Eugene Wigner in physics, Adler and Freud in psychology and the scintillating critic Karl Kraus, whose anti-paper *Die Fackel* (*The Torch*) was dedicated to making its readers 'morally aware of the essential distinction between a chamber pot and an urn'. Kraus was a prophet and satirist determined to expose the lie of Viennese life and warn of the cultural suicide he saw ahead. Joseph recalled the evenings when Kraus would take to the stage for an hour or two of savage reciting and acting. The feeling of impending doom was overpowering, yet the shouting, gesticulating figure on the podium was a figure of despair, powerless to alter what he saw would come to pass.

European culture as it was then, virtually ceased with the outbreak of war. For Joseph, the call-up for military service came in 1915. He joined the First Honved Regiment, a collection of the worst thieves and cut-throats he had ever met. (His wallet and the gold watch and chain given him by his father were stolen from his clothes while he underwent a medical examination in the next room.) He was informed by the Corporal that from now on he had better consider himself as pushing up the violets (no daisies in Hungary?), and that his head was only useful in preventing his collar from sliding up.

The horrors and calamities of those years smashed into his soul: horrific experiences on the battle-front during the war; hearing deserters being shot in the night at headquarters (mostly young men who had gone back to the land to tend the fields); the arrival of Bela Kun, and the tanks rattling through the beautiful streets of Budapest, with Chinese torturers at their helm; the Roumanian invasion, and then Horthy's white terror with countless bodies floating in the Danube.

Somehow Joseph survived, and became the correspondent of Reuter's and the Associated Press of America, as well as several English papers. In the meantime, he had to barter trousers and other clothing for eggs, chickens and similar produce, going into the country to gather enough food to feed his mother and himself. Most of his collection of paintings went in exchange for meat: luckily, he owned some landscapes with cows painted into them for which an art-loving farmer would pay the market price, counting the heads scrupulously.

Those were dramatic years to have lived through, and there is no better way of capturing them, than by quoting from Joseph's notebooks.

Hungary: 1 May 1919

Early in the morning we lined up in the Red Square to join the jubilant procession. Workers, carts, and lorries were coming from all directions and on each cart and lorry glorified in red trappings, were displayed the tools and implements of a trade. Here and there, we saw an armoured car with machine-guns manned by slit-eyed, evil-looking Mongolian terrorists, a present from Russia to the new government. The square and streets were hideous. Cheap red carpets lined the pavements, red flags were hanging from windows, and resting on quickly-built, thirty-foot pillars glowered the huge, plaster-cast head of Lenin. There was one of these monster-heads on every corner. Slowly the procession began to move. We were shivering in the cold morning and with the icy wind came torrents of rain. The carpets and draperies were soon drenched and we were marching through red rain-water and red mud, singing the 'Internationale'. The rain was beating down on us, the singing was loud and cheerless, and the pillars supporting Lenin's head were shaking ominously in the wind. And then it happened.

The monster-head tumbled down and I felt dumb, sickening pain in my right shoulder. Friends were helping me to stand on my feet, my right arm was useless but I managed to bend and pick up a chip of Lenin's head with my left hand, and I put it in my pocket. I was taken home in an ambulance and had to eat Sauerkraut alone for a week. I tried to identify the chip which I had salvaged from the pavement and my nurse thought it was a bit of Lenin's nose. But as it was too round and curved for that, I think I am right when I say that my memento was almost certainly a bit of Lenin's colossal cheek.

In the spring of 1921 Joseph met Dorothy Thompson in Budapest at the house of his friend and erstwhile employer Rustum Vambéry, the man who had been Joseph's law professor at university as well as a cabinet minister. Vambéry used to make sure that Joseph was introduced to whom he thought were the right people. For instance, he introduced Joseph to his own English-speaking wife, and of course Joseph very soon seduced her. For in Hungary, if you did not seduce a good-looking married woman, it was a form of insult. I do not suppose Joseph had to force himself exactly, for he was well-endowed with erotic instincts.

Dorothy Thompson was an attractive and vivacious woman with a quick intelligence, and she struck up an immediate rapport with Joseph. In 1923 they were married in Vienna, with the Vienna Opera Chorus singing at the reception, and Colonel Causey, economic adviser to the Austrian government, giving a banquet for them later in his suite at the Bristol Hotel.

Dorothy Thompson was the dynamic daughter of an American methodist minister, a thrusting, blue-eyed presence who was an energetic money-maker. She had a very strong ego which went marching down publicity street, behind a brass band at times, for she liked to run the show, both domestically and conversationally. She was what Rebecca West later called 'rattling good company', and was formidably self-confident. Even in her teens, she had preached the Sunday sermon when her father fell ill. Her style was simple, direct and unaffected.

Some months after their marriage, the couple went to Rome for a belated honeymoon. It was business as well as pleasure, as Dorothy had been commissioned to cover the International Conference of Suffragettes which was opened by a youthful Duce with words of praise for women who devoted themselves to husband, children and kitchen. These words were carefully mistranslated by the interpreter into praise for international suffragettes, and were received with applause by the largely American audience and with irony by Joseph and Dorothy. Amongst those attending the conference were two elderly spinster doctors, who, hearing of the newly-weds, presented Joseph with a booklet laying down the healthy number and sequence of sexual intercourse, on a weekly basis. This was printed on soft paper, and was later of great usefulness.

In Vienna, Joseph enjoyed the friendship of the painter Oskar Kokoschka, Adolf Loos the architect, and Baron Hatvany, the owner of vast estates in Hungary. Kokoschka was one of Loos's protégés, another artist like Kraus who used his skills to accuse and expose contemporary society. He painted devastating portraits and wrote mystical expressionist plays. Could reason or intellect ever save society from corruption? On the whole, Joseph's experience affirmed the belief that when decay sets in, every member of the body social is affected, no one remains untouched. Consequently, he approached the quarrels raging over psychoanalysis with mistrust, thinking that by lowering Man's status further than Kepler and Darwin had done, the analysts would mortally humiliate Western man's pride. Joseph then envisaged the average man turning round and automatically consulting the nearest ape whenever a problem arose. It was not his idea of enlightenment.

Joseph felt no great personal love for Freud, for around 1923–4 Freud spoiled a promising love encounter between Joseph and an American woman, a dollar princess of Tiffany stature. She asked Freud's advice, and he vetoed the affair under penalty of dropping her as a patient. Evidently the great magician had her in thrall; what an Oriental despot, said Joseph.

Soon after the First World War, Joseph paid a visit to Villa Wahnfried, to interview Cosima Wagner. He was greeted by a stocky figure in knickerbockers and pullover, with very little hair mixed with a few autumn leaves, who appeared from the garden. It was Siegfried, the music of the future, who informed Joseph that since Wagner's fight with Nietzsche, Cosima had withdrawn from contemporary events to live with memories of the past and receive no visitors.

Siegfried Wagner was very friendly and talked about the raging inflation and the contemporary difficulties while entertaining Joseph to tea in his cosy dependance behind the villa. His many children were romping in the garden, and an occasional 'Wolfgang, keep quiet!' thundered through the studio window. The spirit of Houston Stuart Chamberlain – one of Hitler's mentors – seemed alive and at home there, but Siegfried appeared to Joseph as a sympathetic character, in times when hatred was still poisoning Europe's air.

Joseph's life with Dorothy Thompson was happy for the first two years in Vienna; to start with, he was out of Hungary, which had become a nightmare to him, whereas he felt at home in the Austrian capital. But gradually Dorothy became more and more immersed in her journalistic work, and with people coming and going continually, Joseph could not concentrate on his writing. So when a big journalistic job was up for grabs in Berlin and Dorothy landed it, Joseph felt that he had had enough of what Sinclair Lewis later called 'the situation'.

Joseph arrived in London in 1926, and I, from a totally different background, a different world indeed, met this man from what the Romans used to call Pannonia, who was to stay beside me for nearly fifty years.

After that first meeting, we met again several times, and I remember one sunny afternoon in Richmond Park when Joseph told me about his first unhappy love affair. While still at university he fell in love with his sister's music teacher – they must both have been eighteen or nineteen. Joseph's parents were scandalised when they found out and made life very difficult for him. He told me how he used secretly to carry soup in his pocket for Yolan, his girl, when she was living alone and he thought she was ill. When he eventually fetched a doctor to her, Joseph was told that Yolan was pregnant. Joseph's parents must have found out or guessed, for one morning at breakfast Joseph's father roared out; 'Bring him more eggs! He can't do this on one!'

As for us, we met when we could. Throughout a long spring day, Joseph would talk to me in a low, clear, voice with slightly European accent, concerning things both human and divine. Never before had I realised how the voice can be a second face. At the same time, Joseph's manner was so playful, his language so simple, and so affectionate the glance of his brown eye, that though he arrived in England with a Byronic reputation (my family and friends warning this naive young girl to beware of that hedonistic inhabitant of the European mainland), I could not have cared less, for Joseph, to me, was irresistible.

The fortuitous encounter of the two mutually distant realities, beautiful like the chance meeting upon a dissecting table of a sewing machine and an umbrella – such was the meeting of Joseph and myself; the shock effect of a putting out of place, creating the sharpness of a new focus. I could not help realising now that the friendly relationship I had had with Robin had held none of the psychic attraction that existed between Joseph and myself. It was a fresh and potent intoxification, a re-birth indeed.

We do not know what sort of man we want before we know what sort of woman we are. I had never met anyone to match Joseph's vital and courtly personality. A real European, his head overfed and his heart starved, not a good diet for anyone so warm and talkative. But culture-hungry as I was, in some strange exchange he filled my head while I occupied his heart, though I was totally unaware at that time, of my impact on the opposite sex. This may seem slightly unbelievable now when it is the norm to be precocious and self-conscious, but we grew up more slowly then, and I was still intent on enjoying a relatively carefree youth, for as long as possible.

I was a good listener, but rather reticent like my father, while Dorothy Thompson could never stop talking. I felt inarticulate at the time, unfolding only slowly like a plant. Joseph had a ready command of language: his conversation was always interesting and never commonplace, and stimulated by a personal encounter, he could keep a conversation sparkling like a bouquet of *feux d'artifices*. He found it difficult to relate to anything as mechanical as a tape recorder, and even a pen sometimes refused to flow at his command. He was at his best with a human being in front of him, though he was a splendid letter writer, outrageously funny when he knew there was another person at the other end of the envelope, not an impersonal collective body of indefinite shape, known as the reading public. In that sense he was very much a private person, horrified for instance when one of Dorothy's friends exhibited what he called, 'a purseful of sexual objects'. He was offended by this breezy practical approach to the mysteries of love.

I had flu very badly that year, and for a while left Fernshaw Road for a nursing home in Beaumont Street (just off Marylebone High Street) run by Robin's aunt. When Joseph came to see me there, the matron teased me about my good-looking foreign visitor. Robin had arranged the cottage in Varengeville partly as a place for me to recuperate in, so we departed for France. I could not wait to see Joseph again, and so made the excuse that I was needed on family business in Paris.

I stole a week with Joseph in a lovely little arcaded town in the Austrian hills called Feldkirch, where we ate mountain trout straight from the stream. One morning, having decided to get up at five o'clock (we had bedded down for the night in a mountain hut), we determined to scale the mountain, slip down the valley and cross the frontier into Liechtenstein, knowing that it would be an all-day tramp. We had been told that the route, although not easy, was marked. I set off in a cotton frock and tennis shoes. We did not realise that the trek involved rope ladders (already in place I am glad to say) and other neck-breaking experiences. But we had the pleasure of seeing chamois on the icy slopes and cooling our wine on a glacier, besides the rare joy of each other's undiluted company. After having nearly fallen over countless precipices, we dropped down to Vaduz, tired but victorious.

The week's idyll was soon over, and I returned to Varengeville and Robin. I thought of inviting Joseph, but decided that the cottage was far too primitive for his sophisticated tastes. I used to tell him that Dorothy had spoiled him for the simple life, he had got so used to big hotels and endless meals. A top hat and white gloves were more to his taste at that time! To me it was a great relief to be slumming it after the constraints of life with my parents. When my sister Winifred came to stay for a few days and suggested we clear the loo out every day instead of once a week, I drew myself up (to my full height) and said, 'You are not living in the Ritz now!'

Although Robin was not my ideal partner, it was still very romantic in that cottage and I have warm memories of our stay there. Evelyn Waugh used to tell me that one should not own more than can go into a suitcase, but that prospect was too daunting. Besides, my inner life as a painter has been fed by the objects I have accumulated around me.

Meanwhile, Joseph wrote to me from the Savoy in London where he was staying with Dorothy Thompson. Towards autumn I began to feel bored and frustrated at having to entertain Robin's relations; I was also reading Spengler's *Decline of the West* surrounded, appropriately enough, by falling apples. This book made a great impression on me and I planned to escape and meet Joseph at Igls, near Innsbruck, as he had been imploring me to do.

I arrived at Innsbruck before him; in fact, I was in such an emotional turmoil at the revelations of Spengler and the excitement of meeting my surreptitious swain, that I started out for Austria not knowing what day or time of day Joseph's train would arrive. But I was in a telepathic trance, and was on the platform at Innsbruck on the right day and at the right time to greet Joseph as he stepped off the train.

Igls was a small village in a lovely undulating valley, and Joseph at once started a novel, inspired by the peacefulness of our surroundings. We would get up early and both work in the morning, I practising how to capture light on landscape with gouache or watercolours, and he writing in longhand. The novel called *Shipwreck in Europe* was about an American in Paris, and the way he was affected by European culture. *Shipwreck* was dedicated to me, and I was happy that our meeting together for three or four short weeks should have such a brilliant result. Joseph also talked a lot about another idea, much more complex, which was to compose an ambitious philosophical work, to be called *The Mind of Europe*. One chapter was about to be published by *Harpers Magazine*, under their title 'Why Europe Dislikes the Jew'. There were to be other chapters on nationalism, religion in Europe, and on science and art. Joseph was attempting to formulate the historical background of Western culture when it was already changing shape and becoming amorphous, and disintegrating in the process.

I had written to Robin to say that I was not going back to him, but would stay with Joseph. Robin kept sending me distressing telegrams threatening suicide any moment. Joseph, wiser, assured me that the mood would pass – and of course, it did. In the meantime, I inadvertently let the cat out of the bag, a favourite occupation of mine, by sending a postcard to Warren Vinton from Igls. He immediately relayed my whereabouts to Dorothy in Berlin, who already knew that Joseph was in Igls. It did not take much brain power to guess that we were together. Dorothy wanted to come to Igls, but Joseph dissuaded her, and instead they met in Vienna to talk things over.

The Chinese say: 'A woman with a long tongue is a flight of stairs leading to calamity'. Dorothy was dismayed and heartbroken at the thought of losing Joseph. Yet the marriage was obviously breaking down. Dorothy was continuously surrounded by hard-drinking journalists in Berlin, and her friends were hardly aware that she had a husband, he was so seldom seen. When Joseph paid her a brief visit, Dorothy scarcely noticed his presence. His aim was to write thoughtful books, hers to live with sensation and the news of the moment. There were incompatibilities of ambition as well as temperament.

In spite of this unsatisfactory life, Joseph was very troubled by the new state of affairs. He was torn between the intense desire to come to England with me, and what he saw as his duty, which lay in going back to Berlin and attempting to continue his life with Dorothy. She had compromised by this time, in her efforts to keep him by her side, and suggested that they allow each other more freedom. He could see whom he wished (Eileen included) as long as they did not break up altogether.

So at the end of our Austrian stay in 1926, Joseph went back to Berlin, where most of his books and belongings were, to sort things out. On his return he discovered that Dorothy had left a letter saying that to ease her unhappiness she had spent the night with an ardent hard-drinking journalist called Floyd Gibbons. Joseph, angry and disgusted that Dorothy was no Caesar's wife, packed and left Berlin within a day or two. When I met him in London and heard this odd reaction on the part of a wayward husband, I rebuked him for his double standards. It seems the height of hypocrisy, but what a man did in those days apparently did not matter, whereas for a woman of Dorothy's high moral standards her behaviour was shocking. Joseph admitted that his anger was probably an excuse to get away: he said that he could no longer stand forty people at breakfast!

And so a new life began for us in London. In 1927, Joseph and I took a flat in Fitzroy Square in an old Georgian house which had once belonged to the famous opera singer Adelina Patti, and where Virginia Woolf had lived for two or three years. It had one large room running the depth of the house, with windows at either end and an outlook over the square. We divided the big room with a curtain, partly for warmth and partly out of practicality, and I painted most of the portraits I ever did in that room. Just off it was a tiny study for Joseph, and then up a short flight of stairs were the bedroom, small kitchen and dining room; so in fact it was a maisonette.

We went to an agency nearby to find someone to cook and clean the flat for us, and the person behind the desk explained that she had someone but she was dark and would we mind? So out of curiosity I asked; 'How dark?'

'Well,' she explained, 'She's not as dark as the inkpot, but she is darker than the writing desk.'

We engaged this curiously chromatic person with the delicious name of Christina Santanna, and discovered that we had chanced upon a gorgeous negress from Portuguese West Africa, who cooked the most luscious fish dishes and other exotic meals for us. She could never resist a brilliant-coloured scarf or other trifle, and rolled on the floor laughing when Joseph did a painting of her. When our friends saw Christina they would talk of the famous Manet painting of the nude model and the negress with the bunch of flowers, and I was often asked if I had engaged Christina deliberately in order to pose as a latterday 'Olympia', an association which always amused me.

At night Fitzroy Square would be haunted by the shadowy shapes of dark men waiting to take Christina out, but when we asked her to come with us to Paris, she said she had a fourteen-year-old daughter, and would never dream of taking her to such a wicked city. Alas, we lost her, when she joined the Chorus of the Blackbirds at the Coliseum, and we could not match the sum of 7 guineas a week they were offering her.

At this time, 1927, I sat for Cecil Beaton, a family friend who used to love the dancing at our parties. He was starting up as a photographer in his mother's house in Sussex Gardens. His bedroom, which he used as a studio, was full of backgrounds he had painted or thought up. Somehow he turned me into a very glamorous-looking girl with a couple of large eyes and a saucy but determined air.

In May 1927, Dorothy Thompson wrote to Joseph from Geneva saying that if she ever found a gentleman Eileen, everything would be alright, but meanwhile she thought occasionally of suicide. Perfectly idiotic, she said, but she wished very much that I would go to Geneva and meet her. As we had never met, I thought it a good idea, and said at once that I would go. So we met in her large bedroom at the Hotel Richemond and I liked her plump appearance immediately. I found her forthright, putting a brave face on things. She probably expected a battle with me, but she got none.

It seemed the most natural thing in the world to meet someone I had heard so much about, and we both carried off the confrontation with ease, generating a considerable amount of respect for each other in the process. Although I realised I was talking to someone with a powerful personality, Dorothy was so life-enjoying that I knew we could have got on well together if it had not been for the fact that we were both in love with the same man. But was she really in love with Joseph? She had refused to let him accompany her to the States when she went back in 1925 for a few weeks, saying that he would not like America. She had both eyes on an influential and exciting profession at a time when the continent was in chaos after the war; only a small mental squint was reserved for Joseph, until she discovered that she had lost him, and then she became an avalanche of woe.

For my part, I had come to Geneva to convince Dorothy that I was no husband-stealer. At no time did I try to persuade Joseph to break up his marriage – in fact, I had no intention of marrying again – but I wanted to remind Dorothy that it was her profession as a journalist which stood in the way of their continued life together. She was completely absorbed in her work, which sent her all over Europe in search of scoops. She seemed to me to be such a capable woman that even if fifty husbands let her down, she would still control her life admirably.

Dorothy insisted that Joseph misled her as to the person I was. 'Eileen is brave and steely,' she wrote to him after our meeting, 'knowing what she wants, and determined to get it. She is a person of talent and character, of whom I am the least little bit afraid. She is not inarticulate, not naive, and not in the least helpless, but far more of a personality than I had dreamed. I hope to know her better.' Generous words I think from someone who had suffered because I had come into Joseph's life.

Dorothy was a splendid woman, but not to be married to. She loved entertaining and would dominate any gathering with her highly articulate nature, holding forth on the latest political crisis. Writing to Joseph, Dorothy told him that he had meant so much to her that in one thing he stood in a class quite by himself: he made her dumb. This was quite an achievement, she said, and due to his being one of the most terrifyingly articulate of persons. However, Dorothy had more than a touch of the actress in her make-up, as she went on to say that she must do something heroic like swim the Atlantic! Within a year she had married the American novelist Sinclair Lewis, which I suppose was the equivalent.

Joseph had rather a guilty conscience about leaving Dorothy so abruptly, so it was with a sense of relief that he learnt of her engagement to Sinclair Lewis. Also, the tearful flood of recriminations gradually lessened in her letters. Before that happened, Joseph had taken a room in Torrington Square, not far from the flat in Fitzroy Square. We had been warned that proctors often prowled around looking for couples unlawfully living together before divorce proceedings had begun.

For a time our meetings may have been clandestine, but I was quite happy to have it openly acknowledged that we were living together. I was loth to tie myself up again, and despite my mother's extreme disapproval, it was over ten years before I married Joseph, so it can hardly be said that I grabbed him.

One disadvantage of living together in those days in an unmarried state was the way some men reacted to you. I remember Warren Vinton ringing me up one day and inviting me for a drink at Adelphi Terrace. I went expecting another party, but it was champagne *à deux* followed by the suggestion of a weekend away together. I resented being pawed by this ostensible friend of Joseph and made my feelings quite clear. Warren complained: 'You're no bohemian! I thought you'd left home to be more free!' I knew it was time to make my escape, and told a disgruntled Mr Vinton that I had a taxi waiting.

In Fitzroy Square, I painted with the self-assurance that I had lacked when working in Royal Avenue. Then, everything I had done was academic and timid in approach, careful of other men's teaching, not for a moment declaring itself. Now, without thinking, I was free of all constraint and painted almost as naturally as I walked or talked. The work was still of course tied to the model for I had not yet arrived at the country of experiment. Joseph was not too keen to sit for me (except for sketches) since he wished to get on with his own work and needed to be alone and quiet for that. Instead he suggested that I start on a self-portrait, which seemed to be an excellent idea.

I started boldly by outlining in Prussian Blue what I saw in the wall mirror. I certainly felt more positive in my approach than I had at the Slade under Tonks; for I had thrown off the shackles and started a new life, and I painted what may be considered my first successful work. So it was with delight that I heard that the National Portrait Gallery had purchased it from my niece, Jenny Fraser, in 1986.

Looking back I see that my early work, with its broad delineation and vigorous manner of painting, possessed an almost masculine strength. 'Of this period, the solid and well-constructed large head, 'Self-Portrait', is a striking example,' said the *Observer* of 9 April 1933. It is painted in rather thick impasto straight onto the canvas, which gives it a fresh sunlit look. All the forms are slightly different in texture and colour, which adds to their interest, but I seem to remember the hair giving me the most trouble.

After Christina left us we employed an old Italian cook, who made a splendid model with her rugged face, though she was inclined to drop salt tears into the soup while cursing Mussolini. Our life in Fitzroy Square was happy and satisfying even though urchins were inclined to piss into our letter box on the ground floor. We felt sure that this was done for the hell of it rather than maliciously, so managed to forgive them so long as no important letters were damaged.

Happiness is not something one should long for or search for; happiness is an experience like any other, felt when least expected. It is a feeling of being at one with the world, an assurance that you are on the right track. This is what I felt when I first met Joseph: he gave me the feeling that I had grown up at last, enabling me to paint with more self-confidence than I had ever had before. The sense of pleasurable excitement that sent a glow of colour through my life was only enhanced by the tongue-wagging that went on when friends and relations heard that Joseph and I were living together.

Who was this foreign visitor from outer space (they cried) with his courtly manners and outrageous ideas, his good looks and (so-called) bad intentions, indolent yet energetic – an observant, humorous, talkative intellectual who gave spice and wit to any conversation? Who indeed? It was to take me all our life together to learn that with Joseph I would never cease discovering new things.

Many friends, old and new, came to see us in Fitzroy Square. It must have been at this time that I met the top-flight American journalist and interviewer John Gunther, with his wife Frances. They were good friends of Dorothy Thompson but did not seem surprised that her marriage to Joseph had broken down. Another friend of Dorothy and Joseph, from the Berlin days, was the writer Louis Untermeyer who visited us when his own marriage had just collapsed. His son, distraught, had committed suicide. Joseph consoled Louis as best he could, trying to ease his mind through talk. It was an admirable gift that Joseph had – his ability to sympathise with a person in distress, a gift which perhaps was fortified by his philosophical speculations as well as the troubled times through which he had lived.

A new friend was Hamish Hamilton, a dark, good-looking man, who was the first to take Joseph to the Garrick Club in 1927. Joseph's feelings were elated: he thought the place an elegant mausoleum of glass-cases; and the environment tended to increase, if possible, his admiration for English institutions. Joseph had been in love with England since he was twelve years old, when he first started learning the language, though he studied so many others that his father, in a fit of irritation, wanted to know if the boy was keen to be a hall porter! (Today he might have suggested the Common Market as a suitable career.) England for Joseph was the ideal country, and he had great admiration for its institutions and law-abiding ways. Like Rossetti, he always wanted to be taken for an Englishman, and never was. I, of course, longed at this time to live in France, that seat of culture with access to the warm Mediterranean. I would have settled happily in Provence, but Joseph did not feel safe in Europe; and, with the benefit of hindsight, his forebodings were to prove correct.

Later on that year we heard of a small villa to let at Portofino, on the Gulf of Genoa, and decided to spend the winter there. (Joseph's antipathy to Europe did not extend to holidays, thank goodness.) The Casa Signorile was a paradisical spot on the hill overlooking the semi-circle of blue, ochre and magenta houses, which pressed a studded horse-shoe round the translucent limb of the sea. The antique and magical beauty of Portofino lay in the secret of its size. It had the perfect human proportions and everything lay at the right 'nearness', till one felt it almost possible to touch the landscape and feel the beauty with one's finger tips. The peninsula lies like a woman's breasts on the surface of the sea, while at the distance of a kiss, the arm of the mainland stretches and curves away. Although the villa was not large, and the rain came occasionally through the roof, the grounds were spacious with two gazebos built on top of the two conic little peaks in the garden. A grape-hung pergola was our outdoor dining room and we were waited on by Giacinta (another excellent model) whose father, a farmer, used to stride the hillside in bare feet dropping rocks on his enemies below.

We often went into nearby Rapallo, and one day, walking along the sea-shore of that colourful little town, the strange pastasciutta seaweed lining the shore as if the blue sea were showing her brown petticoat, while tall palms waved their fronds in the soft south wind, we traversed the promenade, looking for a café in order to stop and quench our thirst. Having found one which looked promising, we settled down, and ordering two cappucini, decided on a game of chess, with the not too odious proviso that whoever lost should pay for the drinks. We had not been playing long, when a red-bearded Apollo settled down at my side to advise me (I was a novice at the game). He gradually took over, played quick-action chess with Joseph for half an hour, lost four games, won the last, wiped his brow, and said: '*Per Bacco*, the man has a mind.' It was Ezra Pound.

He then dragged us through the back streets of Rapallo, stopping to buy a quantity of candied apricots on the way, and making us admire a large hog's head hanging from a hook in front of the butcher's shop. 'No statesman can ever approximate to such dignity,' he murmured. He was the proud owner of a top floor flat with access to a large roof, from which the Mediterranean could be viewed as a seascape partially framed by Santa Margherita and the hills of Portofino.

Ezra usually wore a black corduroy suit, a present, as he said, from its former owner, W. B. Yeats. Ezra was a fine-looking apparition with sparkling blue eyes, and a certain impersonal sadness mixed with energy and an agility, both mental and physical, which never failed him. In the flat was a large study and a bookshelf with the complete works of Henry James, and on the table a dedicated copy of the first edition of *Ulysses*.

Rapallo in 1927 was a meeting-place for writers and poets from all over the world, but particularly from England. Here is my shopping list of people: Max Beerbohm of course was on his hill (rarely leaving his commodious white villa), but there came W. B. Yeats, Osbert Sitwell, Adrian Stokes, Basil Bunting and a number of younger men, all attracted by the sun and cheap living and by that poetic lode-star, the Mediterranean itself. Yeats is the one Joseph remembered best, striding along the shore discussing literary matters with Ezra and himself. 'Propheten links, propheten rechts, die welt-kind in der mitte,' said Joseph. ('Prophet to the left, prophet to the right, the world child in the middle.)' Ezra, borrowing Yeats' spectacles or pince-nez, handed them to Joseph to try, and asked him: 'Do you see fairies?'

We often went back to Ezra's flat and admired the beautiful Renaissance screen, behind which (appropriately?) hid an American utility wardrobe. Ezra was fond of making pieces of furniture in his spare time, and I found the chair I used to sit in comfortable and pleasing to the eye. Above all things, Pound was concerned with living and dedicated minds, and believed with Machiavelli: 'Gli uomini vivono in pochi, gli altri son pecorelli.' ('Real men are few, sheeplike are many.') He would say quite bluntly: 'I specialise in genius.'

As Ezra was so good at playing the buffoon, I am sorry to say we paid less attention to his true greatness than to the funny side of his nature. On another occasion, walking again along the Italian shore between W. B. Yeats and Ezra Pound (and as Joseph said, not as conscious of the honour as he should have been), Joseph heard Ezra grumbling about the forced continuation of lyrics which sound well enough in a half-lit drawing-room when pronounced by melodious Irishmen, but do not adequately capture the observations and lights of our age. Ezra also spoke frequently of an Italian called Guido, whom we took to be a local friend, only to discover later that he was referring to Guido Cavalcanti, the Florentine poet and friend of Dante.

Pound's parents turned up in Rapallo that year – his ancients as he called them. Tongues wagged that they were brought to Italy to convince the local inhabitants that the first white child born in Idaho (Ezra) was not in fact a Red Indian. They asked Joseph, of all people, to keep an eye on their son.

I remember one weekend when Joseph and I had been staying in a little hotel in Rapallo, on the bay, and I had done a number of paintings and drawings – mostly landscapes and portraits of fishermen. I showed these to Ezra and Osbert Sitwell; the latter said nothing then, but declared later to Pound that I had talent. Another time, Ezra gave me good advice on what a painter should aim for; clarity, structure, and vital energy. 'Don't be a wobbly vagina, not that I think you are,' he added kindly, 'but look at Wyndham Lewis.'

At the beginning of Joseph's friendship with Ezra, Joseph was greatly vexed by emotional problems; his marriage had broken up and he was much perturbed by the despairing letters Dorothy was sending him. Pound, his deep blue eyes full of sympathy, advised: 'Joseph, practise polygamy!' Ezra was always more concerned to save not souls but minds from personal anguish, thus helping them to do the job for which they were intended. 'Be good, and nobody will observe you,' he said. He also read Joseph's bunch of poems, and sent some off to *The Dial*, an American magazine. After a few weeks, Ezra greeted Joseph happily with a cheque for £100, *The Dial* having chosen to publish 'Aurea-Mediocritas' a long poem. 'But,' Pound added, 'do not think your troubles will be over; the same happened to me ten years ago and I have not sold another since.' In retrospect, I believe Ezra often put on the jester's rags in order to avoid the danger of growing pompous and snobbish, the latter quality which he hated with an almost savage hatred.

The only time we heard Uncle William (as Pound called Yeats) laugh, was when he told us that, as a Senator, he had received a delegation of Indian revolutionaries. They had come to ask for a dozen Irish assassins because the Indians lacked moral courage. Yeats laughed and laughed; the word 'moral' tickled him. Ezra was often less than kind to Yeats. To Joseph he whispered that Uncle William wrote some fine lyrics in his youth, but had long since lost his way. Yeats seemed slightly afraid of Pound, very much on his guard, and whenever possible, avoided being drawn into discussions on modern poetry. Joseph found Yeats melancholy, sweet and with an inbuilt kindness. 'To be a true poet,' said Yeats, 'you must turn with the whole wheel of existence.'

The three of us together took many more walks in Rapallo and met often in restaurants, and Ezra would sometimes come over to Portofino and partake of our pigeon pie which he enjoyed immensely. Watching him after lunch feeding any stray cats on hand was a Jamesian pastime. He was always very serious during this performance, and, as the ravenous cats fell on the residue of his meal, he watched them as an augur might have watched his sacred chickens pecking at the corn. Pound was very concerned one day, when sea anemones were plunged into fresh instead of salt water by mistake. Later, in Paris when Joseph was in bed with flu, I brought him a goldfish to cheer him up. When Ezra saw it, he admonished me, insisting that fish go mad having to swim round and round a small bowl. Ezra might have cursed itinerant carpet-sellers, but he was certainly considerate to animals.

Ezra was fond of playing tennis. He used to say that it was a sculptor's game, as the sweep of the racquet had something in common with the movement of the sculptor's arm. Ezra was a menace at the net, but it was at the back of the court that the sweep of the arm came fully into play. Occasionally we played in a foursome, with Dorothy Shakespear, Ezra's wife. We knew of Olga Rudge, the musician-mistress of Pound, but rarely caught a glimpse of her.

I was debating one afternoon with Joseph and Ezra what I should call the painter that I aspired to be. I was completely happy about my surname Agar, but had never thought that Eileen was a suitable name for an artist. It was too feminine, and anyway I wanted a first name that was shorter. Joseph, who was a great admirer of Byron, suggested 'Allegra' since it seemed to encapsulate both names. I agreed at once, and from then on – at least for a short while – Joseph and Ezra called me Allegra. My architect friend Rodney Thomas, when he came to stay with us for a week or two, was not so impressed. He thought Allegra was a silly name, and that I ought to stick to Eileen. When Joseph and I returned to London two years later, the name faded in the foggy realities of a big city for it somehow belonged to the Mediterranean and golden light; it disappeared like the ghost of a young girl.

Rodney had been having marital troubles, and as he had never been to Italy, we invited him for a break in Portofino. He arrived at Rapallo station and, as we had told him to, he hired a horse-cab to drive him along the coast road to our villa. He tried to explain to the cabby that he had no money for the fare, but the cabby only repeated 'domani, domani,' meaning tomorrow. Rodney however thought he was demanding 'de money' and arrived at our front door panting and alarmed, convinced the cabby would cut his throat at any moment.

We stayed longer than we had anticipated in Portofino, enjoying the brilliant company and the beautiful landscape. For us it was a sort of honeymoon and remained always a treasured memory. Dorothy Thompson still wrote regularly to Joseph, and one letter hilariously described her recent experiences in renting a villa in Naples, ending with an invitation to stay for Easter. Dorothy's letter reminds me of the occasion when another Naples agency swore to me that they could recommend 'a bitch in Sicily in the family way'. Had I then been a card-carrying Surrealist (not that I ever was), I should no doubt have felt it my duty to investigate that beach.

After rejecting a dilapidated forty-room barracks of a place, Dorothy and Sinclair had settled into a little guest house in a huge park. There was a salon, and a great glass verandah looking over Naples and the sea; the kitchen was on one floor, with a not very desirable bedroom (being parkward, green and cool, instead of seaward, blue and warm), and up above, three bedrooms in a row; and the whole resting on a big stone terrace. Hal, as we called Sinclair, was hard at work on *Dodsworth*, using the villa Galotti (of which this guest house was a tiny appendage) as the setting for parts of his novel. Tall, with brushed-back carrot-coloured hair, a global forehead and informal rubbery face, he was an intelligent octopus, with large pop-eyes, an electric vitality and long lanky limbs which spread everywhere like tentacles.

As we were still in Portofino, it did not seem far to hop across the water from Genoa to Naples, and we accepted their invitation hoping that things would go as smoothly as the crossing. For the first few days, everything in the garden was gorgeous, including the panoramic view of Vesuvius across the bay, even though we were woken up at seven o'clock every morning by the insistent tapping of two typewriters. Both Dorothy and Hal were hard at it, their mechanised muses demanding to be fed. But then one night at dinner all hell broke loose. Dorothy got up from the table saying that she must find some missing pages from the manuscript she was writing for a syndicated newspaper. Lewis was very drunk, and obviously feeling that his work was of more moment than Dorothy's, he erupted bitterly. After all, he said, he had written a few books himself in his time that were somewhat more important than her bloody manuscript. He was completely plastered and ended up by stalking out of the room into the garden, where he tripped in the dark amongst the rose bushes and fell into an intoxicated sleep. It was Joseph who had to rescue him, pick him out of the thorns and plant him in his ex-wife's bed. Apparently, Dorothy later recorded in her diary that she felt Hal had denounced her to Joseph that night.

Sensing that we might be making things more difficult, we decided to return to Portofino next day. But the little contretemps was soon forgotten, and we continued to be on good terms with this oddly-assorted couple, and except for their wedding-day in May 1928 we saw them whenever they came to London. In fact they blew in to Fitzroy Square one day just before their marriage, when I was back in Portofino, and Joseph was in London on publishing business. He recalled how they came to London to buy the motor caravan in which they were to spend their honeymoon touring England, a happy and energetic American edition of Romeo and Juliet.

Joseph claimed they made his life unsafe for two full days, dragging him to theatres and introducing him to their friends. He spent an evening with Frere-Reeves, a director of Heinemann the publisher, and saw again how the English lose their proverbial cool in the presence of Americans. Frere-Reeves told a story about the day when T. S. Eliot's naturalisation was celebrated, and he had quietly remarked: 'You are, of course, no Englishman, only a British subject, which is quite different.' This was meant to insult Hal – with full results. Later when Hal said: 'I would love to write a book called *Mother England* to emphasize America's indebtedness to England,' Frere-Reeves responded: 'We don't need your protection, my dear fellow.' As Joseph said, he felt like setting himself up as a diplomat charged with restoring sympathy between the two countries.

Dorothy and Hal missed their train and Joseph had to put them up for another day. He said they were all smiles and friendliness towards both of us, charming and uncomplicated.

In the same letter he told me he rather liked Hal this time, though he still thought him neurotic and unsure of himself. He recognised Lewis's courage, and his brilliance as an interpreter of America, but feared he had nothing to offer as an alternative to the stupidity he exposed. Joseph wrote to me that he saw Lewis as a weeping interpreter, whose mouth would grin and scold and ridicule, but whose heart wept because all the time he was exposing his own self. He probably drank to ease the ache, for later, reading another Lewis novel, Joseph remarked: 'You can smell the whisky between his lines.'

Mixed feelings about Hal were the order of the day. Joseph recalled a time when he had been reading Lewis's novel *Mainstreet* aloud to Dorothy Thompson (they were still married then). She tore the book out of his hands and stamped on it. 'I hate that book,' she said. A few years later she was Lewis's biggest admirer. Sinclair was often criticised for his meanness, but at one point he offered to support Joseph for a year or two so that he could get on with his writing. Joseph never accepted this generous offer, but he certainly appreciated it.

While Joseph was in London for two or three weeks seeing about his novel *Shipwreck*, I stayed in Portofino, and one day, wanting a book or some paints from Rapallo, I thought I would walk in along the glorious coast road. Halfway there, the bus passed me going to Portofino, and who should I see in it but Ezra, coming over to visit me. Luckily he saw me and got out, and we returned to the Casa Signorile, where we spent a very enjoyable afternoon wandering about the grounds. Pound tried to persuade me that England was finished, as far as literature was concerned – and probably art too – but I would not agree with him. When I added that I enjoyed talking to Apollo in Rapallo, he gave me a quizzical look.

Joseph, hearing that Ezra had been over to see me while he was away in London, came tearing back to Portofino, sitting up all night in the train to reassure himself that I had not absconded with Ezra. I assured Joseph that the visit had been purely friendly, but his possessive nature was immediately aroused, and perhaps he was not so misguided. Geoffrey Bridson, a friend of Pound as well as us, told me years later that Ezra would have liked to have been more intimate with me, but feared my passionate Hungarian lover. Joseph had been a boxer when young and a fine fencer – fencing being a national sport in Hungary – and kept his splendid physique long afterwards.

Shipwreck in Europe was published in 1928. Dorothy Thompson had tried to stop Joseph publishing it as she saw too many close parallels between the character of Nausicaa in the book and herself. But I heard that John Gunther persuaded her to drop this pressure for it would do her no good. More amusingly, two of the typists engaged to copy the novel for *Harpers* refused to type what they considered indecent writing. Even then this seemed incredible, now it is simply hilarious.

The novel had many excited and appreciative notices, especially in America, and it was translated into French and published in the thirties by Gallimard. *Why Europe Dislikes the Jew* had come out in March 1927, and Joseph had plans for other books besides the massive project he called *The Mind of Europe*. It was a very creative period for him, and discussions were going on with Harper and Brothers, his publishers, about a new novel *Puppets in the Mirage*, as well as a book of poems. Joseph wanted the poems to be illustrated in colour, and had me in mind as their illustrator: unfortunately, the poetry project was altogether too adventurous and nothing came of it.

Returning from Rapallo one evening, Joseph and I discovered to our dismay that the father of our Italian maid had shot an Ibis (that sacred bird) and nailed it to the front door. Although the Italians seemed to shoot at anything, and this one was only proving himself a good shot, it seemed an omen of change, as if the smiling world was about to become grim. The old atmosphere was gone, and almost abruptly we returned to London, letting the Casa Signorile to an Englishwoman (who turned out to be dishonest, for the beautiful carpet designed by Marion Dorn disappeared, as did other small items).

The Warren Gallery opened in Maddox Street, near Hanover Square, at about this time, and Henry Moore had one of his first shows there. Joseph had known the gallery's founder, Dorothy Warren, in Vienna, and we naturally went along to the most sensational show of the time – when some of D. H. Lawrence's paintings were exhibited there in 1929. The police confiscated many of them, but I saw the show before it was circumcised, and I must admit that what I remember of the large paintings seemed to be mostly foreskin in close-up. I met the Russian artist Boris Anrep through Dorothy Warren and he came to the flat in Fitzroy Square to have a look at my paintings. He liked my work, especially the portraits of the old Italian cook and of Mouma, a Russian child of twelve and niece of Tchaikovski. We had met this girl in an hotel in Birling Gap, near Eastbourne, and I had asked her to sit for me. Anrep suggested that I go to Paris since art in England was far too provincial. He was convinced that I needed to study the 'new' continental disciplines. According to him no one in England was doing anything worthwhile. Who is Paul Nash? he asked dismissively. I was to find that out later.

I thought it a good idea to study in Paris. Joseph agreed to move once more as we only planned a short stay and he had many literary friends in the French capital. He took a tiny flat in the Quai de Bourbon on the Ile St Louis among the tree-tops, with pigeons galore and a fine view of Notre Dame. I found a studio in the Rue Schoelcher opposite the cemetery, and so we moved in. Neither of us liked being too much on top of each other, but the right porcupine distance is not always easy to achieve.

While in the rue Schoelcher I was a frequent visitor to the Jardin des Plantes, fascinated especially by the bones of that proto-bird, the Archaeopteryx, which I felt should be painted life-size. I was enthralled by fossils, their muted colour and embedded beauty. They reach us as signals in time, isolated objects which take on the importance of a problem resolved at some moment far back beyond the mists of human memory. I learnt about the secrets of animal structure, and from there my thoughts led easily to the problems of human structure. It cannot have been simple coincidence that at this point I met the Czech painter Foltyn.

It was through Adolf Loos – another contact of Joseph's from the Vienna days and a visionary architect – that I met Foltyn. I decided that since I had come to Paris to study, I had better get on with it, instead of wandering around museums. Foltyn was a protégé of Loos, and recommended by him as a teacher of painting. Foltyn was a short very thin fellow, due, as he said, to the diet of milk on which he was living. He said he could not afford even the cheapest restaurant and could not be bothered to cook for himself. He spoke not a word of English, and his French was almost unintelligible because of a thick guttural accent, but he spoke a certain amount of German so that Joseph could converse with him and translate his more esoteric phrases for me. Foltyn had studied the Cubists very thoroughly in a sophisticated and analytical way, though I do not think this was finally to benefit his own painting.

Foltyn, with his large, almost bald head and thin figure in floppy trousers much too big for him, looked very much the East European refugee. He had very blue prominent eyes and a ruddy colour in spite of the diet of milk. He told us that when he was called up to fight in the First World War he certainly did not want to be killed, so on the battlefield, when no one was looking, he shot himself in the leg. Then he waited for the Red Cross to carry him away so that he might continue painting.

In spite of his linguistic disadvantages, and perhaps because this forced him to demonstrate rather than talk, Foltyn was a good teacher. Moreover, he dismissed all the 'isms' of the time – except Cubism or Abstraction – but especially Surrealism, which had recently surfaced in Paris. So he took me on as a willing pupil, and I learnt much more about sensitivity to form whilst trying to cultivate colour, planes and composition. This was altogether a more stealthy advance in comparison to my usual direct approach to what was before me.

One afternoon we ran into Adolf Loos in the Champs Elysées. He was with Knize, the famous Viennese tailor who had a magnificent collection of modern paintings. Loos introduced his friend simply as 'my tailor', and then started fingering the material of my blouse, admiring it, and asking Joseph where he got such a treasure from. Loos always said that to be really modern one must not go around looking like an artist. His great model was the English gentleman, and he would insist that another of his protégés, Kokoschka, was always dressed beautifully even when he was penniless.

Ezra Pound came on a short visit to Paris and Joseph lent him his flat in the Quai de Bourbon. I remember walking down the Avenue de l'Opéra one day with Ezra and Joseph, when we ran into the lanky figure of Aldous Huxley, whom neither Joseph nor I knew. Huxley stopped to greet Ezra, who then introduced us. We chatted for a bit and then walked on, and I asked Ezra what he thought of Huxley as a writer – he had had a great success with *Point Counter Point* recently published. To my surprise, Ezra did not answer, he simply turned his head aside and spat into the gutter; an answer which was clear enough though unexpected.

It was on this Paris visit of Ezra's that, walking together in the Jardin du Luxembourg, we came near to the faun fountain. Ezra maintained that it looked exactly like James Joyce reading the first pages of *Ulysses* to some chosen friends. When so much was being written in all lands and all languages, Pound must have been right to concentrate on works which displayed an unusual or higher degree of intelligence. But unfortunately in his case, this choice was also associated with a mortal hatred of all average beings, an emotion which tended to distort rather than strengthen his judgement.

Before Ezra returned to Rapallo, he took us on a memorable visit to Brancusi in his studio in the Impasse Jésu Christ. My first impression was of whiteness: marble dust and the white coverings which seemed to clothe everything in the small studio. It was an impressive sight to see those golden phalloi unveiled, one after the other, with a religious simplicity by the white-bearded Roumanian sculptor who seemed deliberately to knock his slender bronze birds to make them vibrate. Ezra had a fine feeling for form – witness his book on Gaudier-Brzeska – and was a tremendous admirer of Brancusi, and one could feel Brancusi responding with warmth to our collective admiration.

Ezra also gave me letters of introduction to the artists Louis Marcoussis and Tristan Tzara, who were supposed to be in Paris at the time. Marcoussis told me that my work was all very interesting but that I must show it at all costs. Unfortunately Tzara was out of town and I never had the opportunity to meet him. I took one painting of an Italian peasant which I had done at Portofino, to the gallery which exhibited Modigliani's work. I had admired the melancholy sculptured heads in Modigliani's paintings and set myself to learn from copying them. His influence on my work was limited, but the gallery accepted my peasant portrait and I have never heard of it since. It was in a party in another gallery at around the same time that I met André Breton, who introduced me to Paul Eluard, both of whom I was to meet a few years later, when they came over to London for the International Surrealist show.

Many of Ezra's introductions have formed themselves into the very gems of memory. Such was our entrée into Natalie Barney's salon in the rue Jacob. She lived in a sixteenth-century villa behind St Germain des Prés, believed to have once been occupied by Racine, and there she held her literary gatherings, welcoming Rilke, d'Annunzio, Rémy de Gourment, Pound, Hemingway, Scott FitzGerald and many others. Natalie Barney was a well-known Amazon of letters who became leader of a brilliant coterie of lesbians; 'In England,' she wrote, 'nothing is for women – not even the men.' In 1926 she had tried to set up a bilingual magazine which she was to co-edit with Sinclair Lewis (of all people), but the project never materialised. Life came before art with her – and what a life! Ezra remarked that he thought she got more out of life than was perhaps in it. Among other excitements we were taken to see the *temple d'amour* and watched chubby Salomon Reinach, the art historian, taking saccharin from a book-shaped *étui*, much to Joseph's amusement, in order to sweeten his tea.

Ludwig Lewisohn, the well-known American writer, another friend of Joseph's from Vienna and Berlin, was living in Paris at that time. He was married to a would-be singer called Thelma, and I remember at one of her dinner parties that she entered the dining room carrying a large soup tureen and announced in a triumphant voice that the cook had had a miscarriage. Thelma used to say: 'I am my husband's virgin,' and when asked what she thought of some American law called the Mann Act, replied: 'I love it'.

Joseph and I spent the early spring of 1929 in the Basque country, near a tiny village called Biriatou on the river above Hendaye. It was here that Joseph wrote *The Tale of a Child*, later to go into the collection of the world's greatest stories (he is sandwiched between Leo Tolstoy and Karel Capek, which pleased him). It is a lovely story of childhood in Hungary, conveying the authentic smell of small boys, and full of wonder and disbelief at the strange ways of grown-ups.

It was wonderful country. We could bicycle down to Hendaye and bathe in the great rollers that came in with a thunder across the smooth sand, then visit the flesh-pots of the famous hotel, before bicycling back to our roomy pension where nothing disturbed writing and painting. St Jean-de-Luz was not far off, and we even visited one of my mother's favourite haunts, Biarritz; there was such a thunderstorm at the time that I felt I could hear my lioness of a mother roaring her disapproval as forked lightning played all around us.

I had to return to London to attend the final legal proceedings surrounding my divorce from Robin, and in the meantime Joseph returned to Paris. He seemed to enjoy himself there, entertaining Harold Laski and meeting Ezra Pound's parents once more. Joseph wrote to me: 'The father is a nice old country Americano, she from the brand where twelve make exactly a dozen, and at the same time the spit image – shall I say years' ago image – of Ezra's wife. It is some story to see Ezra performing his filial duties.'

I rejoined Joseph in Paris where he was busy sniffing the political air and already growing suspicious and worried over the future of Europe. We moved out of the hot depressing city and travelled down to Bandol in the south of France. We used to see D. H. Lawrence moving around there restlessly. He looked ill, otherwise I would have approached him since I knew both Frieda, his wife, and Barbara Weekley, his step-daughter, quite well. Frieda was rather an overpowering woman: vital, fat, with wonderful red hair and flamboyant clothes. She tried unsuccessfully once or twice to persuade Barbara and me to go out to Mexico. Barbara had been a student with me at Underwood's and later had taken us to see her father in London, when Joseph and Professor Weekley had spent an enjoyable afternoon discussing words and exploring their meanings.

Mindful of my resolution to continue studying, we soon returned to Paris despite the summer heat. Edna St Vincent Millay, the American poetess, turned up one afternoon with her Dutch husband Eugen Boissevain, to surprise Joseph in his tiny flat on the Ile St Louis. Joseph and she had been lovers in Dorothy's day back in 1923 in Budapest. According to Dorothy, Edna was the toast of half the town, with her little white body and green-gold eyes, and she captured every male she could. With Dorothy away in Vienna, Joseph, true to his Bohemian tradition, was a willing victim.

In Paris in 1929, Edna sent her husband ahead up the three or four flights of stairs to knock at Joseph's door, and demand as an outraged husband where Joseph was hiding Edna. Joseph, for once innocent, protested that there was nobody in the flat except himself. Nevertheless Boissevain made a show of searching, until the panting poetess, Edna Millay, arrived on the scene amid laughter and relief. She also came to see me in my studio. I think she wanted to have a look at the girl Joseph had left Dorothy Thompson for. She seemed satisfied as she stayed all afternoon. I remember Joseph reading out some of his poems, and Edna chiding him: 'Beware of bastard words' – whatever that may have meant.

At this time Foltyn moved to a flat with a large 'cocotten' bed – as he called it – of which he was inordinately proud. Previously he had been using Adolf Loos's bath as a sleeping apartment, until one night, coming home late and rather drunk, Foltyn fell fully dressed into a bath brimming with water. Loos appeared to cultivate protégés in groups of three. In Vienna, he had befriended and helped Kokoschka, Schoenberg and Peter Altenberg the poet. In Paris, there were Foltyn, a Persian architect and another musician, who were always known as the Three Musketeers. Foltyn was an abstract painter obsessed with minute colour changes, but he knew a great deal about technique and the history of Cubist painting, and thus possessed the sort of expert knowledge I was seeking.

After working in Paris for some time, Foltyn suggested that we go down to Menton, as the light and painting possibilities were so much greater in the south of France. We agreed, but to our surprise, meeting Foltyn at the station, we found a Czech painter friend of his (who called himself simply the Kunst Maler, or Art Painter) also included in the party, as well as Foltyn's Polish girl friend. 'She will cook for us,' explained Foltyn. As the others were short of money, we all travelled third class, uncomfortably but companionably.

Foltyn divided painters into three categories: Vaugirard (the intellectual avant-garde), Stella Bella (the trite and academic) and Homopopo. This perhaps needs some explanation. In Paris, the rue Vaugirard was the home of the galleries which would show accepted avant-garde work, whereas in Menton, every other villa was named Stella Bella, and this seemed to sum up the whole school of Sunday painters. Today, Foltyn's third category, Homopopo, might be interpreted as the gay scene.

After looking around, we eventually found part of a suitable villa where we could work. It must have been at this time that we went to view Sarah Bernhardt's villa. I remember seeing her on the stage, a living legend with an amputated leg.

I thought she was rather dreadful. Her villa in the south of France was stuffed with carpets and hangings and contained a huge bed covered with moth-eaten furs. It was a mausoleum of a place super-stuffed with junk.

The Polish girl's idea of cooking was to make mountains of meatballs, which were supposed to last a week or a month; it was like eating ammunition; in the meantime she could relax, and read her Polish novels in the garden. This was not Joseph's idea of paradise, for he was an adept in the art of living, so he hunted about until he found a small but attractive (though newly-built) villa, in the middle of an old olive grove at Cap Martin. The rent was £70 a year unfurnished, so, nothing daunted, we sent for the furniture from Fitzroy Square, said goodbye to Foltyn and his compatriots, and in January 1930, moved in.

It was a curious little villa with rather a naked look about it, built by a committee, the estate agent informed us, with only an outside staircase leading to two large terraces, one on each floor, and as an afterthought, a few rooms in the middle. We christened it at once the Casa Allegra after my new name, and of course the locals thought it was a cat house. As it was so easy to break into, we thought we should have a guard dog, and seeing an advertisement in the paper for an alsatian whose father had been a wolf in Corsica, we went to have a look at this ferocious animal. What was brought out for our inspection was a tiny puppy, not more than a week or two old, and utterly captivating, so we called him Brutus and took him home to guard the house.

A little while later, Alec Waugh (whom we had met through his old school friend Hugh Mackintosh) brought his younger brother Evelyn to visit us. Brutus had grown and I remember him eating Evelyn's shoe laces under the dinner table. Evelyn was not amused. (As Thérèse, who came down from Roquebrune every day to cook for us, said: 'Ce chien ne veut pas être raisonable.' 'That dog doesn't want to be reasonable.') Evelyn was full of complaints. There were spring onions on the table (with a few other things) and he said: 'You don't expect me to eat those, do you?'

Evelyn then was still a slight boyish *après-midi d'un faune* figure, giving no hint of the overweight monster he was to become, though the serpentine tongue was firmly in the cheek. He was very attentive to me, and seemed to dismiss Joseph as the boyfriend of the moment. To my surprise, he admired one or two abstract paintings I had done at the Casa Allegra, and even threatened to buy one but for a detail that displeased him. The painting was 'Movement in Space', which was more abstract in intention and muted in colour than most of my work at the time. I was torn between the abstract and Cubist lessons I had learnt from Foltyn, and the representational work I had done spontaneously in the portraits. Evelyn objected to a certain area of pigment in 'Movement in Space' which he thought inappropriately thick; otherwise he said he would have bought it.

At Cap Martin we were near Monte Carlo, so could go in to see the Diaghilev ballet, which was a most stimulating and exciting event. Rupert Doone was dancing there at the time, and often came over to see us. I must have first met him in London through Middleton Murray or someone at the Slade, some time previously. Rupert was not very tall, with a slim but muscular build, a large head and closely-cropped fair hair. He was a beautiful dancer who made seemingly effortless leaps, and had something compelling about him which held all eyes when he was on stage. He became a brilliant choreographer and was much in demand, while still later he produced the *Agamemnon* and other plays for the stage. I saw a spell-binding performance of this at Morley College where Rupert directed the Theatre school. Perhaps he will be best remembered for the essential part he played in founding the Group Theatre, and collaborating with Eliot, then Auden and Isherwood in the thirties. Joseph used to tease Rupert by asking him to tell us how he drank champagne from Isadora Duncan's navel.

In the meantime, Brutus the dog was growing up. We tied him to the gate one day when we went to play tennis, then hearing a thunderous noise, looked back to see him tearing along the road after us, towing the gate behind him. Our sojourn in the South of France was coming to an end. The double taxes were straining our resources, and Joseph in particular wanted to be back in England. The local butcher at Cap Martin took on Brutus as a guard dog, and before the end of 1930 we had returned to London.

In Italy and France I had grown up, both as a painter and as a person. I had won my freedom from Robin and had no intention of tying any more knots just yet. My impish ex-music master, Horace Kesteven, told me that Napoleon was also quick to change his mind once he knew he had made a mistake; a curious remark, I thought. At the same time, largely thanks to Foltyn, I had begun to free myself from the cul-de-sac of representational painting, by learning the principles of abstract painting, and experimenting with content as well as form.

I had understood the lesson the Cubists were driving home, and Juan Gris had particularly impressed me, though I always had the urge to develop more strange ideas. An early work of that time, (now in the Tate Gallery and called 'Three Symbols') which I dubbed 'The Flying Pillar' is a good example of how I was beginning to change. In it, a pillar stands for Greek culture, Notre Dame is a symbol of Christianity, and a bridge built by Eiffel (the Tower man) symbolises modern technology reaching into the future and expressing time to come. It was my first attempt at an imaginative approach to painting, and although the result was in some ways surreal, it was not done with that intention. However, Surrealism was in the air, for painters and poets in France, and later in England, were kissing that sleeping beauty troubled by nightmares; and it was the kiss of life that they gave.

When I left Robin, I had taken his advice literally (alas for him!) to strike out for myself. I remember going back a little later to the studio in Fernshaw Road to collect the last of my things. In a drawer, looking most macabre, was a skull. By some sleight of hand, Robin had managed to acquire this object at the Slade during one of Tonks's anatomy lessons. I picked it up, packed it, and sent it to his home address, in Prince of Wales Terrace. Robin was in Scotland I think, and by misfortune his mother opened the package. She was horrified, and automatically assumed it was a practical joke on my part. She wrote a furious and indignant letter saying that she had no intention of keeping such a horrible thing in the house, and was forthwith returning it.

I must have already been in Bramham Gardens with Joseph when the package came to rest again with me. (It must have kicked around a bit through temporary or old addresses, though I do not suppose it went abroad – think of the Customs.) I decided that I could not allow poor Robin's skull to ricochet backwards and forwards like this, so I determined to keep it, and I still have it here in Melbury Road. It lives in a small trunk which used to belong to Dorothy Thompson. One day I painted the skull golden and began to decorate it with small sea shells. 'Those are pearls which were his eyes.' Trawling for objects became a favourite working method of mine, and although this found object has remained unfinished, it was nevertheless the first to be started. It has survived, and somehow it has defeated time.

CHAPTER FOUR

Through the Broken Glass

I had kept in close contact with Rodney Thomas since we had been students together at Underwood's, and we had often discussed architecture and design. Already in 1929 I had asked him to think about how he would lay out a studio and small flat for me, so when Joseph and I found our pair of flats in Bramham Gardens I immediately asked Rodney to start work. I had wanted to settle in France but Joseph could not feel safe anywhere in the European landmass for any length of time. England was the centre of civilisation for him and he was not happy until we had planned our return to London.

For a few weeks we lived in short-let rooms in Half Moon Street, just off Piccadilly, and while we were there Evelyn Waugh came to see us. He was a man of strong convictions and a clear mind. He himself had wanted to be a painter, and I heard later that he was drawn towards Catholicism by his devotion to art. He was attracted, in other words, by a sense of beauty, just as I remember being much moved as a young girl by the beauty of Rio at dawn when arriving by ship. But on this occasion, Evelyn had come to inform us that he was off to Ethiopia to attend the coronation of Ras Tafari, the Lion of Judah, and he tried to persuade us to go with him, enlarging in a lively way on the horrors and delights that would be in store for us. I told him that we were going no further than Kensington, whereupon he said: 'Oh, but you can't live in Kensington!' as if it were the last word in degradation. Evelyn kept on teasing Joseph, asking him what he meant by living with an attractive young woman and keeping her all to himself; he obviously intended to have a slice of her himself if possible. But I had no desire to be eaten by white ants, or carved up for a cannibal feast. So saying goodbye to Evelyn, we departed our different ways.

Joseph took a small flat on the top floor of a corner house which used to be the Persian Embassy in that much-despised Kensington. Of course, to be the true English gentleman, Joseph wanted a country residence as well. He always dreamt of a little country cottage, but if we were to live in England, I was determined to stay in the city. Besides, neither of us could drive, so I made out that I could find nothing suitable in the country and instead took another flat in the same block, almost underneath Joseph's. In this way we moved into Bramham Gardens, again managed to find the right porcupine distance, and stayed there, on and off, for many years. Rodney Thomas designed the furniture for my flat, and Joseph got Duncan Miller – who worked at Curtis Moffat in those days – to build bookshelves and lighting for his flat, much of which we took with us when we moved to West House in Melbury Road.

We spent the summer of 1930 in Sark with my sister Winifred and her husband Hugh Mackintosh, whose breeding ground it had become; from honeymoon to stamping ground, they were faithful to this tiny island for years. Winifred had married Hugh in 1925, some four months before Robin and I married. I had been a bridesmaid – though not much of a maid – and it had been one of the few public family occasions I attended after leaving home. Sark was beautifully peaceful since no motor cars were allowed on the island, and this added greatly to the pleasure of our visit. If Joseph had no country cottage to retreat to, at least we often got out of London.

On Sark it was enchanting to swim through caves open to the sky, their walls clustered with sea-anemones. But Joseph eyed the sea-crossing with dazed apprehension, and one time returning to Guernsey in the small, smelly cockle-shell of a boat, packed with sheep, hens, humans and other impedimenta, on a rough and stormy day with the waves breaking over the boat in great cascades, he asked the captain if it would not be wiser to turn back. 'What for?' returned the captain, spitting into the sea as everything on board got drenched for the fifth time.

Joseph was intent on making his mark as a writer in London, and soon met some of the leading personalities of his time. He recalled, for instance, going into Harold Monro's Poetry Bookshop in Great Russell Street and meeting T. S. Eliot there. Eliot had arrived in order to tell Monro that he had not enough money to take him out to lunch, which seems rather curious. Joseph had an ingrained dislike of Americans, and the poet's meanness did not endear Eliot to him. However Joseph's main project of this period was *The Island*.

The Island was a magazine which I helped to found, which had Leon Underwood as art editor responsible for the practical layout, and Joseph as overall editor. We began working seriously on the idea in 1930, intending the magazine to be a quarterly devoted to the plastic arts, poetry and the imagination, priced at half-a-crown. The title we took from Prospero's island, not Robinson Crusoe's. As we wrote in the publicity handout, *The Island*'s purpose was,

> to strengthen the creative life of the individual struggling under the weight of the industrialised and standardised spirit of the age. It is endeavouring to form a centre of artistic and literary activity that shall represent a line of continuity with the past and, at the same time, build from contemporary poetic imagination immune from post-war disillusion and fatigue. . . .

Among the contributors were John Gould Fletcher, the American poet who had contributed to the first Imagist anthology, my friends from Underwood's school, Gertrude Hermes and Blair Hughes-Stanton (they married in 1926), together with the literary critic R. L. Megroz, Catherine Carswell, Naomi Mitchison and myself. Henry Moore contributed some wood engravings, as did Underwood himself. I had kept up my friendship with Leon since leaving the Brook Green school and had become godmother to his daughter Jean just after I had left. Mama was typically caustic, implying rather unfairly that the only reason I was asked was in expectation of the expensive gifts I would give.

Ezra Pound, hearing about our venture, sent us innumerable letters and postcards, offering advice and insisting that there was ample room for a decent quarterly in London. However, *The Island* was run on a shoestring, and had a homespun atmosphere about it. Joseph's sophisticated intelligence contrasted sharply with Underwood and his colleagues' more primitive and otherworldly approach. There were continual disagreements about what were to be the aims and contents of the magazine. Meanwhile, Pound, knowing what was going on in Paris, wanted Joseph to get in touch with Cocteau, Tristan Tzara and others. Ez said: 'Give them the good European stuff and make 'em match it . . .' But he did not take into account the fact that such luminaries were unlikely to contribute without payment, and we could not afford to pay our contributors. One postcard I particularly remember was brought up on a showy silver salver by the live-in porter at Bramham Gardens, and said in large letters: 'Back we are to the shitten-arse shepherds,' signed simply EP. Pound was incensed that we did not recruit better (and less pastoral) contributors.

Time and chance have always figured greatly in Ezra Pound's strategy of making an impression, making something felt in the very midst of his contemporaries. There is a time when a new magazine can be started and a time when this is impossible. But a united strategy is essential from the beginning. There does not have to be agreement over all the details, but in our case, even the necessary basis of agreement was lacking. *The Island* folded up after four numbers, for a major split had developed between the contributors. Joseph said that editing the magazine was like being inside a large sack of fleas.

Joseph wanted to turn *The Island* gradually into a more intellectual magazine, but Underwood disagreed, believing more in the noble savage approach. Underwood carried quite a lot of weight, and was vociferously supported by the American writer, Velona Pilcher. She wrote sentimental poeticised prose and loudly maintained that *The Island* should remain unsophisticated and as isolated intellectually as England was geographically. At the same time, Joseph's publishers, Harper and Brothers, were encouraging him to drop *The Island* and concentrate on more sustained writing. There had indeed been a long gap since any work had been done on Joseph's great project, *The Mind of Europe*.

In fact, Joseph was disillusioned with this master-work. Fired with the enthusiasm of new friendship, he had shown his notes for *The Mind of Europe* to Ezra Pound when we were in Rapallo. Pound, excited by Joseph's outline, but convinced that his approach was misdirected, made copious suggestions as to how Joseph's book should be changed. As a result, Joseph's own ideas were so muddled that he was discouraged from ever attempting to finish the book. Besides, the mood of Europe was fast changing as the balance of political power shifted; as it turned out, events superceded Joseph's ideas.

The last number of *The Island* came out in December 1931, containing a whole section on religion and art. I contributed a short piece proclaiming the new reign of womb-magic, the dominance of female creativity and imagination, but the star turn was Mahatma Gandhi. Joseph had been to interview Gandhi at a house in Knightsbridge next to the Hyde Park Hotel, where the prophet was living with his goat. Joseph came back rather shaken from this meeting between the 'welt-kind' and the saint. However, he sat on the floor cross-legged as Gandhi himself did, while an American sculptor was busy with clay, modelling Gandhi's nose. It was the living skeleton of this man with the burning eyes, wrapped in what looked like a shroud, which both fascinated and repelled Joseph. Jo Davidson, the bulky sculptor, dropped the lump of nose he was holding when Gandhi referred with disgust to the amount men eat; they should be thinking about God instead, said the sage.

In this last number of *The Island* there was also an interesting contribution from another new friend, C. R. W. Nevinson, who wrote about 'The Adventure of Modern Art'.

The press response to the magazine was mixed, as it usually is. *The Times* remarked on our earnestness, but Stuart Gilbert, who was co-editor of *Transition*, asked if he could reprint some of Joseph's one-line philosophical speculations as apparently they expressed with wit and vigour exactly what *Transition* stood for. Henry Moore wrote a lovely letter hoping that *The Island* could live up to its manifesto, and agreeing with Joseph's aims. Alas, *The Island* was sinking beneath waves of discord, so it was providential that at this time Ezra Pound asked the famous editor, A. R. Orage to call on Joseph.

Orage was a landscape of a man, 'the full of a door', with an expansive and benevolent Yorkshire nature. He hated writers who made a cult of genius, but admired brilliant common sense. Bright-eyed, of great presence of mind, he bore out Ezra's promise that 'he will talk to you from the shoulder'. Joseph was still editing *The Island*, and Orage too advised him to drop it in order to concentrate on short stories. Orage, who had edited a brilliant periodical called the *New Age* until 1922, had been abroad and had just returned from New York to found another paper, the *New English Weekly*. Joseph was greatly impressed by Orage's balanced judgement, his intellectual freedom, and his experience in literary matters. He exacted a full response from his contributors, who included Pamela Travers (a jobbing journalist before she wrote *Mary Poppins*), Dylan Thomas, Arnold Haskell the great ballet critic, D. G. Bridson and Alec Waugh.

Joseph submitted several short stories to the *New English Weekly*, including 'The Tale of a Child', which Orage in a letter called 'a classic of its genre'. He went on to say that he was sure that Joseph would one day write a modern *Journal to Stella* packed full of the deadliest of innocent satire.

Orage was a Fabian who first elected Nietzsche as his god and then moved over to the Douglas Credit Scheme (an idealised system of controlled prices, dividends and social credit intended to increase everyone's purchasing power), before eventually joining Gurdjieff, that enigmatic and larger-than-life sage who had a school in Fontainebleau outside

Paris. Orage was a firm believer in Indian mythology and Vedanta philosophy, which he thought would take the place of Greek. He extolled the *Mahabharata* above the *Iliad* or the *Odyssey*, and believed it should influence the Europe of tomorrow. Religion for him was the study of perfection.

As editor Joseph had obviously been more involved in *The Island* than I had (though I also contributed some woodcuts besides a little writing), and while he had been busy, I had set about making for myself an environment which would serve as a living space as well as a studio. From the outside, the front door looked normal, but from the inside it was a mask-like face: the letter-box forming its mouth, a plaster hand the nose, and twisted ironwork as eyes and hair. In the studio itself, was a beautiful serpentine marble inlay for the fireplace (in a lovely variegated pattern of sea-green and white), chosen with Rodney Thomas from a stone mason's yard, and then the chromium dish-clock he designed (now in the Victoria and Albert Museum) over the mantelpiece. This has a frosted glass back-plate, pierced with the hours of the day: electric light shines through the apertures of Father Time. Around the clock I made a huge collage of images – small drawings and postcards mostly. Other objects were constantly changing: drapes and sculptured plaster heads, textures, fabrics, stone and metal shapes – throughout the thirties my studio transformed itself, it seemed, at the blink of an eye, one day suggesting Magritte, the next de Chirico, and this was before I had been 'identified' as a Surrealist. Julian Trevelyan, in his memoir *Indigo Days*, described the room as a work of art in itself, art and life approaching and forming one pattern. I was collecting and storing all the time, surrounding myself with the raw material which would be transmuted into paintings and objects.

Indeed the Bramham Gardens décor must have changed like the seawrack cast up by the tide. The bathroom had a particularly nautical flavour, being at one time decked out with rope, propeller, chart and lifebelt. There was even a toy swan mounted on a Bath Oliver biscuit and the curtains were made of fine fishing net.

I started to show my work, and in 1932 exhibited with the National Society of Painters, Sculptors, Engravers and Potters, at the Royal Institute Galleries in Piccadilly. My first press cuttings are from this show, and I was at once ambitious for more. My work was changing and beginning to assume a more lyrical and imaginative presence of its own. As I grew in confidence I was impatient to have my work seen by a larger public. When Henry Moore suggested that I join the London Group in 1933, I was more than willing, and it was about the same time that I had my first one-man show, at the Bloomsbury Gallery in Bloomsbury Street. The London Group was an exhibiting society of artists founded in 1913 as an alternative way of showing work without going through an establishment selection committee. Thus it had a reputation, at that time, for showing exciting new work.

The exhibition was a retrospective of seven years' work, and showed my paintings developing from the realism of the early portraits through the abstraction learnt from Foltyn, to what I hoped was a new synthesis. Henry Moore came to see my work at the gallery, and I remember showing him one painting on an easel which you could rotate through 360 degrees. Henry looked at it, and obviously not liking the fact that the painting could be viewed sideways or upside down, said: 'Eileen you are wrong to let the spectator decide; you should decide for yourself which way up the painting should be shown, and then stick to it.' This was another example of Henry's famous practicality and tidy-mindedness, but I was just getting into an experimental mood and still trying to find my feet – whether they turned out to be pointing sideways or even upside down, I still had to discover.

In the early thirties Joseph and I used to go on walking tours with my sister Winifred and her husband. Hugh Mackintosh was the life and soul of every party: the singer of songs, both business man and raconteur, he must have been the model for Stephen Potter's one-upmanship as well as Nicolas Bentley's 'Mr Can'. (Mr Can and Mr Can't were the two faces of the advertisement for Eno's Fruit Salts.) J. B. Morton, who wrote as 'Beachcomber' for the *Daily Express* and was also 'Dr

Strabismus', accompanied us, striding over the whale-backed downs of Sussex reciting the poems of his friends Hilaire Belloc and G. K. Chesterton ('two buttocks of one bum'), and more often than not, bound for that shrine, The Swan at Fittleworth, to down pints whilst swapping songs with the natives. Beachcomber was a jovial lunatic, even funnier off the stage of the *Daily Express* than he was garbed in newsprint. A short, tubby man, a convert to the Roman Catholic Church, his blood bubbling with beer and wine, he was a walking fund of agreeable absurdity, funny to his fingertips. For both of us, this walking and pub-hunting was a new experience, but particularly for Joseph.

Hugh Mackintosh, who was chock-full of limericks, ballads and bawdy stories, was good company in those far-off sing-song days. He was so in love with books that he would prop one up beside his shaving mirror and read whilst shaving, which must have been a hazardous occupation. Winifred, who could never resist the chance of swift repartee, had a tendency towards the acid comment. It may have been a reaction against this which made Hugh forever pull out his own ballads from his pockets and read them to anyone present, hoping to get a sympathetic hearing.

In 1933 we stayed with Alec Waugh and his new wife, Joan, at Oswalds in Kent, where Joseph Conrad had once lived. Alec always reminded me of something very English, a sturdy mixture of cricket and roast beef. He had kindly, quizzical blue eyes which were always ready to give you the benefit of the doubt, unlike his brother Evelyn, who seemed to rejoice in thinking the worst of everyone. Alec had been a schoolboy at Sherborne where his greatest friend was Hugh Mackintosh. In several school-day letters kept by my niece, Miranda Mackintosh, Hugh reproved Alec for being so fond of boys. Alec asked – who else was there to be fond of at school when you are brimming over with passion? When he had left school, Alec wrote *The Loom of Youth* about precisely these problems, and it caused a sensation. He left for the South of France with the money he made from the book, and then it was girls forever after; whether chamber-maids or wealthy women, Alec adored them all. He told me once that he would rather see his name on a bus than seek immortality. Making money was his prime aim, so he was never jealous of the more critically respected Evelyn.

We spent an amusing and quick-witted long weekend at Oswalds, in company with Evelyn and Eddie Sackville-West, and I remember, amongst other things, listening to Alec's account of how Evelyn had warned him not to marry until he had examined his prospective wife's teeth and ankles. Alec's Australian wife, Joan, complained that Evelyn must think she was a horse, talking so much of teeth and ankles; 'not a horse, a mare,' he said. Evelyn was fond of Alec's mare, but was aghast to hear from her, while lunching together at the Hyde Park Hotel, that when he had sinned and then confessed like a good Roman Catholic, he was supposed to stop sinning. Joseph said that at Alec's wedding, Evelyn had been like a malignant demon with a red hot poker, announcing in a loud voice to all and sundry that I was to be his next target. My mother had also been invited to the wedding, and seeing Joseph, asked, 'Who is that good looking man?' She refused to meet him however, because we were still living together and were not married.

'We young people who are bright, but are not to be confused with the "bright young people"' was Joan Waugh's description as she pointed a camera at us in the garden at Oswalds. The author of *Vile Bodies*, the tempestuous young demon with a keen eye and a dictionary under his tongue, stepped carefully in front of Joseph, to claim as much, if not more, photographic attention as my six-foot lover. Evelyn renewed his acquaintance with me at Oswalds by trying to lure, charm and finally push me into the bushes on our walks through the woods. I riposted by explaining what jealous Hungarians did to men who tried to steal their girlfriends – although I knew Joseph was sublimely unconscious at that moment of Evelyn's attempt to flush a wild duck and that in Hungary stealing each other's girlfriends was a national pastime. However, Evelyn had a persevering nature, and that evening after dinner, when I had retired to our room earlier than the others after many exhausting games of tennis, I heard him calling me outside the bedroom door. Evelyn had evidently been into the room earlier on in the evening, and since it was the habit in those days to have one's night gear laid out lovingly on the bed, he had apparently inspected it and been most intrigued by what he saw: instead of a lot of frills and furbellows, a very simple shift, more like a nun's night-dress. It certainly excited his – shall I call it, curiosity? But at the time I was not in the mood for a demon lover. Next morning at breakfast Evelyn asked me if I had made my mark yet as a painter. With those kidney-shaped eyes you should have, he said, stabbing a kidney in two. It was during this visit that he told me he thought Eddie Sackville-West was the writer with the greatest future. An opinion which now might be considered wide of the mark.

Piqued by our encounter of the evening before, Evelyn also prophesied that in a couple of years I would have broken blood vessels, swollen ankles and that my hair would probably fall out. I asked him if this was wishful thinking, which left him without a reply. The night before I had given him a coconut kiss and told him I was already booked. A coconut kiss is really a small tea cake, but wondering how to describe the goodnight kiss that I gave Evelyn, I expropriated the name which had intrigued me when I saw it in a baker's shop window. A chaste kiss on the brow, cool as a coconut, but with perhaps a hint of indulgence – this was all that Evelyn got.

My sister Winifred said that Evelyn was enamoured of me, but I must admit that I thought he simply wanted to amuse himself at a weekend party. I was quite happy with Joseph, my calm and steady lover. I had no desire to rush into a passionate and agitated affair which would leave me no chance to pursue my all-consuming interest – painting. For Evelyn, it seemed to be all or nothing, and he refused to be a friend though we did bump into each other from time to time. One wet afternoon we encountered him at the Movietone News in Shaftesbury Avenue, and he proceeded to give us a running commentary on the film we were watching. I remember a feature about Mesopotamia and Evelyn remarking that the small children milling about in the picture's foreground were already prostitutes.

I met the painter Richard Nevinson through Alec Waugh, and went to many of the parties he gave in his Hampstead studio. He insisted that Joseph join the Savage Club, and he wanted to put me up for the Royal Academy. I refrained from such an establishment move, yet Nevinson was himself much more of a bohemian than these conventions might suggest. Paul Nash called him 'the Minotaur', which gives some idea of Nevinson's instinctive energy and lack of restraint. At one of his social gatherings, a pretty Savage Club hostess withdrew with H. G. Wells to an alcove, emerging flushed half an hour later to be asked if she liked doing funny things with H. G. Wells and vice-versa. She grasped her head in horror and shrieked: 'H. G. Wells! I thought it was Edgar Wallace!'

Nevinson as a painter I considered something of a split personality. Although he was extremely interested in modern French painting and frequently visited Paris (he was instrumental in persuading Derain to come to London) he veered between a certain academicism and a more free approach. He was a staunch Royal Academician who seemed to think that the English were too conservative to be dragged into modern art. Much of his wildness must have been released in his entertaining, for he was a great (if overpowering) talker, an excellent cook and a wine connoisseur.

In 1933 we found a small house for the summer at Wittersham in Kent, and as Orage and his wife Jessie were at nearby Winchelsea, they often came over to visit us. Henry Moore and his wife Irina came to stay with us, and as there was not room for a tennis court on the lawn, we used to have hectic games of battle-dore and shuttlecock. The house was called The Orchard and belonged to a chicken farmer, so we were never short of eggs or cocks crowing. I remember Henry mending a bit of wall for us, knocked down when we had been playing darts too enthusiastically. And when I apologised to Henry and Irina for there being no double bed in the house, Henry replied cheerfully: 'That's all right, we slept in one of the single beds together.'

One afternoon we found ourselves in Henry's studio in Parkhill Road, Hampstead, surrounded by his sculptures. (Was it Leon Underwood who took us up there?) There was one very large carving, but all of the sculptures were impressive, whether in wood or stone, impressing through their tactile strength and rounded forms, as if one could stroke them with one's eyes and feel them in the dark. It was an exciting experience, for Henry's sculpture released instinctive reactions in us and we bought a carving – a bust of a woman with folded hands and eyes inset (now, I believe, in the Israeli Museum) – as well as a couple of drawings for 7 guineas each.

We used to play tennis with the Moores either in Belsize Park or Hurlingham. I was a member of the Hurlingham Club (near Putney, on the river) until the 1940 war, and when I met Henry many years later at the Tate, he reminded me how I had beaten him on the court. He also took us one afternoon to tea with Jacob Epstein, though Henry was never happy with the exotic women Epstein surrounded himself with. In Epstein's studio I seem to remember seeing bronze heads of children as well as one of Augustus John. With Henry again, we watched Alexander Calder, the American sculptor (famous for his mobiles) manipulate his toy circus in Ben Nicholson's studio, also in Parkhill Road, for a group of admiring friends who sat round on the floor.

It must have been around this time, 1933 or 1934, and everyone was in evening dress, *chez nous*, when in walked two delightfully refreshing youngsters. Both were poets: one was a shy sensitive plant, the other a ruddy-faced cherub with a snub nose and no chin, at home in any scenery. Dramatically, as they entered the crowded room, all the lights went out, but Dylan squatted on the floor and in a jiffy was reciting limericks in the dark which made everyone present sit up and take notice. This was long before the poet became famous, and he was gay and carefree that evening and hooted when the lights went up again. Then we greeted his companion, David Gascoyne, who had brought Dylan along. David was the image of quietness and reserve which yet held such strong poetic promise: two sides of the poetic persona were with us that night: the limelight and the starlight.

While Dylan Thomas was deep in a flow of bawdy nonsense that kept everyone enthralled (reminding me of Jung's saying: 'The pendulum of the mind oscillates between sense and nonsense, not between right and wrong'), I managed to grab a pencil and paper (never very far away) and did some lightning drawings of this ugly suckling. Later on, I worked from one of the drawings on a painting which was bought by the Tate Gallery in 1962. The National Portrait Gallery would have liked one of my original drawings, but I had destroyed the two or three I had done so quickly.

In the summer of 1934, Joseph and I took a coastguard's cottage at West Bay, near Bridport in the west of Dorset. Bridport's high street was long and straight because the local rope-making industry required space for the new rope to be laid out to dry. Bridport supplied both the Royal and the Merchant Navies with rope, and I purchased some odds and ends for later use. Our cottage was right on the seashore and I always wondered why it did not get inundated at high tide. In fact, the only flood we suffered was one of my doing. For some reason, known only to the local council, the water taps were shut off every evening. One night when the taps annoyingly refused to give water, I went to bed forgetting to turn them off again. We woke in the morning to find the downstairs sitting-room swimming, the carpet afloat and the cushions learning the breast stroke. We hauled everything out on to the beach and hoped for the best.

In 1935 we took a house for the summer in Swanage. I had always remembered going to Swanage and Corfe Castle as a child and many other childhood memories (less clear, more like feelings) were sunk in Dorset. A nameless something prompted me to dig up my past and visit that part of Dorset again, having already reconnoitred at Bridport. So we set off with Joseph's bulldog Dandy and my white cat Bella (with one blue eye and one green) and installed ourselves at Clarence Cottage, Chapel Lane, Swanage. We had not been there long before Ashley Havinden rang from the Grosvenor Hotel in Swanage, asking us for a drink to meet Paul and Margaret Nash, who, unknown to us were also living locally at the time. Ashley Havinden, the poster designer, had the reputation of being the best-dressed man in London, drove a magnificent car and had been introduced to us quite recently by Rodney Thomas. Paul Nash was an artist I had come to respect but knew little about; the idea of meeting him, somehow mixed up with my feelings for Dorset, was exciting.

It was a lovely summer afternoon when we greeted Ashley and his wife Margaret on the hotel lawn in Swanage. A small, trim, raven-haired man with an acquiline nose, distinctive allure, and a triangular look about him, was introduced as Paul Nash. His wife Margaret was buxom, also dark-haired, and more motherly-looking than I had expected. The sparkling sea beneath us, and in the distance the white cliffs and Old Harry Rock, it was the perfect setting for the beginning of a friendship that lasted till Paul's death. He seemed to know my name, though I had exhibited very little, and with the exception of the London Group and National Society, only at the Bloomsbury Gallery. When Paul heard that we were in Swanage for the summer and not just birds of passage, we agreed to meet. The Nashes were living on the front, at No. 2 The Parade. Sir William Crawford and his friend Florence, a sister of Margaret Havinden, were also of the party at the Grosvenor Hotel, and later that summer he invited us on a trip in the *Titania*, a small yacht in the millionaires' berth in Southampton, as he proudly told us.

Bill Crawford was a big sturdy Scot who had made a lot of money with his advertising firm. I remember how we all fore-gathered below deck on *Titania*, while Crawford instructed us on how much we should tip the crew at the end of the week. He was an engaging man ready to tell stories against himself. Once he had been invited by Lord Northcliffe to spend a weekend in the country. Never having stayed in a big country house before, he bought a book on party manners, packed it and duly arrived at the house to be greeted by his host with a couple of drinks before they changed for dinner. Imagine his embarrassment, on retiring to his bedroom to change, at finding his clothes beautifully laid out by the valet but also his new purchase propped conspicuously on the mantelpiece, the book *How to Behave in a Country House*.

The other guests on the *Titania* were the Havindens and Peter and Clifford Norton. (Clifford Norton was later Ambassador to Warsaw and Athens.) We all became amphibious: the more hardy amongst us diving overboard, the others climbing down into the calm sea. Then we took turns at the helm; having driven a Rolls (when we lived at Balfour Place), and looped the loop on my own, I felt that the chance to steer a yacht should not be missed. We passed the awe-inspiring battleship *Revenge*, not once thinking she could ever be sunk. With the Isle of White and Needles as a background, it was impossible to imagine that she would go down, drowning hundreds alas, in the 1940 war.

Paul and Margaret Nash came over to Clarence Cottage many times, for Paul was interested in my work, and we got on famously. He used to bring me curious stones that he had picked up on the beach, and as he said, he felt rather like a penguin, laying them metaphorically at my feet. Joseph eyed the penguin warily, but they were both witty fellows, and even their birthdays were only a week apart, though Paul was three years older. He gave Joseph a copy of *Nightmare Abbey* with a note inside referring to the binding paper which was his own design. Joseph, who was a very knowledgeable man, had never read Peacock, and was delighted with the discovery of a new author.

Paul also introduced us to Archibald Russell, Lancaster Herald at the College of Arms, who had built for himself a house called Scarbank on the cliffs above Swanage. It was full of fascinating objects and paintings, including a most touching drawing by Jacques-Louis David of Marie Antoinette going to the scaffold. Archie was a great connoisseur and a most cultivated man. He kept a Doge's hat under a glass case. It was of yellow silk and fashioned in that delightful shape which recalls Bellini. He told us that the maid invariably referred to it as the 'Dowager's Hat'.

There was a life-size painting of the Lancaster Herald in his heraldic dress in the drawing-room, and I felt as if I had been transformed into Alice in Wonderland as he opened chest after chest of drawers full of moths he had collected on the Downs. He even had a small moth room built on the flat roof of his house, completely empty save for an electric light bulb, which used to burn all night long to entice the moths in. He went about on summer nights with a miner's lamp on his head, wearing very little else during the hot weather, collecting midnight moths and startling the loving couples in the grass. His wife, Janet, ran a shop in Swanage, full of treasures her husband did not think worth keeping in his collection. I still have one or two small terracotta heads which we acquired from her. She sold Greek vases, Etruscan bronzes and all sorts of Roman odds and ends. Archibald Russell was a fine man, lean and tall, with an aristocratic manner. He was to lose both his sons in the coming war, and he never recovered from the blow.

But the war was not yet even a presence on our horizon, and during that wonderful summer at Swanage, we dined often with Paul and Margaret, or with Archie and Janet. Paul was talking of building a house on the Downs, and had in mind a piece of land belonging to Archie. There was a shed already on this land which Paul thought might be convertible. When he returned to London he wrote asking me to measure the shed, but the idea was eventually dropped as there were too many difficulties in the way. Paul used to suffer from bad bouts of asthma and was concerned to be near the best doctors.

Paul opened my eyes to the strange poetic atmosphere he identified in Swanage: the two Greek columns (recalling de Chirico?) standing for no apparent reason on the drive of the Grosvenor Hotel, the lonely love swan buffeted by the waves, and countless other details he delighted to observe. Joseph and I went over the Lulworth Cove one day, and walking along the beach of that geological wonder, I saw something which aroused my curiosity. Digging like a child hunting for treasure, I unpebbled a long snakey monster with a bird's beak. It was clothed in stones, shells and all sorts of other marine accretions which gave it body and turned it into a remarkable object. It was an old anchor chain, metamorphosed by the sea into a new creation, a bird snake, or as Paul Nash called it, a 'seashore monster'. The sea and the land sometimes play together like man and wife, and achieve astonishing results.

I did a watercolour of the monster, and Paul took photographs of it, later using it in a photo-collage entitled 'Swanage' (now in the Tate Gallery). Photographs were an important visual aid for Paul, and occasionally he would even consent to being photographed himself. That summer, Paul, Joseph and myself were photographed separately by a young local photographer called Helen Muspratt. There is one particularly effective photograph of me, a solarised portrait, which, fifty years later, has cropped up in books and magazine articles. As for the sea-shore monster, it is as well that it was recorded elsewhere, for when I brought it back to London, it did not survive the Blitz.

We returned to Bramham Gardens and Paul Nash came to see us often when he was in town, admiring what Rodney Thomas had done to a very ordinary little flat with some ingeniously designed built-in furniture. In fact, to some extent Rodney built me into the flat with the furniture, because it was many years before we dared move. We were attached to our home like snails, being quite sure the landlord would claim such a monumental triple piece as the wardrobe with curved mirror and small cabinet, if we did move. But eventually, when we departed for West House, all I had to leave behind me was the serpentine marble inlay of the fireplace.

But all was not peace and harmony, for when I met Paul Nash, another love element entered my life. We spent time together in Swanage, gave each other ideas for work, and enjoyed an artistic understanding which became an emotional attachment. In February 1936 Paul wrote to me as his 'fair collaborator', mentioning an exhibition space at Charing

Cross Underground Station, and also a mural. I have no precise recollection of this show, and can only assume that I may have helped with some suggestions and advice but that I did not put work into it myself. However, as our collaboration became more intimate, Paul and I became lovers.

When someone puts their hand through a window, the shock of smashing the glass often makes them pull the hand back too quickly. Often this is how arteries are severed. My relationship with Paul was causing great unhappiness to the others concerned – to Joseph, and to Paul's wife, Margaret. In July 1936 I felt that I had to break off our affair. Paul wrote to me, anguished but still marvellously eloquent, desperate to meet again.

He wrote: 'This year we have had together has given me something I don't feel I shall have again while I live . . . In you is embodied for me some essence of life which I have desperately enjoyed as often as I possibly could because it fed me and gave me new energy and poignant joy. In you it remains.'

It was too painful not to see Paul, and we continued to meet, though in a more clandestine fashion. Neither of us could bear any more rows with our partners, so we arranged to meet secretly – at the bookstall outside St James's Park Tube station, or in Kensington Gardens. We vowed to destroy each one's letters to the other, but I could not bring myself to do this – for which I am very glad today. The obstacles to our friendship may have added poignancy to our feelings, but there was too much broken glass about for there to be no pain as well.

CHAPTER FIVE

Am I a Surrealist?

Surrealism came from France to the shores of Albion (to mingle with our native roots in Blake, Lewis Carroll and Edward Lear) largely through the efforts of two remarkable men: Roland Penrose and David Gascoyne. In 1924 on Roger Fry's suggestion, though against his father's wishes, Roland had gone to Paris, and as a student he began to realise his affinity with certain of the young Surrealist painters and poets. In 1925 he married the striking French poetess Valentine Boué, who moved also in the Surrealist circle of the late 1920s and early 1930s. Her earliest poem was an aborted flight to Paris in order to join the Folies Bergères. André Breton admired her utterly personal intransigence and she always retained the devotion of Eluard. The homage of Max Ernst, Picasso, Paalen, Miró, Man Ray, Tapies, Roland and myself is evidenced by the engravings, lithographs, paintings, drawings and photographs reproduced in the posthumous *Poems and Narrations* by Valentine Penrose.

Valentine was much given to Eastern mysticism, and persuaded Roland to accompany her to India in search of enlightenment. Roland was soon yearning for the stimulus of Europe once more, and returned to France while Valentine stayed in the land of the gurus. Soon after his return, Roland met Lee Miller, the beautiful American model, photographer and one-time companion of the great Surrealist Man Ray. Roland fell deeply in love with her, and eventually married her. Luckily, Valentine was able to remain a friend of Roland, but her relationship with Lee was not as easy as Roland fondly imagined; however, some sort of truce was maintained.

The prodigious young poet David Gascoyne had also gone

to live in France and was deeply involved with the Surrealist movement. Anaïs Nin described him as looking just like an English poet should look. We saw little of him because he stayed in France, translating Valéry and Rimbaud. He had very blue eyes and a most engaging manner. He was painfully shy, and did not seem to have enough confidence in his own poetry. Paul Nash used to call him 'a violet poet, born to blush unseen'. Gascoyne managed to combine an intellectual approach to Surrealism with intuition and commitment to the cause. It was a crucial day for English art when he and Penrose met on a Paris pavement, for they decided then and there to launch an international show of Surrealist work in London.

Early in the spring of 1936, Roland Penrose and Herbert Read came to the studio to see my work, and to decide if they should choose something for the newly-organised International Surrealist Exhibition to be held in the New Burlington Galleries in June. André Breton and Paul Eluard were to be on the French committee, and Paul Nash with Penrose and Read were on the English committee. I think Paul Nash had suggested my name to them as a potential exhibitor, but the sudden attention took me by surprise. One day I was an artist exploring highly personal combinations of form and content, and the next I was calmly informed I was a Surrealist!

It was through Paul Nash that I met Roland Penrose and Herbert Read, but Paul played no part in the selection of my work for the 1936 exhibition. Read and Penrose together chose three oil paintings and five objects, and I became one of the English representatives of Surrealism amongst the thirteen other nations which contributed to the show. The English contingent also included the powerful biomorphic sculptures of Henry Moore, the inspired linearity of Bill Hayter and the sinister creations of Edward Burra. Some of the artists I knew better than others. Hayter was another francophile and so not much seen in London, whilst Burra was a recluse. John Banting was a much more colourful figure who lived up to everyone's idea of a Surrealist, although apparently he was not the only one to dye his hair green. Lee Miller told me that when she met Roland for the first time in the early summer of 1937, he also had green hair! However, this was altogether more explicable than Banting's behaviour, since Roland was going to a fancy-dress party. As in so many other things, the punk rockers of the seventies and eighties were anticipated in their peacock plumes by the Surrealists, some forty years before.

John Banting was certainly more extreme than Roland when he cut off the tops of his shoes in order to show his painted toe-nails – as well as doing homage to Magritte, of course. Banting was very conscious of dress in his paintings which often included rather flimsy yet lyrical floating figures, and for a short time he had even worked as a window-dresser in a big store. He once borrowed a lovely golden chainlink triangle that I sometimes wore as a choker, though I do not know whether it was to wear himself or to put on one of his mannequins. Like the rest of us, he had difficulty in selling his work, but I remember that at some point Eddie Sackville-West commissioned him to paint a screen.

Banting's work was intuitive and likely to contain musical references since he himself played, or pretended to play, several instruments. Perhaps it was the drums he played – that would have been in keeping with the loudness of the checks he wore! A short, rather stout man with a witty face and not much hair (no doubt the green dye did not help), Banting was quite unpredictable. His flat was always in complete chaos, dishes getting washed up once a month, borrowed clothes lying around in disorder. He was a great friend of Nancy Cunard, and also of Julian Trevelyan – another artist who was elected a Surrealist overnight. For many years Banting was a member of the Communist Party, but finally could not reconcile his belief with Soviet repression in Hungary in 1956.

Roland was the guiding force behind the exhibition in England. His years in France had led to acquaintance with all the great masters of Surrealism, so he was well-cast in the role of co-ordinator. Roland himself was a Surrealist in his life as in his art, a polymath who was a famous collector as well as a writer and an artist, a Quaker who was gentle and courteous. He had known some wild men and women in his time and

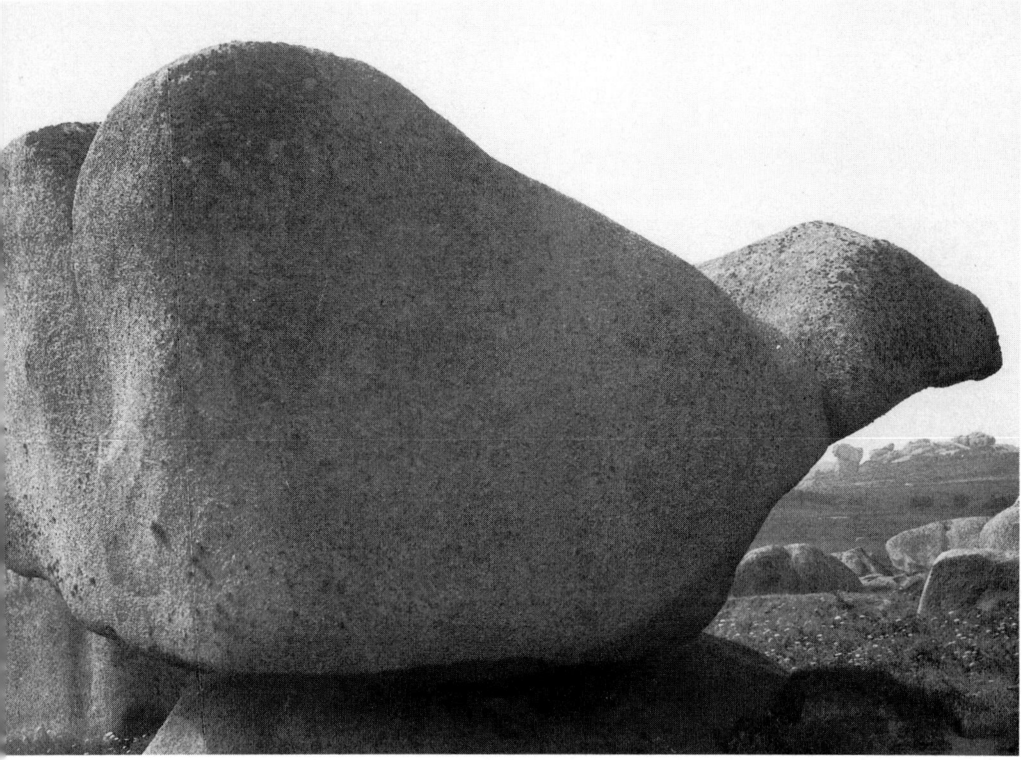

9 Two images which haunted me for fifty years: 'Bum and thumb rock' (top), and 'Rockface', Ploumanach, Brittany, in 1936.

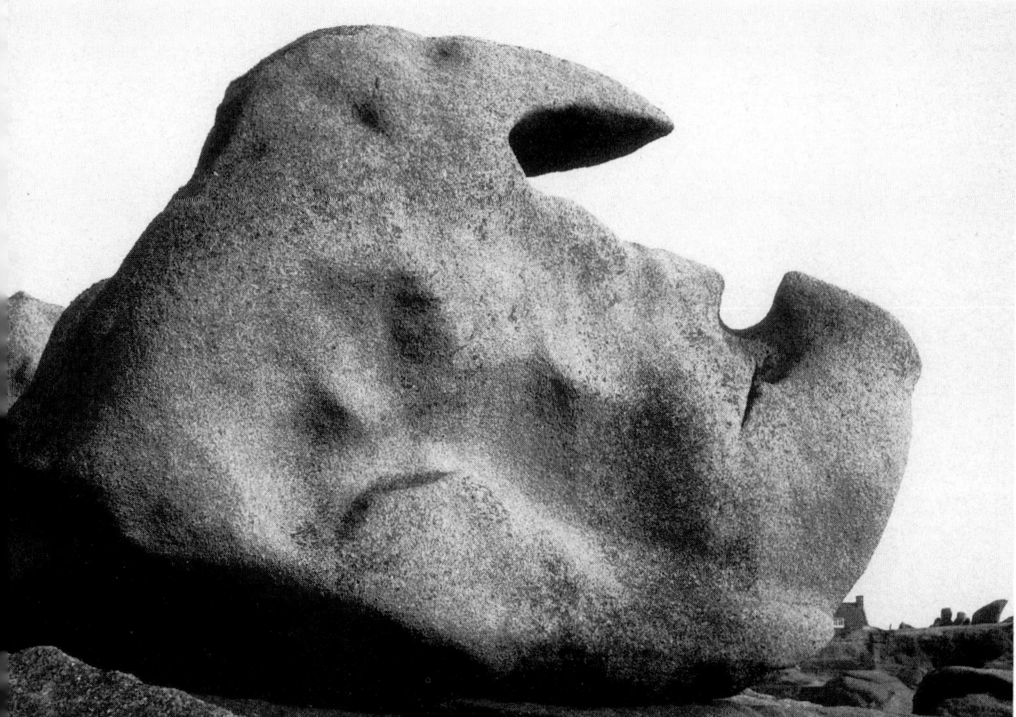

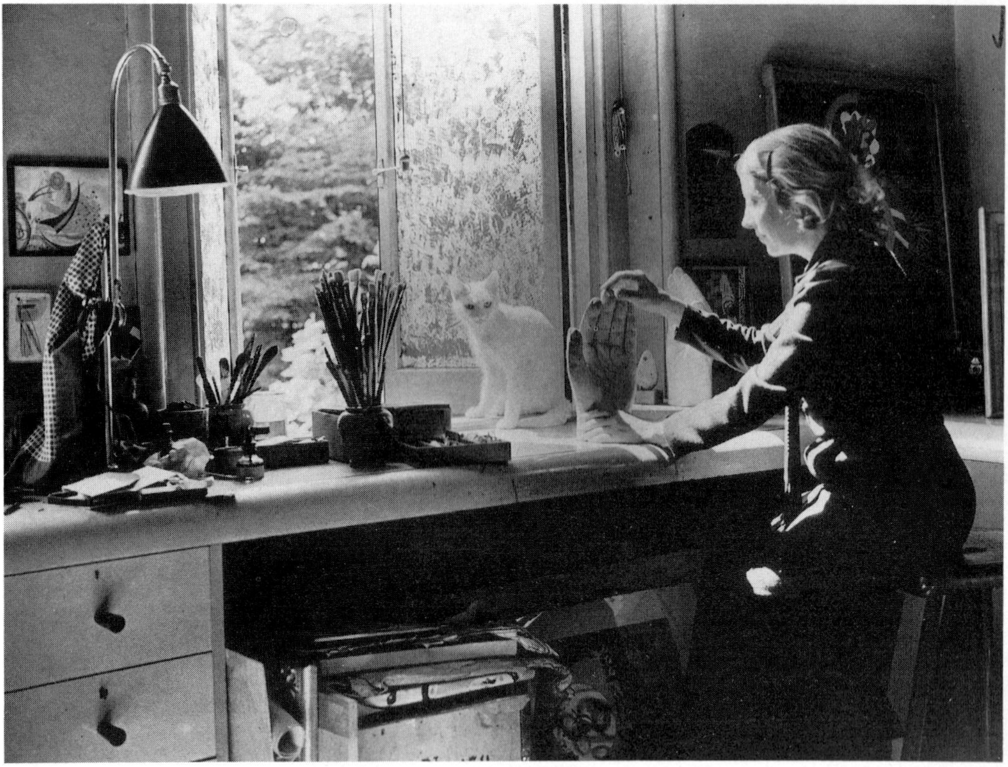

10a Self in Bramham Gardens studio in 1936 with Bella the cat.
Someone had certainly given me a hand . . .

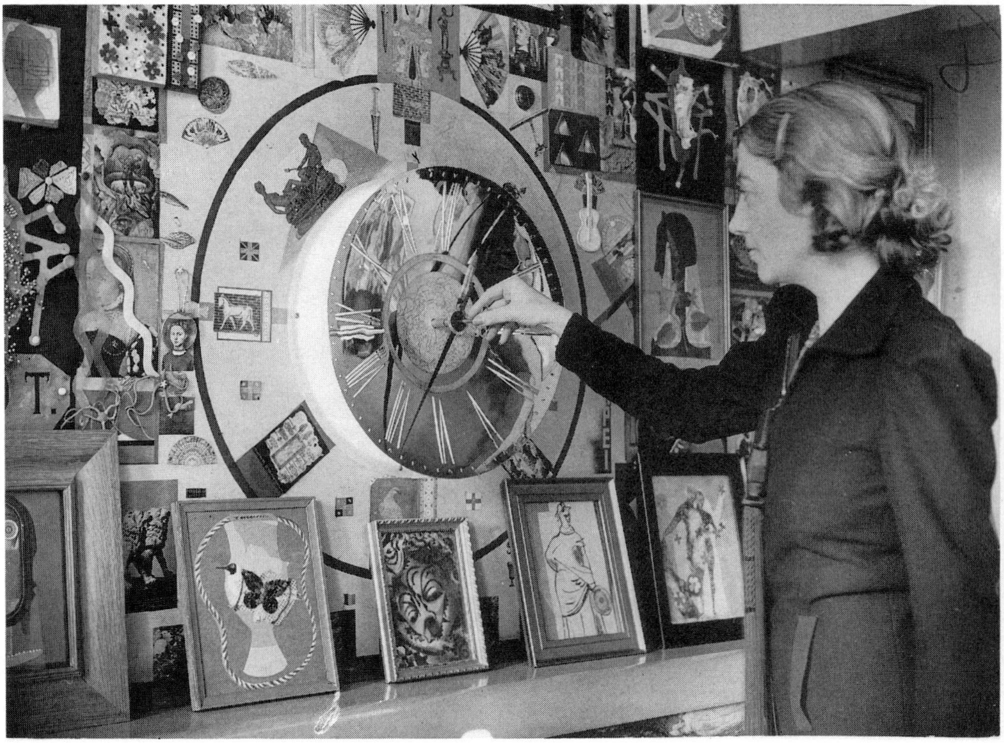

10b Self in studio at Bramham Gardens in 1936,
showing Rodney Thomas's clock embedded in my collage arrangement.

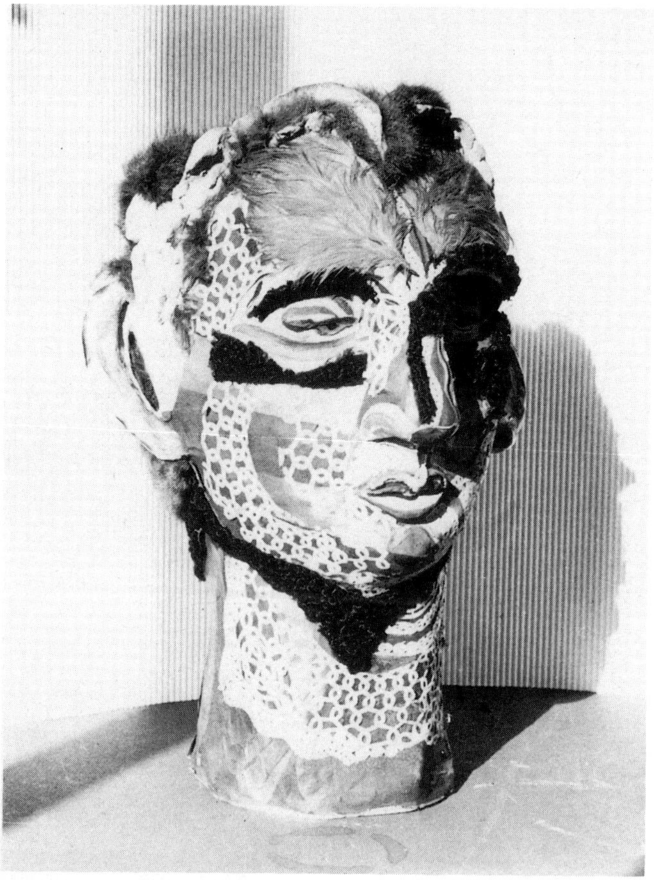

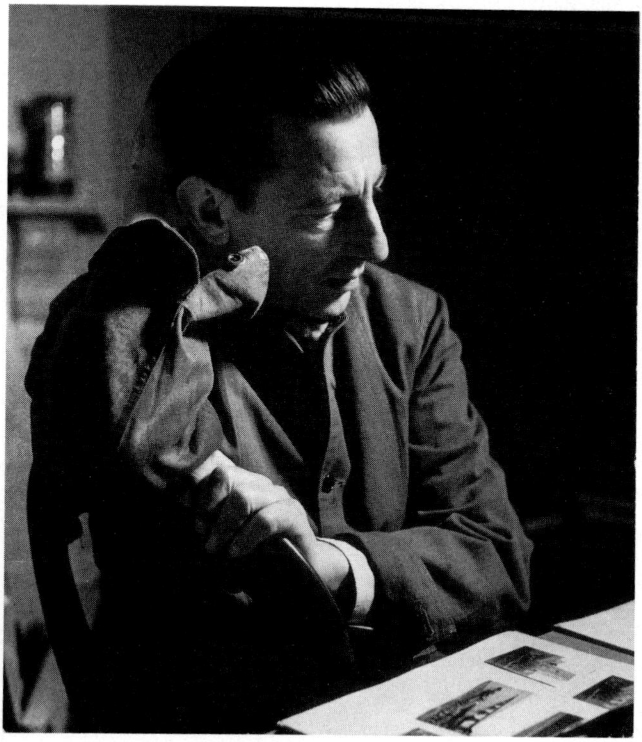

11a 'Angel of Anarchy', 1937, the first version which went missing. Paul Nash showed this on television.

11b Paul Nash at Swanage in 1933.

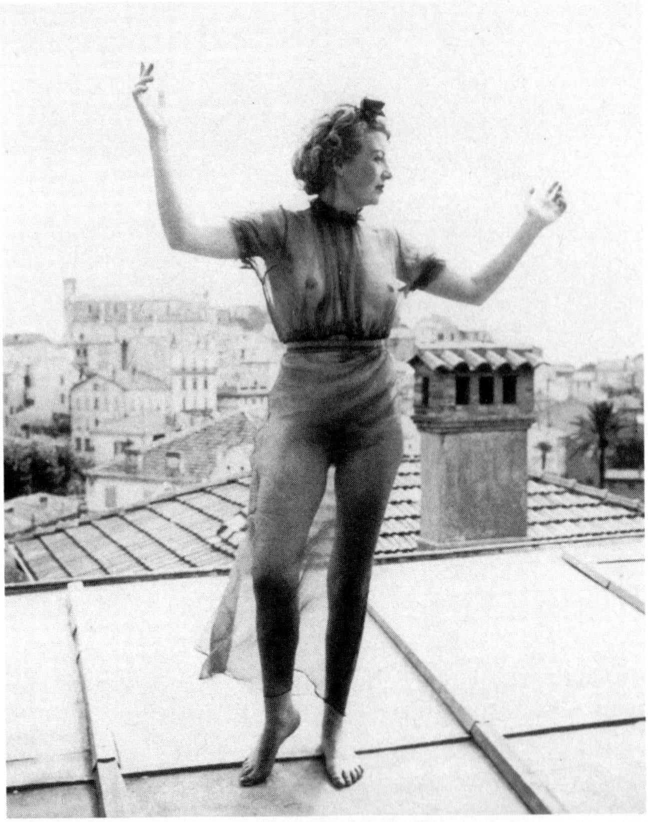

12a Self dancing on a roof outside Mougins in 1937. After a bat-infested night, a dance of freedom.

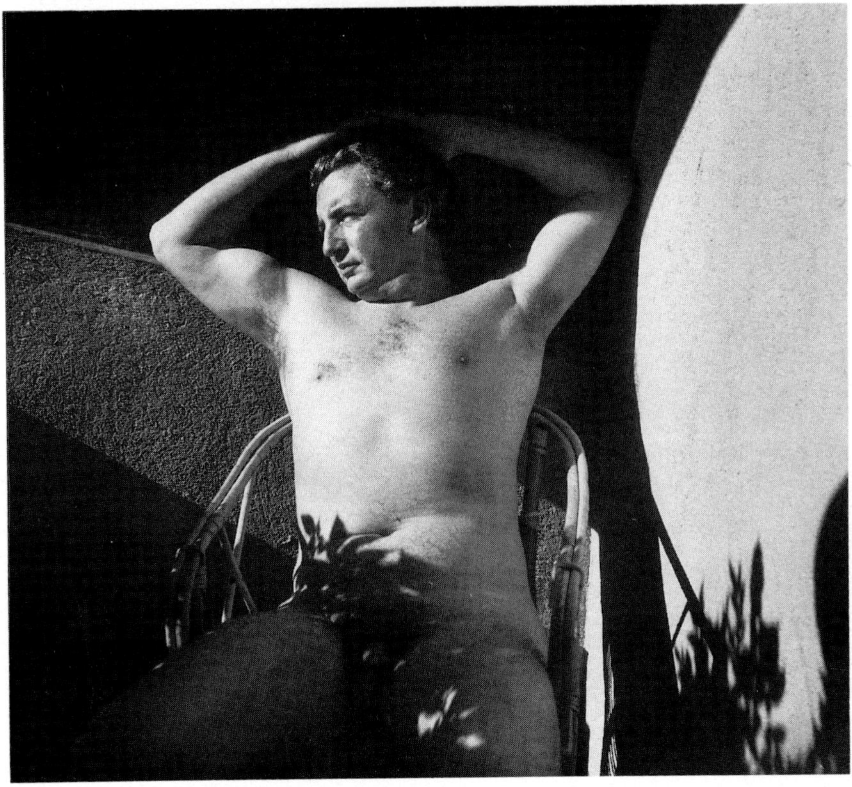

12b Joseph on Picasso's balcony (after he had left), at the Hotel Vaste Horizon, Mougins, 1937.

13a Man Ray on the beach at Juan-les-Pins, 1937.

13b Paul Eluard and Picasso on the beach at Juan-les-Pins, 1937.

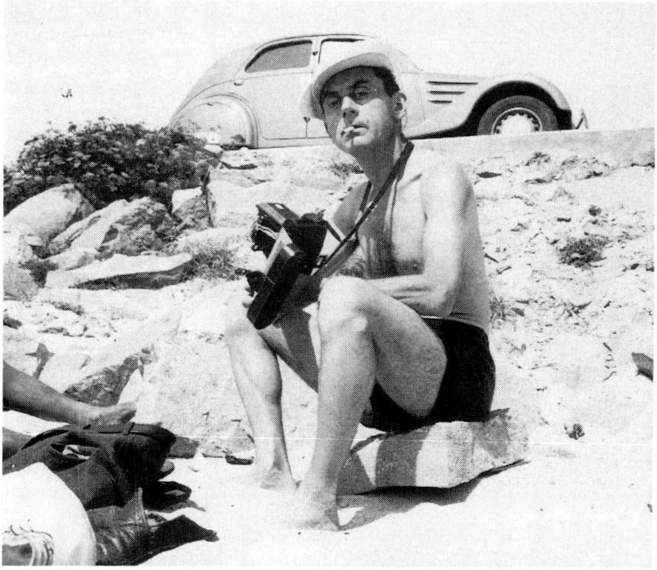

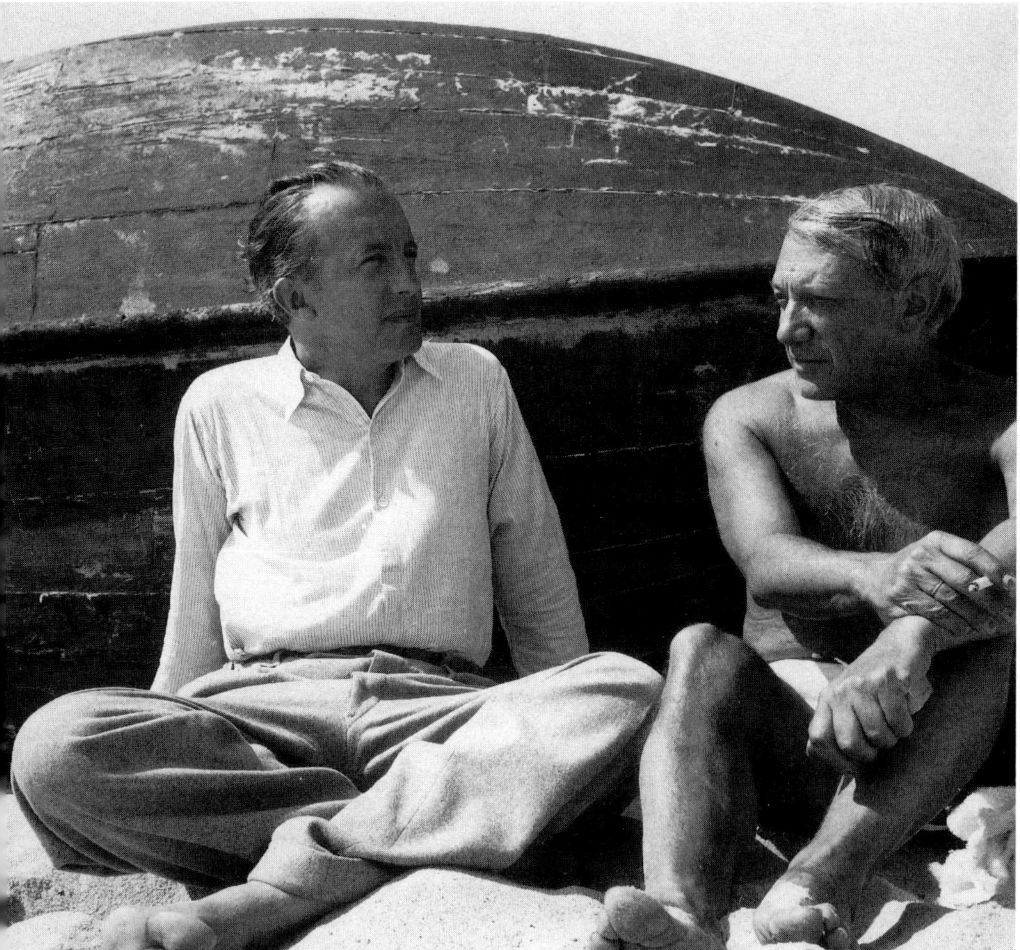

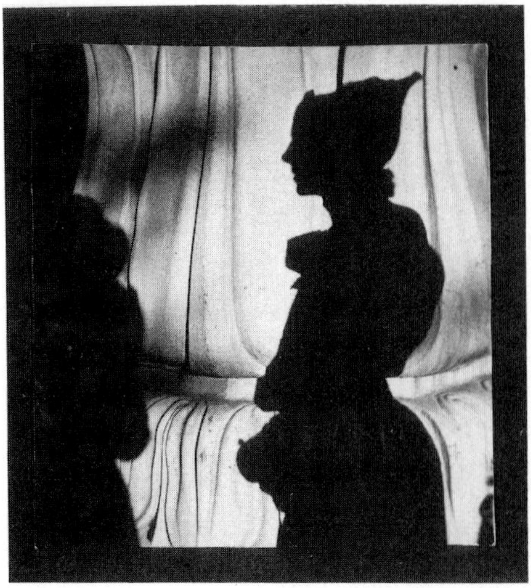

14a Lee Miller's photograph of me at Brighton Pavilion, 1937. As Picasso said, 'Eileen pregnant with a camera.'

14b Roland Penrose and Lee Miller (wearing my hat), on the beach at Juan-les-Pins, 1937.

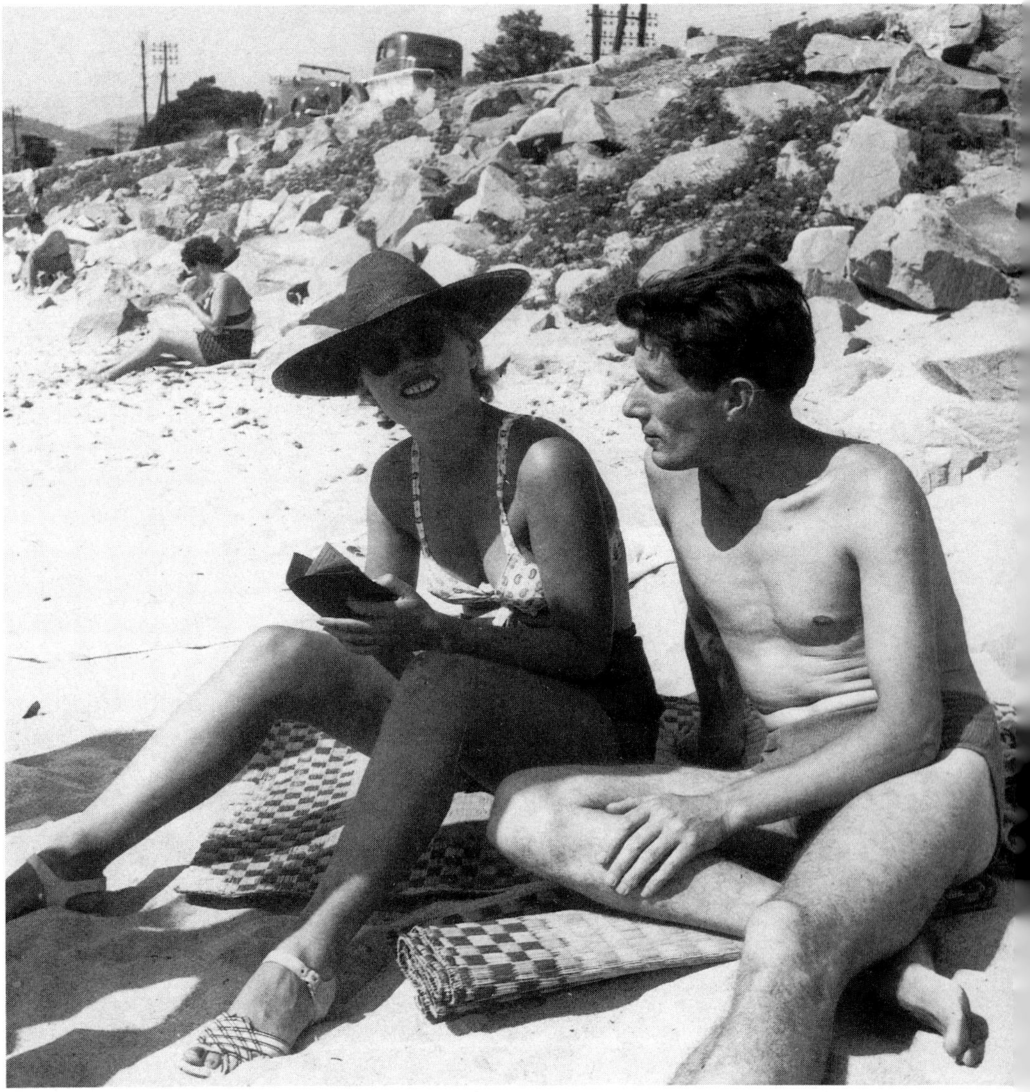

15a Picasso leaving Mougins, cases at the ready, with Marcel the chauffeur in the background.

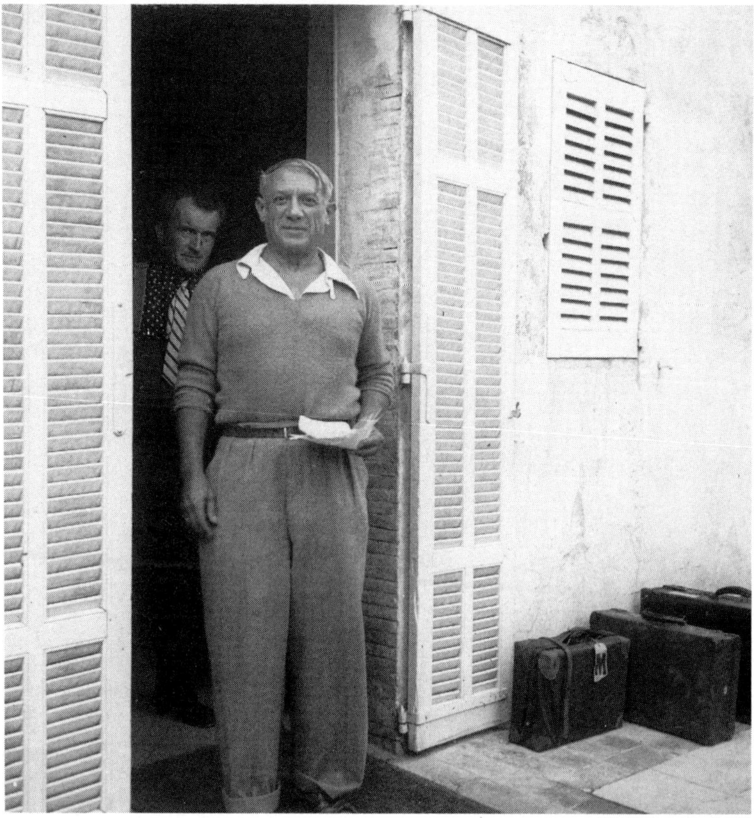

15b Hotel Vaste Horizon with Joseph on the terrace, 1937.

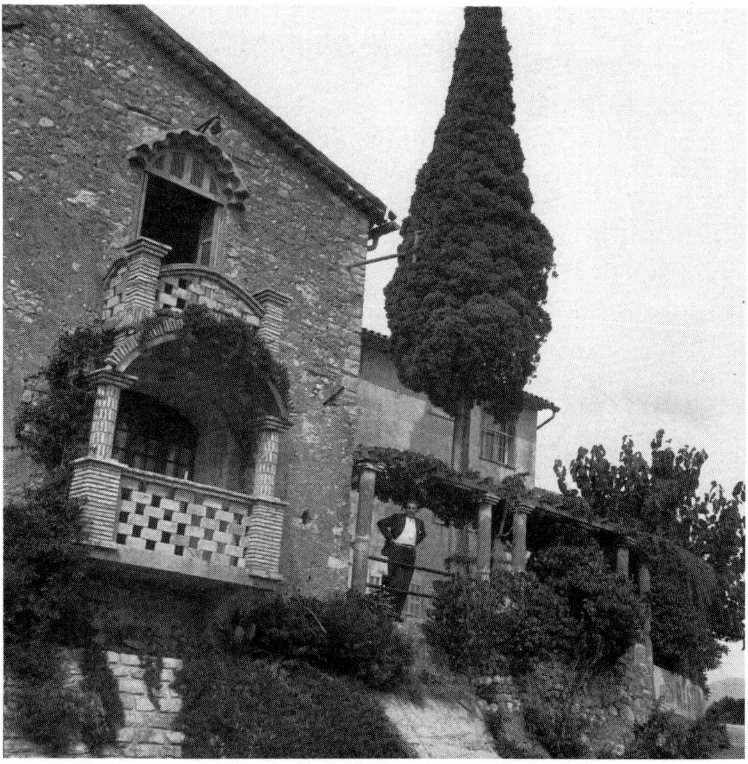

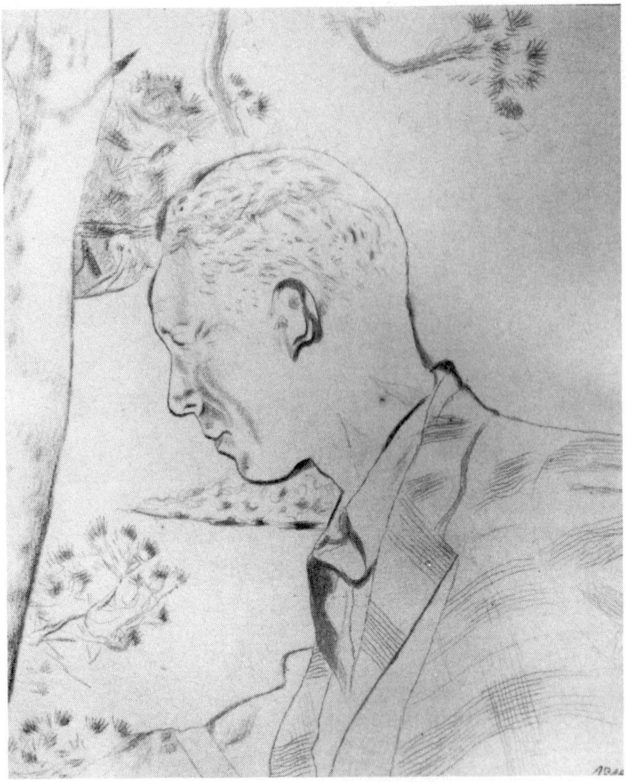

16a My drawing of my brother-in-law, Hugh Mackintosh, at Hyères in 1939.

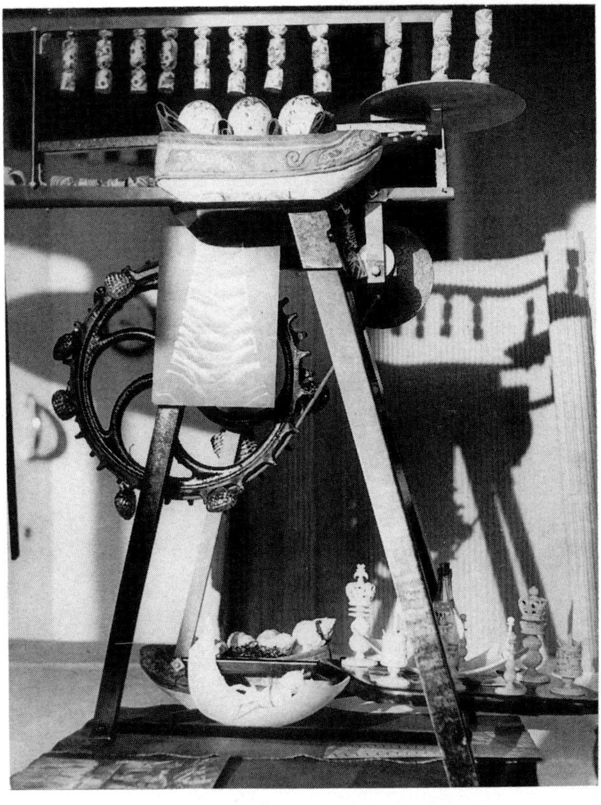

16b Surrealist party-piece. The pedal-operated fretsaw which decorated the table at our Surrealist dinner party in 1939.

never been provoked. But perhaps he sometimes felt the tension between the free, uninhibited and occasionally violent world of the Surrealists, and the *douceur de vivre* of the Society of Friends. But Roland was bold and far-seeing and set the Thames on fire with the organisation of the dream world of 1936.

The International Surrealist Exhibition was well-timed, and that very hot summer the New Burlington Galleries became a new source of wonder as we made living contact with the materialisations of strong spiritual forces, and sought to hunt down the mad beast of convention. You turned into Burlington Gardens, symbolically between the Royal Academy and Bond Street, and took the lift to the third floor of an ordinary-looking building. After that the spectacle began. The large rooms were crowded with the works of de Chirico, Dali, Duchamp, Brancusi, Giacometti, Klee, Miró, Picabia and Picasso amongst others. There were many notables present as well as many respectables, and they acted as people usually act when observed in an 'immoral place'. They tried to be invisible.

Roland was a close friend of the poet Paul Eluard, and it was their inspired enthusiasm and combined doing which led to the success of the exhibition. It attracted large crowds, and, sensational and exciting, was the great event of the year, causing much controversy; it burst on London like a many-faceted flower, sending its petals all over the world, and its seeds fell in many countries. Indeed, Breton envisaged England as the stepping-stone for World Surrealism, although events were not to bear out his optimism. Record crowds were drawn to the New Burlington Galleries on that June day, and some two thousand people saw the exhibition officially opened by André Breton.

Joseph mentioned that his outstanding pleasure was to see T. S. Eliot come in with Herbert Read, and linger in front of Meret Oppenheim's tea-cup and saucer covered in fur, obviously moved by this super-objective correlative of the female sex. There was a ferment of stimulation everywhere, for the sight of nearly four hundred paintings, sculptures, objects, collages and drawings, in a completely new visual language, was overwhelming.

Across the room, an incredulous smile was staring at a melting watch hanging on to its memory. A fantastic painting of a Paranoic Head was watching a mask insulting aesthetes, while a painted man was executing a dance of liberty. ('If you don't like Max Ernst you're a stupid bastard!') Arguments, agreements, forthright with hatchets or with love, I was proud to be among them.

Before 1936 there had been very little information available in England about European Surrealism, apart from articles in obscure periodicals. But however many the shocked disapprovals of the exhibition, nearly everybody behaved well. Only when Paul Eluard delivered his poetry lecture on 24 June and talked of de Sade, that holy martyr of freedom, did Augustus John, until then sitting quietly in the audience, get up noisily and exit dragging his blonde companion with him, slamming the door behind him. A thousand visitors came each day, mostly stunned and puzzled by what they saw, except for those few who were aware of the international significance of this new approach to art. My sister Winifred visited the show, but the strangeness of the work disconcerted her, and she always remained a bit frightened of the Surrealists. For some, the liberation was too much.

Miró's large painting 'Carnival of Harlequins' was a wonder of gaiety not only in the comedy of detail but in its fantasy and fascinating rhythm laid out upon a soft skin-coloured background, enlivened by reds, blues and yellows against black and white – the tiny wasp-clowns, poles, snakes, starfish-wheels, animals and musical instruments all busy with an evident enjoyment of existence. With this painting Miró made a tumultuous entry on to the London scene.

André Masson set a universe in motion with his menacing insect ballet in green, yellow and blue, whilst I could hardly forget Max Ernst's powerful image of 'The Elephant Celebes', with its sombre colour and enigmatic headless female with the pointing finger. I believe that the composition was based on an enormous round grain container which Ernst saw in Celebes, Indonesia, an object the size of an elephant which stuck in his creative memory. Salvador Dali's 'Aphrodisiac Jacket' was always surrounded by the curious. It consisted of a well-tailored dinner jacket hung with small liqueur glasses, each filled with a different beverage. The level of alcohol kept going down, but Dali never seemed the worse for wear . . .

In the last week of the exhibition Salvador Dali, that astonishing super-Surrealist eccentric showman, on a sizzling hot day lectured in a diving helmet and suit procured for him by Lord Berners. Dali was to lecture on 'Authentic Paranoic Phantoms', the last in a series of talks which had included André Breton speaking on 'Limits not Frontiers of Surrealism', Herbert Read on 'Art and the Unconscious', and Paul Eluard on 'Surrealist Poetry'. Dali made his entrance holding two white Russian wolf-hounds on one leash, with a billiard cue in the other hand, a jewelled dagger in his belt, and of course the diving helmet on his head. He strode on to the stage like a bug-eyed monster of the underworld, and proceeded to try to lift the helmet off in order to begin talking. Unfortunately for him it had been bolted down ready for the deep-sea dive he was to take into the unconscious, the proper depth of experience. The audience waited almost as breathlessly, unaware that Dali was suffocating and about to faint. Gala Dali and Edward James, the 'Humming Bird Poet', rushed on stage to the painter's rescue. They tried hammering the bolts to make them turn, but Dali thought his head would burst, for each hard blow was like a gun-shot. Meanwhile the audience howled with laughter, and applauded what they thought was a deliberate pantomime, but Dali was nearly dead when he was released. The man who wanted to plunge deeply into the unconscious mind almost died on the way. Later Dali was convinced that it was the violent eccentricity of this lecture which paved the way for his already growing reputation in New York.

The press had a field day, though their taunts must have

often fallen on deaf ears, for people, mostly young people, came in their hundreds and thousands, not to sneer, but to learn, to find enlightenment and to live. There was much to see and admire in the show, not only the courage – east of the Rhine, at that time, every item would have been burnt or condemned as degenerate – but the revolution in thought, for Kant, that Chinaman of Konisberg, had eternally narrowed the German imagination and sense of freedom, if not that of the rest of Europe.

The Surrealists themselves were a proud, elegant and unforgettable group. They all seemed to be very handsome, Max Ernst with his startling bird-like face, eagle presence and blue eyes; Eluard, tall and classic-looking, sensitive and romantic in emotion; Breton with his Roman head (always slightly tipped back) and small stature, had something leonine about him; Yves Tanguy, nervous and excitable, the most bizarre Bohemian, though extremely disciplined in work; Dali, given to doubts and explosive tempers and never-stilled paranoias, conspicuous by his moustache and his cravates; little Miró with his lovely face, immense childlike talent and spontaneity, a true poet of painting.

The Surrealist women, whether painters or not, were equally good-looking. They were elegant and dressed with panache, caring about clothes and their surroundings, however strange the interiors. Our concern with appearance was not a result of pandering to masculine demands, but rather a common attitude to life and style. This was in striking contrast to the other professional women painters of the time, those who were not Surrealists, who if seen at all, tended to flaunt their art like a badge, appearing in deliberately paint-spotted clothing. The juxtaposition by us of a Schiaparelli dress with outrageous behaviour or conversation was simply carrying the beliefs of Surrealism into public existence.

Amongst the European Surrealists double-standards seem to have proliferated, and the women came off worst. Breton's wife, Jacqueline, was expected to behave as the great man's muse, not to have an active creative existence of her own. In fact, she was a painter of considerable ability, but Breton never mentioned her work. The men were expected to be very free sexually, but when a woman like Lee Miller adopted the same attitude whilst living with Man Ray, the hypocritical upset was tremendous. Perhaps the English, ever discreet, managed to avoid such obvious confrontations . . .

Abstract art and Surrealism were the two movements that interested me most, and I see nothing incompatible in that, indeed we all walk on two legs, and for me, one is abstract, the other surreal – it is point and counterpoint. Surrealism for me draws its inspiration from nature. I recall the account of Tanguy walking along the beach noting the tiny marine forms, studying the seaweed and the rocks. Then he would go back to his studio and create a painting which made references to what he had seen, yet nature would only be the starting point for his imagination. I adopt a similar approach, though at the same time, abstraction would also be exerting its influence upon me, giving me the benefit of geometry and design to match and balance and strengthen the imaginative elements of a composition. Outer eye and inner eye, backward and forward, inside out and upside down, sideways, as a metaphysical aeroplane might go, no longer classical or romantic, medieval or gothic, but surreal, transcendent, a revelation of what is concealed in the hide-and-seek of life, a mixture of laughter, play and perseverence.

You see the shape of a tree, the way a pebble falls or is formed, and you are astounded to discover that dumb nature makes an effort to speak to you, to give you a sign, to warn you, to symbolise your innermost thoughts. Chance is not a neutral but a distinctly positive force; the Surrealists believe that you can get on good terms with chance by adopting a lyrical mode of behaviour and an open attitude.

The piece of work which I had in the New Burlington Galleries which aroused most interest was my painting 'Quadriga'. I had long admired a photograph I had of a horse's head on the Acropolis, and wondered in what strange way I could make it into a painting which would fit into the twentieth century, which could bridge the gap between the centuries. I knew that there was a fountain in Boetia sacred to the muses, which first rose from the ground when struck by the feet of the flying horse Pegasus. Then there was Selene, the pre-Greek goddess of the moon who was given horses to drive across the sky. And I had ridden a lot as a child, in that exalted innocence the Surrealists so admired. In other words, the fountain sacred to the muses was also the horses' fountain which in turn reflected the moon, so I said a private prayer, invoked the childhood drumbeat of hooves, and started on my painting.

One horse's face became four ghost heads, agitated, beating rhythmic cabbalistic convoluted signs expressing movement and anxiety, each square a different mood. Were they the four horses of the Apocalypse? War was encroaching on the selfish peace of England: the Spanish Civil War acted as a kind of distant prelude to the Second World War, and it was to be many years before the Four Horsemen allowed their steeds to return to my frame.

One morning during the Surrealist Exhibition, Paul Eluard rang me up to say that a few of the exhibitors were being photographed in the gallery that afternoon and would I come along? I happened to be lunching that day with Paul Nash, so naturally I suggested that he should join us, as he was on the English committee and had been instrumental in getting Herbert Read and Roland Penrose to come to my studio in the first place. But Paul was on his high horse and refused, saying that nobody had rung him up and asked him to come.

It seemed that nobody had asked Henry Moore either, or Graham Sutherland. As a consequence, proud Paul did not figure in what was to become a famous photograph, although at that time, he was as dedicated to Surrealism as any of the others. It is a curiously selective photograph, organised by the continental contributors without giving the true Surrealist mixture. In the photograph reading from left to right in the back row are: Rupert Lee (Secretary), Ruthven Todd the poet, Salvador Dali, Paul Eluard, Roland Penrose, Herbert Read, E. L. T. Mesens, George Reavey the poet and translator of Russian, and the Surrealist novelist and theoretician Hugh Sykes Davies. In the front row are: Diana Brinton Lee (our secretary's wife), Nusch Eluard, myself, Sheila Legge – the legendary Surrealist phantom who walked around Trafalgar Square with her head covered in rose petals and ladybirds, an idea Gascoyne adapted from Dali – and finally an unidentified friend of Salvador Dali.

I think it has to be admitted that the English committee hunted with some urgency for a reasonable quota of 'Surrealists' to represent Britain in the International Surrealist Exhibition. Charles Howard, for instance, was an American abstract painter, and yet he was included because his work often incorporated what could be read as 'biomorphic' forms. In fact, Conroy Maddox refused to exhibit in 1936 because he felt there were too many hangers-on, people jumping on the prestigious band-wagon without a full commitment to Surrealist principles. However, he later consented to exhibit with the English Surrealists, and has continued to produce Surrealist work of distinction ever since.

One aspect of Surrealism that provoked controversy amongst its English supporters was the political dimension. Under the French definition we were supposed to be political activists, adhering to the cause of proletarian revolution, yet in reality Communism and Surrealism did not go together so easily. The French poet and war-hero Louis Aragon felt he had to leave the Surrealists in order to dedicate himself to the Communist Party; in England, John Banting was almost unique in being able to ride – at least for a time – the two spirited horses of Surrealism and Communism.

I have always described myself as apolitical, but as a humanist there were important issues which I felt the need to endorse. A number of us reacted strongly to the threat of fascism, and there were demonstrations and petitions to sign. The Spanish Civil War was being shamefully ignored in England. Roland and Valentine and David Gascoyne went to Barcelona to support the Popular Front and to speak against fascism. I used to have arguments with my mother, who thought Franco was a marvellous person. She knew nothing about the real situation, for whenever she went to Spain (after the fighting, of course) she only talked to friends and they were all in favour of Franco. A lot of wealthy English people thought like that. Somebody even said to me in 1936, referring to 'these minor Spanish upheavals' – 'it's so far away, what do we care about it?' The Surrealists tried to make people think a bit, but I am sure that in most cases their political beliefs were never very deep or committed. Fundamentally, the English turn everything into a social gathering, they do not try to upset anything, and I think the Surrealists suffered from that kind of apathy, despite the efforts of a few.

After the exhibition ended in July, Joseph and I went for a holiday to Brittany, and landed up at Ploumanach. We chose this stopping place by looking out of the train and trusting to chance, like all good Surrealists. Before us were the most fantastic rocks. They lay like enormous prehistoric monsters sleeping on the turf above the sea: a great buttock ending in a huge thumb, or a gigantic head tuned with organ pipes, a crowd, or a foot rearing up like a dolmen, all sculpted by the sea, that master-worker of all time. Our surprise and delight at the discovery came as a bonus after the excitement of the exhibition in London. It was as if nature had arranged a show of sculpture in the open air, just to prove that she too was keeping her hand in . . .

A camera became a necessity, and so, in a day or two, we took the train again and travelled to Brest, the nearest town, and after a deliciously drunken meal (what soupe à l'oignon!) I bought a Rolleiflex, my constant companion for many years. For me, photography has always meant truth to the objective image of reality, while painting should lean towards the beauty or ugliness of the subjective idea or symbol. The photographs I took in Brittany have now come to fruition, acting as both *aide-mémoire* and starting point for a series of paintings. Pattern and chance, fate – these things have determined my life, and continue to do so.

While we were at Ploumanach, I heard from Roland Penrose that the Museum of Modern Art in New York wanted to borrow my painting 'Quadriga', which he owned, for their show in December of 'Fantastic Art Dada Surrealism'. I was very pleased and felt I had begun well this time. I had hardly ever shown before, but now I had made my mark. Could I keep it up? The doubt was healthy, but I had no wish to rush into conveyor-belt creativity, to feed a demand. I hardly believed in automatism, let alone automation.

Automatism, the process of automatic artistic creation, so beloved of Breton and the French Surrealists, was supposed to bypass conscious control and draw directly upon the deep springs of the unconscious. It was a method of working similar to dream inspiration, another favourite and apparently sincere practice. I agree wholeheartedly with the Surrealist belief that we must somehow avoid the constricting influence of too much accumulated civilisation: we must indeed learn to breathe in a different way – too many have choked on the musty air of established culture. But I am suspicious about the whole idea of working from dreams. I find that daytime dreams can be inspiring, but not night-time ones – they are too confusing.

My own method is to put myself in a state of receptivity during the day. I sit about sometimes for a quarter of an hour or more, wondering what on earth I am doing, and then suddenly I get an idea for something. Either it is the beginning of a title or just the germ of a visual image. Later on, if I am stuck with a half-finished painting, I might take a snooze and after that it comes together quite simply. It may well be that we hunt too much when we are completely on the alert. Too much awareness can be as inhibiting as too little. Of course, there are different ways of tapping the unconscious, but I think it is just an attractive but rather fanciful idea to say that the Surrealists work so often directly from their dreams. I am convinced the majority of them did not.

Automatism is also impracticable. Over the years I have made various attempts to produce automatic painting – so many people have asked me about it – but I have never yet been successful. The last attempt began with spilling enamel paint on to canvas, but instead of being dominated by chance the forms became calligraphic and representational, my conscious mind hardly relinquishing control at all. An earlier attempt at automatic art was 'The Battle Years', a piece I made in the period of increasing violence leading up to the Second World War. I covered parts of a tin tray with melted lead, which I had heated easily over a small burner, and let the fluid metal form its own shapes. I watched fascinated, but when it had cooled and fixed itself, I began to criticise the result, and decided that I should improve upon it. I juxtaposed various disjointed images with the lead shapes, using paint and plaster to try to catch some of the atmosphere of those years. A face, an eye and some teeth, hands and a sword, a small skull and a star. The end result was a mixture I found satisfying, but which could hardly qualify as pure automatism. For me, intuition combined with controlled emotion and intellectual consideration produce the best effects.

The problem with the International Surrealist Exhibition was that it was something of a Nine Days' Wonder – the brilliance and momentum and intensity of it were impossible to sustain. However, a number of people dedicated themselves to organising the Surrealist cause in England, and the London Gallery was set up at 28 Cork Street with the financial support of Roland Penrose. E. L. T. Mesens had been the Surrealist representative for Belgium in the 1936 exhibition, but he was increasingly attracted by England, settling here in the winter of 1937, and in the following year becoming director of the London Gallery. Mesens thought that England offered a more creative environment for artists than remaining among the Belgian bourgeoisie, although his great friend Magritte never abandoned their homeland. Mesens bought Magritte's paintings for very little before they became so popular, but he was always trying to influence Magritte. Mesens insisted Magritte should make his paintings more commercial and understandable. Luckily Magritte would not compromise, which rather neatly shows who in fact was the more bourgeois of the two!

Mesens was a short, fat, baby-faced man with popping blue eyes and continental manners. After lunch he would invariably say: 'Alors, maintenant le love-making'. Neither Lee Miller nor I ever came forward, so the little man would disappear to make a new baby with someone else, or a new collage – I never found out which; perhaps they were much the same. Amongst the Surrealists he was known as a mischief-maker, or *tricheur* as some called him. He was adept at harbouring grudges and besides quarrelling with his one-time great friend Roland, he also brought about a split in Surrealist ranks some years later by alienating the painter and writer Toni del Renzio. But Mesens was a clever collagist, though he did few paintings; conceivably, he will be more remembered for his expertise in public relations (as opposed to private friendships) in support of English Surrealism.

The next exhibition in which I showed work was at the London Gallery, entitled 'Surrealist Objects and Poems'. It was opened at midnight in an appropriate atmosphere of mystery and play. Julian Trevelyan was costumed as a blind explorer to emphasise the importance of searching through the inner life. Herbert Read made a speech which began: 'Approach, for we have names to sell – angels of anarchy and machines for making clouds . . .' Trevelyan had indeed produced an object like a mincer: a mannequin's head poked into it, and clouds emerged. I exhibited my first 'Angel of Anarchy', which began as an ordinary plaster-cast head. When Paul Nash saw it, he claimed that it looked like him. 'Rubbish!' I replied; for the head was initially modelled on Joseph. Paul could only respond that I was evidently attracted to men with prominent noses!

In fact, when I got the plaster head back from the workshop, I was so dismayed by the deadness of the material that I first clothed it in paper and then applied bits of white doyley to the surface. In order to bring out the contours, I added black fur for shadows and green feathers for the forehead. The black fur gave it the slightly sinister look which Paul seemed to share (and recognise) – with his dark hair and curiously weather-beaten eyes. Certainly he liked the object, because he showed it on television just after the show at the London Gallery.

I had called it the 'Angel of Anarchy' partly in tribute to Herbert Read, who had called himself an anarchist in one of his books. However, the head is in no way intended to be a portrait of Herbert, as is sometimes suggested. Anarchy was certainly in the air in 1937, the fighting in Spain was far advanced, and I sincerely hoped that the Angels or revolutionaries would win. Furthermore, I liked the alliteration of my title, it seemed rather aptly to combine Heaven and Hell. Unfortunately, my object was anarchic enough to go missing after an exhibition in Amsterdam, never to be seen again. I was forced to make another version, which is now thinking its own anarchic thoughts in the safe custody of the Tate Gallery.

Herbert Read was the head of propaganda for the Surrealists in England. He had edited a book, with contributions from Breton and Eluard amongst others, which was simply called *Surrealism* and was first published in 1936. One of the illustrations in this book was of another object of mine, which I made from an old-fashioned carpet beater. I pulled this cane contraption to bits and reorganised it after my own fashion, so that it became two standing personages, one with a transparent leaf head and the smaller one with a gourd head. The whole object was a form of aerial or open sculpture which has always fascinated me.

The triangular face had the slightly worried look of a landscape full of thoughts – tall, with deepset blue eyes and a quiet voice, Herbert Read, the elder statesman of art, was an enigmatic figure to some, though to me he was always a good friend, ready to spare time which he did not really have, to help with an introduction or preface to a catalogue of one of my shows. Herbert in his life wrote hundreds of such catalogue introductions, and apparently had a large room in his house lined solely with the catalogues to which he had contributed. He sincerely believed in helping artists, particularly his friends, and he tried through his writing to establish without doubt the crucial role of the artist in society. Later he complained that his efforts had turned him into a copy-writer, but that moment of bitterness was more a reflection of his disappointment at the lack of recognition he received as a poet. He wanted to be thought of as a more creative writer, but perhaps he lacked the necessary self-confidence.

Certainly, a large determining factor was economic necessity. Herbert remained a committed art commentator, and although he was sometimes disparagingly referred to as 'the broken reed', he was a man of idealism and enthusiasm. But as he said himself, if there was a book to write, he would write it – simply because he had a wife and four children to support; because of this, it was sometimes difficult to see where Herbert's sympathies lay. He was a silent man and difficult to talk to, saying that writers should not give away what they were thinking. He liked observing and being thought something of an enigma, but although he was very much the intellectual, he was not cold as some thought. He did a tremendous amount to make the ideas behind modern art accessible to a wide audience, but on the way, he often seemed to involve himself in controversy.

A man not given to surprises, Herbert surprised everyone and delighted few when he championed both abstract art and Surrealism, for he got caught up in the isms and schisms of the different art movements. A friend of Ben Nicholson and Naum Gabo, Herbert supported their work and ideas and wrote a great deal about abstract art. Then in 1936, when the English Surrealists surfaced, both Ben and Gabo attacked him because he could write with conviction about such a different kind of art. This the journalists and critics also did not like; 'what about integrity?' they cried. Of course now it is seen that abstract art and Surrealism can live side by side, that they are different facets of art, not opposite poles.

How dull to live in a standardised world, how right Herbert was to write about what interested him. André Breton said in one of his manifestoes that the Surrealists accepted abstract art as something strange and new, and I am sure they would have shown a Ben Nicholson if he had been willing. But Ben worked to a tight formula and was too puritanical to see as Herbert did that the Surrealists were opening up a new approach to art which would indeed stir sluggish minds.

What did enrage Breton particularly was to learn that Herbert's wife Ludo went to Rome to have an audience with the Pope. As the self-styled 'Pope' of Surrealism, perhaps

Breton resented this threat to his authority. Paul Eluard, on the other hand, said that he would not object if his wife Nusch wanted to do anything so eccentric as to see the Pope.

Perhaps 'Ludo's Monks' had something to do with it, for near the Reads's Georgian home in Yorkshire was a monastery or retreat. Ludo was alone very often, when Herbert travelled to London, so she got to know some of the monks and used to ask them over to the house for a beer or a whisky. However, Herbert put his foot down, because he said her monks (they were always known as 'Ludo's Monks') were drinking the house dry. In future they were only to be invited when Herbert himself was at home. But then he did not know what to talk to them about since they had never heard of Henry Moore or Barbara Hepworth.

Herbert worried the Surrealists as much as the Abstractionists by what seemed to be his double-standards. Even his great friend Henry Moore told me that he had sleepless nights at first when he heard that Read was prepared to support Naum Gabo, whose work was so completely different that it seemed to cut at the base of what Henry stood for – solidity and form. Such were the battles of the thirties and forties, when Herbert found himself the whipping boy amongst angry artists; he fought well, knowing that Naum Gabo and Ben Nicholson who attacked him in print were simply guarding their territory for more or less the same reasons that he was championing Surrealism.

In 1937 Paul Eluard was again in England and he came to see us in London. He was a tall good-looking poet, with a fine forehead and a sensitive face; Paul said of Joseph that he resembled André Breton 'mais mieux proportionné', for Breton was short in stature. Joseph took Paul to the Savage Club for lunch, but first he arrived at the flat, and ensconcing himself in an easy chair rolled off Rimbaud:

> Jeanne-Marie a des mains fortes,
> Mains sombres que l'été tanna,
> Mains pâles comme des mains mortes.
> – Sont-ce des mains de Juana?

(Jeanne-Marie has strong hands,
Hands dark with summer tan,
Hands pale as a dead man's hands.
Are they Juana's hands?)

He did it to the manner born, his voice vibrant with feeling. Joseph had said something previously about the Abbé Bremond and his book on contemporary poetry, which was summarily dismissed by Eluard: 'C'est un idiot'. He then discovered Rimbaud's *Oeuvres Complètes* on Joseph's shelves and demonstrated his points *viva voce*. It was excellent to hear a good poem properly read.

A week before, the Irish writer O'Riordan had told Joseph that Lord Tennyson on a Paris visit called on Baudelaire, and as a compliment read him 'Le Voyage' from *Les Fleurs du Mal*. Baudelaire stood it for a while, but when 'O Mort, vieux capitaine, il est temps! levons l'ancre' was reached, he took over his own poem pronouncing all the 'e' mutes which the Laureate had omitted, and smiling happily said: 'C'est comme ça, vieux masturbateur!' Eluard liked this tale. Dandy, the bulldog, sniffed him with manifest approval and then it was time for lunch at the club. Eluard first wanted to ring up Mesens and asked Joseph if he had any rusty chains which he could rattle during the conversation, as Mesens was very susceptible to alarming noises. Joseph replied that he had left all his chains in Hungary, and that he had spent the previous ten years transforming himself into an English gentleman, so there was not a single rusty link to be had in the flat.

So they climbed unfettered into a taxi and were soon at the Savage Club, where Paul admired the early collection of African sculpture scattered among the rooms, and disliked the paintings hanging on the walls. He became quite excited when presented at the end of the meal with an orange jelly which shook and trembled like a breast, most erotically, for he could give a sensuous existence to the curvatures of his pudding by merely touching it with his spoon. He contemplated it for some time before deciding to devour this object of his desire.

The story, as related to me by Joseph, reminded me of the time we were dining with friends at the Café Royal and, fooling around, I had picked up a couple of bread rolls and popped them into my bosom where they warmed themselves. Then I took them out and put them on a plate, and hey presto, before I could say a word, a waiter had picked them up and offered them to the theatre critic James Agate, who was sitting not far away. What could I do? I hardly dared call out give me back my breasts!

In July 1937, I found myself once more in Truro, this time not alone, as we were on our way to stay with Roland Penrose, the best of hosts, near Lamb Creek in Cornwall in a beautiful Georgian house belonging to Becus, Roland's brother. Lee Miller and Paul and Nusch Eluard were already there. Lee took snapshots and looked most alluring. Nusch was Eluard's second wife, a French peach much painted, loved and admired by Picasso. She was sweet, gentle and dark-haired, light in spirit and laughing. She was the daughter of a circus artist, who performed in a travelling show in the French provinces. Her part of the act was to be chained up by her father, and by invited members of the public, and then in some mysterious way throw off the chains and perform a little dance in triumph at her freedom; a career which was to prepare her well for her later life with Eluard. She was a delightful being who could never be permanently tamed.

I was walking with Paul one day in the grounds of Old Kea, the house near Lamb Creek, and it was then that he confessed to me that he had taken a long voyage to the East in an attempt to exorcise the image of his first wife Gala, whose presence was always with him, although she had left him to live with Dali. I remembered this many years later, when in 1984 I read Eluard's passionate love-letters to Gala, which for twenty years flowed from his pen. He wrote to her almost every day, never once blaming her for her behaviour.

But on this Cornish holiday, Eluard was a fountain of joy and faith in life, a living Eros; he and I had become very attracted to each other, and we had some delicious days and nights together, brief but exciting. Paul Nash was aware that Eluard admired me, and was overcome with jealousy at the thought of me in the arms of a perfidious Frenchman. His letters to me were full of distress and anger that I should throw him over so lightly, yet I had done no such thing. Ours was a lasting companionship of like minds, similar to Goethe's *Elective Affinities*; indeed, Paul spoke of such relations in his own work as well, saying for instance that he tried to solve the mysterious equation between a stone and a moon. I had no intention of being 'solved' by either Eluard or Paul Nash, and though I liked and admired Eluard a great deal, I knew that to Frenchmen love affairs are frequent and their importance is slight.

However it was a delightful Surrealist houseparty that July, with Roland taking the lead, ready to turn the slightest encounter into an orgy. I remember going off to watch Lee taking a bubble-bath, but there was not quite enough room in the tub for all of us . . . The Surrealists were always supposed to be immoral monsters, but I for one did not go to bed with everybody who asked me. When would I have had time to paint? I think if love comes your way you should accept it, as I did with Paul Nash and Paul Eluard; I have never been able to believe in complete fidelity. But that special attraction does not spring up between most people, and I could never love Roland, for instance, except as a friend. Lee once threw a glass of water over me because she thought I was flirting with Roland, and Mesens the mischief-maker (why did Breton call him 'our silent friend'?) told Lee afterwards that I had designs on Roland. That was completely untrue, but I was not surprised to discover later that Lee hated Mesens.

In fact, we all got on together so well (Joseph liked Eluard and avoided being jealous of him, perhaps because he was himself enjoying a liaison with Nusch) that when Paul suggested we adjourn to Mougins in the south of France for September, the chance was not to be missed. News of this further holiday with Eluard made Paul Nash even more jealous, but to me the thought of our visit to Mougins where we were to stay in the hotel Vaste Horizon with Picasso and Man Ray was enchanting. Who wanted to go back to care-worn London after such a sojourn in Cornwall? Eluard gave me a copy of Edward Lear's *Book of Nonsense* in which he had written a poem, and we parted with the warm knowledge of a swift reunion.

The poem that Eluard inscribed for me runs as follows:

Le 'non-sense'
de la prononciation française

Les poules du convent
Avec candeur convent
Les oeufs sacrés du Fils
Et tissent les longs fils
De la Vièrge qui parent
Leur déplorable parent
(Convent tarts
Hatch with candour
The sacred eggs of the Son
And weave the long threads
Of the Virgin and avoid
Their deplorable parent)

Roland was very much in love with Lee, who had arrived in Paris from New York in the mid-twenties and persuaded Man Ray to tutor her in photography, although as a rule he took no pupils. Hers are the gigantic pair of lips floating in the sky – the image that spread over the world in that classic of Surrealist painting 'Les Amants', which Man painted in 1934. Lee also appeared as a living sculpture in Jean Cocteau's film *Le Sang d'un Poète* (1930), leading a cow with the map of Europe painted on its bovine body. In repose she had an Hellenic beauty, but when active was full of *élan vital*, and very uninhibited. I still have a vivid memory of her, trouserless, dancing in front of the headlights of the car in which we had gone for a midnight drive in the south of France. She was then married to an immensely wealthy Egyptian called Aziz, with whom she lived in great style in Alexandria, but in 1937 she had escaped for a time to Europe.

So in September, Joseph and I found ourselves en route for the small hill-top village of Mougins to join the others. We stopped at a small hotel on the outskirts of Cannes, where we spent one hectic and startling night invaded by bats from a nearby derelict church which must have been given over to the Devil or haunted by visiting vampires. Joseph stood up stark naked and swiped at them with a newspaper, while I cowered under the bedclothes. Next morning, Roland and Lee rescued us, and drove us up to Mougins, Roland telling us on the way how inadvertently he had nearly killed Picasso in a motor accident. It was delirious meeting Paul and Roland again, in fact it was a happy gathering of artists, and became the most memorable holiday, engraved like a gem in the encrustations of the mind.

It was presided over by le Peintre Soleil himself, Picasso the Master, who was indubitably boss of the roost, his thoughts and moods somehow setting the ruling temperature. Man Ray had already arrived at the Vaste Horizon, a hotel of beautiful simplicity overlooking a courtyard and vineyards, while way below could be seen the roofs of Cannes and the dark sea. Man had with him Ady, his exotic girlfriend from Guadeloupe, to whom he held forth on the advantages of a saltless diet, and whom he teased with, 'On mange les chevaux en Guadeloupe'. Man was American and although he made his home for some years in Paris, obviously did not take kindly to a diet of horse flesh. His teasing evoked a fierce protest from Ady, who defended Guadeloupe's claim to a cultured cuisine. The argument dragged on until it was ended by Picasso's thunder: 'Fâites-moi la paix – on mange les bicyclettes en Guadeloupe!' ('Give me some peace – they eat bicycles in Guadeloupe!')

Ady was a charming creole, very young and attractive and full of laughter; unfortunately I rather over-exposed my snapshots of her, and she looked considerably darker than she was, much to her chagrin. To pacify her, we asked her to lunch with us in Cannes. She accepted and of course ordered Riz Creole, and ate it daintily with her fingers, rolling the food in handy little balls. We tried to do the same, but failed, and messed up our hands, faces and clothes; humbly we returned to fork and knife.

Apparently, when Ady first met Picasso, she went up to him, flung her arms around his neck and said: 'I hear you are quite a good painter.' But there was a serious and thoughtful side to her as well. She was to be seen now and again in cemeteries, measuring graves. It was not that she was particularly pessimistic, but rather that graveyards gave her a great feeling of peace and calm. She probably needed a respite from the high spirits of the Vaste Horizon.

Our first morning we awoke early to a noise in the courtyard, and looking out we saw Picasso and the hotelier's small son of about ten, looking at the boy's bicycle. 'Monsieur Picasso, vous avez abimé ma bicyclette' ('Monsieur Picasso, you have ruined my bicycle') shouted the boy, shaking his fist at him. Picasso was squatting on the gravelly ground and doing his best to make the thing work, and this was the only time we saw him dismayed or apologetic.

One afternoon, after lunch sitting around the table in the courtyard, Picasso broke a matchbox into small bits and pieces, and built them up again into an equivalent of the landscape which lay below us, with the rooftops of Cannes in the distance. The model was like a house – or rather town – of cards, manipulated in an astonishing fashion; it was not that Picasso was showing off, but that he was showing us what could be done with the slightest means.

Dora Maar, who was Picasso's companion at the time, was a highly intelligent photographer. She was very dignified, and yet something critical and unexpressed lurked in her. According to Joseph I was truly happy in Mougins, taking photographs and sporting in the sea, yet while our garden of poets enjoyed life and the warmth and love of art and poetry . . . one could almost feel the throb of war machines being built everywhere to destroy our world. We knew it and assumed we were sheltered.

The days rolled by most pleasantly and excitingly. Bathing on the sandy beaches at nearby Juan les Pins was delightful, and Joseph remarked on the beauty of the women, and the powerful build of Picasso. I had met him first lying on his tummy on the beach. I had been for a wander along the shore, and came back with an armful of bits and pieces, mostly shoe-heels and other strange flotsam and jetsam, which I laid as a tribute at his feet, while Paul Eluard introduced me as a friend. The shoe bits amused him, there were so many; he said he had noticed them and also thought of collecting them.

The Vaste Horizon was a perfect place for us, simple but good in every way. Its hygienic arrangements were also simple – there were few of them. One morning, Joseph was wending his way to the end of the corridor, when turning the door handle of the loo, out came Picasso with the beaming face of one who could do it. It was no small matter to follow the minotaur to his secret lair, and Joseph tried to back away in order to return later, but no, Picasso caught him by the arm, bowed him in with mock solemnity, pulled out a large silk handkerchief and wiped the seat. Then he made Joseph sit down, and laughing and bowing, closed the door behind him. Joseph said that he felt rather foolish and somewhat costive for a day or two, but that it was an event of which to be proud.

Indeed, there was no mistaking Picasso's sense of style. Another time, we were all at lunch around the same courtyard table, when an enormous hornet started angrily buzzing round us, and we women, scantily clad, shrank into our bikini skins. Picasso got up from the head of the table, and with one stroke of the carving knife cleft the flying hornet in two. It was no mean feat, and we all applauded, while he bowed, beaming.

For a photographer, Picasso was a monumental work of art, waiting to be snapped sitting on his haunches in the sand, with his steady brilliant black-and-white eyes and sculptural build, compact as some Mexican god but vitally alive, whether serious, amused or intent. Lee said that Picasso always smiled for me in photographs, but I have studies of him in many moods and poses. A bull-nosed head on a powerful body, Picasso was not tall, but short in stature. Another agate in fact, whose feet were so well-planted that they seemed to grow out of the ground. While his untiring genius devoured ideas, a volcanic imagination unleashed them again, but transformed, and feeling hands and well-articulated fingers proclaimed the result on canvas, paper, stone, metal, collage, engraving or pottery. He had in superabundance two of the many qualities needed in a painter: authority and magic. He liked to startle and amuse, and his physiognomy was the constant chart of an expressive temperament, showing the weather of his inner world.

There was a slight wariness, he told us, of 'les anglais'. On a visit to England, he was invited to a dinner party, and when he arrived, he was shown into a dark dining-room lit by candles placed on a long table covered with a black cloth. Only his hostess was present, in a black nightgown, and on his appearance, she started blowing out the candles one by one, ordering him to do the same. Picasso was so frightened he could not blow! No wonder he was uneasy with Anglo-Saxons, but such a Proteus should merely have changed himself into a candle and her into a moth, and he would soon have been rid of her.

Picasso in fact loved women and his drawings and paintings of his many mistresses reveal great tenderness. But he had nothing feminine about him, he belonged to the school of Roman emperors who did not believe in the androgynous nature of man. He was not a great flirt, being more gallant in his attentions, and I was struck by him less as a sexual being than as a powerfully male physical presence. A small warm friendly man to most people, he lived surrounded by his famous friends. To others he was a fascinating monster, but the reality was that he lived an exceedingly simple life, drank nothing but Evian water, took great care of what he ate, and allowed only a few people close to him. He was a very hard worker with a prodigious output, and I remember his cry of, 'au travail, au travail!' after lunch while we dozed or lay in the sun.

Picasso was surrounded by a chaotic amount of possessions in his many houses. There were treasures of all kinds, shabby, forgotten or beloved, boxes full of old iron shards or bones, trunks of stones awaiting the day when they would be turned into masterpieces. Lee told me that he had dozens and dozens of hats of all kinds as well as beards, false noses and costume jackets from God knows where, all hoarded away in his villa, La Californie, in Cannes. His friends were encouraged to dress up, for he liked to see them transformed. He asked Lee for a copy of a photograph she took of me at Brighton Pavilion: he liked the idea of me being pregnant with a camera, transformed by Rolleiflex.

Picasso evidently enjoyed games as much as he liked transformations, especially when they turned out to be the same thing. When we were at Mougins with him, we played the game of changing names for a day. Pablo Picasso became Don José Picasso, Joseph became Pablo Bard, I became Dora Agar, Man Ray became Roland Ray and so on. I think we had to pay a fine of one or two francs if we forgot. Picasso rarely complimented people, but said of Joseph: 'This is a man. This is a charming man.' It was an even greater seal of approval when Picasso took Joseph's name.

But not all people liked or admired Picasso. Some thought him incredibly mean. I never saw him in a rage, but I heard about them. There is the famous story of the drawing-pins. He stormed into a room one day in a vile temper, accusing everyone in the house of stealing four or five drawing-pins that he had left on a table. Could he not leave anything on a table without it being stolen? He made the whole house miserable with his lamentations, until about four hours later he discovered where he had really put them. Eluard, who seemed to me the most peaceable and lovable man, also got into rages. I think he even cracked a chair over someone's head once in the midst of an argument.

Picasso seemed to be thinking about his work all the time.

Yet when we were at Mougins, he must have just finished painting 'Guernica', and he did not say a word about it. But I think he was deliberately keeping quiet then, since he was not at all sure how it would be received. The only thing he did say was that he would never go back to Spain; apart from that, it was scarcely noticeable that he had been working on such a masterpiece. Picasso did ask Eluard to let him know what prices his paintings were fetching at the Parisian auctions. He was very competitive, and wanted to know whether Braque or other painters were outstripping him.

Roland, Lee, Man and Ady, Paul and Nusch went fishing in a large boat one day early in the holiday. I am a very bad sailor, and decided that I would rather stay on terra firma. Luncheon came, and we were surprised to hear that Picasso and Dora Maar had not gone fishing either. They came to the table a bit late, scared perhaps of being left alone with 'les anglais', but when Picasso discovered Joseph originally came from Hungary and that like Dora Maar I had lived in Buenos Aires and could speak a bit of Spanish, the insular ice was broken for the rest of our stay, and Picasso was reassured that we would not ask him to blow out any candles! Joseph told him of my admiration and added that I looked towards Mougins as Moslems did towards Mecca. Picasso laughed and pulled the cork out of a bottle standing on the table, and handed it to me saying that I should put it between my teeth to stop them chattering when the bombs started falling. We had talked that day of the threat of war, but in spite of the increasing Teutonic fury, we could still bathe and ignore it, bask in the sun, eat and have a merry heart.

Another time, Picasso surprised and delighted me by coming into my small room to see some objects I had made out of the shoe bits and driftwood, collected while swimming or from the beach. The Blitz in London took its toll later, and like the seaside monster in Dorset, they were demolished by Hitler's boys. However, the Surrealists made objects out of whatever turned up, believing that they came at the behest of chance and went that way also. Objects were ephemeral, sometimes even made in order to be destroyed. A lot of objects I have made in the course of my life have disappeared like that, and have escaped my memory.

The object is an even more typically Surrealist creation than the collage, and at once comes into competition with sculpture. I am mentioned in Alexandrian's book on Surrealist art as one who stood out amongst others with my poetic objects. The found object had a special significance for me, for the selection of one particular thing from amongst a host of others, whether stones or bones, has often provided the solution to a creative problem, or provoked its own separate inspiration.

Joseph mentioned his bulldog to Picasso, who replied that he too once had a bulldog which he liked, but he could not put up with him 'because he was barking at both ends'. Finally he presented the dog to Braque, who, blissfully unconscious of the drawback, jumped at the gift. Picasso could be most amusing as a raconteur when he wanted. He told us that one evening he felt he just could not continue painting, so he turned to writing poetry. But he said he found it too expensive: he had to keep a mistress, go to good and elegant restaurants, and as he could not afford it, he was forced finally to go back to his *métier*, and be satisfied with being a painter. He knew the Sitwells, and said of Osbert: 'On commence comme Lord Byron, après ça on va voir.' ('He comes on like Lord Byron – after that, wait and see').

Every now and again we went into Picasso's room, at his invitation. In it was a black trunk purchased in Cannes, full of treasures, *objets trouvés*, strange stones, wood picked up, pebbles, shells and broken shards. On the balcony, I remember him opening up a white handkerchief to show us stones most beautifully incised, into which he had carved designs. Dora Maar wore a heavy wide African ivory bracelet which Picasso had gloriously enriched by a minotaur sporting with maenads. These unusual pieces of jewellery were much cherished, and the engraved shard which Nusch wore on her neck was a sign of great affection.

Picasso was very fond of Nusch, but there is still controversy about whether she became his mistress. Eluard kept offering his wife to Picasso as a gift, presumably as a measure of his friendship, though at the cost of treating Nusch like an *objet trouvé*. Did Picasso accept? It hardly seems to matter. Whatever their actual relationship, Picasso insisted that after the Eluards had returned to Paris, he could still hear Nusch's voice on the stairs.

Alas, the red-letter holiday was coming to an end. Soon the Hispano-Suiza was at the door, waiting for Picasso and Dora Maar; while the paintings were loaded onto the back seat, Pablo and Dora sat opposite on the strapontin seats, uncomfortable perhaps but happy, watching over their precious cargo. Perhaps it was not all that precious. Picasso was much less reverential towards his work than his admirers were, and knew well when he had fallen short. As the famous story relates, a fan once expressed admiration for a painting that was leaning against the studio wall. 'Oh that,' said Picasso, 'my cat painted that.'

When they had gone, Joseph and I inherited Picasso's large bedroom and balcony looking out over the countryside. I can truthfully say that I slept in Picasso's bed, though not when he was in it. There was a very small bright green frog leaping about the bedroom, and I wondered if Picasso had kept it as a pet. Drawing-pins had been left in the walls, so remembering the story, I kept them as trophies. The brown paper palette was gone, but an ox skull had been left behind. I could not look at it without seeing a Picasso drawing or painting.

Roland and Lee also left for London, but we lingered on, wanting to digest all we had seen and heard in that Mediterranean setting, a setting which is constant, and according to Joseph, holds an assurance that its scale, humanity and values cannot be destroyed. It may go underground, but it will re-create itself, like the ancient olive trees that will surely sprout and blossom once again in the sun. No artificially projected environment could ever do the same, it would lack the vitality of the natural world of the Mediterranean. So much of Picasso's Mediterranean texture lives because of that constant; Joseph found it 'hitting his inner box' much more than the sentimental baroque of his friend Kokoschka. As far as I was concerned, although I admired Picasso more than any other painter I could think of, that holiday in Mougins had left me more cautious of his influence than ever before, seen as it was at such overwhelmingly close quarters.

When I look back on the year before the outbreak of the war, I remember it as a time of uncertainty and apprehension, dismay and despair, mixed with determination that life should be as full as possible. Joseph and I spent the summer of 1938 in Somerset, with my white cat and his bulldog, in a cottage lent us by Enthoven the architect, the first person to buy a painting of mine. On our walks through the fields, the cat Bella used to move unconcerned beneath the cows, while Dandy did everything he could to provoke them.

It was a period of more travel than work, for the international political situation made it impossible to concentrate on anything for long. In September we had a holiday in Europe – in case it was our last – visiting amongst other places Knokke, a seaside town in Belgium. We revelled in the sun and the bathing, and Joseph took some photographs of me for a change. We visited Bruges, where I remember seeing the old ladies like wax dummies outside their houses, eternally doing their crochet work.

In the spring of 1939 we went to France, determined to have a last fling on the Mediterranean coast. We were also pretty hard up and it was cheaper to live in France than London. Our friend Mary Oliver took over the Bramham Gardens flats, as she had just adopted a Chinese girl from Limehouse, ordering clothes for her from Doucet and Balenciaga, as well as enough toys to fill both flats. We rented a flat with one large room just outside Toulon. I discovered one day, returning from the town where I had been shopping in those wonderful cheese shops in the back streets, that a sailor had turned me into a *Poisson d'Avril*, or April Fool. No doubt thinking that I had too carefree and happy a face for such troublesome times, he had stuck a paper fish on to the back of my coat. Joseph discovered it when I returned and was highly amused, while I decided that I must retaliate by pinching the red pompom off a sailor's cap. The chance came in a cinema, but – alas – no scissors, so I could not take it.

We often went to the nearby village of Carquieranne, where we used to watch the boats come into the little port in the evening. I always had my eyes open for objects, and was delighted to see a Greek amphora being disentangled from the fishermen's nets one night. I immediately went up to one of the men, and asked him if I might buy it from him. 'Have it,' he said, 'I find them tearing our nets too often.' It was already in two pieces, and so, adding a ram's horn that I had picked up in Cumberland to the encrustations already there, it was short work making 'Marine Object' – though in fact it took me and the amphora a long time to attempt such a conjunction!

We went over to Port-Cros for a few days to stay with Winifred and Hugh (who had forsaken Sark for once), and quite by chance we ran into Geoffrey Grigson in the only hotel on that small island off Hyères in the south of France.

Grigson was a tall man with gnostic eyes and acid tongue. He was a deep thinker given to both mischief and mysticism, and was well-known for his sharp remarks about poets and writers. He believed that the English were sliding into soft sentimentality, and in doing so were losing their intellectual inheritance. He was an eighteenth-century man, admiring the fierce intellectual battles which were frequent at that time. For him, the British were too fond of a comfortable life, which seems difficult to believe considering our conduct in the war which was steadily approaching.

Geoffrey was also a nature-lover with a keen memory for all the trees and flowers and anything that flies. He must have agreed with the notion that language owes a greal deal of its meaning to the eye, since he thought that the English were philistines, unawakened to visual pleasures in comparison to the French or other continental people. He insisted that we should go for walks together in the lovely landscape, and it was then that he told me how francophile he was and enlarged on his belief that England would never regain her former greatness. Both he and Joseph were good talkers, both like-minded in thinking about the destinies of nations, so we discussed everything from politics to art. Geoffrey was fascinated by Surrealism, and had even contributed a found object to the International Surrealist Exhibition of 1936, though I do not know if he ever produced any painting or sculpture.

The waterfront at Toulon in those days was magnificent, with the old houses which must have looked as they did in Napoleonic times, excellent restaurants and groups of sailors moving about in slow motion. But the news front was not good, and one morning late in July, we looked out of our window to see rows of Senegalese soldiers creeping along, well-armed, in the road beneath us, while others were sharp-shooting not far away. We decided it was time to get back to London, before events overtook us. Most people had already fled to their respective homes and we found it easy to book seats on the train. So, laden with canvases, drawings and other equipment, we travelled back to London.

We decided we still had time for a few farewells before the holocaust, so with a couple of friends who had a handy car, we moved around the South Coast calling on old friends like Alec Waugh, whom we found imperturbably playing cricket on the village green.

As war appeared more and more certain, refugees from the continent – many of them friends and acquaintances – arrived in London. Walter Gropius and Marcel Breuer, also Moholy-Nagy, stayed for a while on their way to America. Just before war broke out we invited them to a farewell dinner. We rigged up a ping-pong table in the studio, and had a light-hearted 'surrealist' dinner with a few strange objects scattered amongst the dishes, and a pedal-operated fretsaw as a centre-piece hung with fruit and flowers and crackers. The menu was a curiosity I have unfortunately lost, but we ate unusually coloured dishes, like Huysmans' character Des Esseintes, and I have a feeling that pink potatoes featured among the vegetables. The complexion of the dinner party was rather more abstract and architectural than Surrealist, but our guests took it all in their stride, and Gropius told me he was pleased to learn more about Surrealism. Herbert Read and Roland Penrose were among the guests, and we managed to have a marvellous evening before the refugees left for their new life in America.

Marcel Breuer lived for a time very near us in Tregunter Road, and he came often to see us. I remember him telling me that he thought that women are or should be the real Surrealists because of the metamorphic changes in the womb when they are pregnant. Strangely enough I do not know of any Surrealist literature which mentions such an idea; although the Surrealists have explored many avenues of thought, the biology of the embryo does not seem to be among them.

In the late thirties the Surrealist group in London used to meet about once a month in a Spanish restaurant called the 'Barcelona' in Beak Street, Soho. Among those who came were Roland Penrose and Lee Miller, Henry Moore, Conroy Maddox, John Banting, Paul Nash, Edouard Mesens, Humphrey Jennings, myself and a few others. There were no coffee houses in those days and no cafés as in Paris where we could meet to discuss ideas and make plans, and so a dinner seemed the next best thing. They were enjoyable get-togethers, for English artists are notoriously self-contained as a rule, and do not have either the desire or opportunity to meet as often as they should. Some meetings were stormy, some merely cloudy, all lively and tempered by Spanish wine and good company. In art as in life, nothing reaches us pure. We cannot decide that our daily experience must be either aesthetic or practical – Art or Life: it is never either/or, it is always both.

There were some personality clashes in the group. Mesens complained that no one was sufficiently motivated at the meetings. In comparison with his continental behaviour, we may have appeared too easy-going, but certainly I remember arguing with him. I recall one occasion when I got rather furious, but Mesens was delighted. 'At least Eileen contradicts me,' he said, 'she makes a controversy out of it!' Other disagreements were more personal. Henry Moore complained that Gordon Onslow Ford, the Surrealist who was soon to leave for America, was rude to a waiter. Henry, of course, would always stick up for the working class, but he may have been too sensitive in this case; Onslow Ford claimed that he did not insult the man, but merely said that he had forgotten the bread. The English are not very good at groups: an art movement easily becomes a social club, and then class is drawn in. Looking back on it now, it could be said that English Surrealism was doomed by the English character.

It may seem that in contradiction to the well-established reputation of Surrealist artists, the English Surrealists were not particularly notorious for outrageous behaviour or conversation. We were unconventional, but as Roland said, we had no wish to exhibit ourselves as clowns or monkeys. No, it was to the work, our paintings and objects and poems, that we directed the public; there they would find their surprises and the best scandals.

There are various distinctive signatures of Surrealist art, and collage, although invented by the Cubists, became a key to our work. I have always thought of collage as more of an urban art form than frottage; both are dictated by your surroundings, and I tend to do less frottage simply because I do not have access to the materials. (Frottage, of course, is the technique of placing paper over interesting raised surfaces, then rubbing over the paper with wax crayon or graphite, to take an impression of the patterns and textures.) Roland, on the other hand, had a room full of bits and pieces he had picked up and which he could rub to produce weird and beautiful patterns. But then he had a place in the country and the opportunity to collect the raw materials. Nowadays I can only make objects from what I find, and beachcombing is a thing of the past. The found object is another distinctive signature, together with the made or interpreted object, but I still think that collage is one of the more important additions to twentieth-century techniques. For me it is a form of inspired correction, a displacement of the banal by the fertile intervention of chance or coincidence.

The Surrealists and Picasso have taken what lies around them and turned it into art. And that is what I attempt to do, which is why I surround myself with fantastic bric-à-brac, in order to trigger off my imagination. For it is a certain kind of sensitive chaos that is creative, and not sterile order. The revelation of the inexhaustible aspects of things is one of the great delights and one of the deepest charms of art.

The Surrealists have seen that the universe is at root a magical illusion, a strange, mysterious, fabulous game, and that is how they play it.

The subterranean kingdom of the Surrealists is difficult to assess, for I am often asked what I think of Surrealism now and where it is going. The work of Magritte, Max Ernst, Miró and Dali is famous, highly priced and hangs prominently in museums all over the world. There is no doubt that Surrealism is a cultural and artistic success. But the Surrealists' aim was not to establish a glorious place for themselves in the annals of art and literature, but to change the world. To transform life itself, this was the essential purpose of the group, but alas the form of the flower is unknown to the seed, and the goal has not been reached, for the great transformation has not occurred.

The place of Surrealism in the world now may be infinitesimal, but like a small dust cloud which penetrates the corners of the universe, it has changed many things, and the call to the irrational is now listened to even by scientists. Surrealism spread its wings slowly but inexorably all over the world, invading the domains of advertising, theatre, design and ballet, not to mention photography, which was originally of especial importance to the Surrealists. In unforeseen ways, it has affected our sensibilities; on a wider and more popular level it has quietly achieved a distinct modification. It has helped to break down barriers, but in the process it has become more diffuse. Although there are Surrealists painting and writing all over the world, the impact of Surrealism now, is not, and cannot be, as explosive as that first bombshell in Zurich or Paris or London. Surrealism has settled down to a comfortable middle age, recognised by the Establishment as a major art form of the twentieth century, like Cubism or Abstract Expressionism. As André Breton said shortly before he died: 'It is no longer possible to scandalise anyone.'

CHAPTER SIX

'All the Gods are Dead except the God of War'

Then on 3 September 1939, war. Again, war; this time to touch me more deeply and lastingly. I was older, my life was more easily affected by outside events, and the massive scale of the hostilities left few undisturbed. In due course, but all too soon, the bombs were falling on London. Discovering that we were still alive after the first air raid, we went to Torquay for a few days to decide on our next move. The prospect of instant annihilation tends to put a new complexion on all relationships, so it was not just to make up the seemingly endless feud with my mother, but also to affirm my love for Joseph that I decided we should get married. I proposed to him and he accepted. We chose Leap Year Day 1940 for our wedding, as this way we would have fewer anniversaries. We had been living together for twelve years in a state of unmarried (and so-called sinful) bliss.

After we had visited the registry office and made ourselves respectable, my mother gave us a lunch party at Claridges; as she had been reassured by Lady Smiley, a society friend of hers, that he was an asset, she took to Joseph and found him delightful but rather foreign. (In fact he spoke immaculate English with only a slight trace of accent). Mama would have done well to remember that life itself is a foreign language that we all occasionally mispronounce.

Dorice Fordred, the South African born actress, threw a less formal party for Joseph and me in her lovely flat on the Embankment at Chelsea. A lot of people came, including Winifred and Hugh, Henry Moore and Robert Helpmann. Dorice was a friend throughout the thirties and forties, and we first met her at Alec Waugh's house one weekend. I lost touch with her when we moved to Melbury Road, I am sorry to say. Her Chelsea flat was a delight: Rodney Thomas had done the interior decoration, and to complement the river view she bought a fairly large painting I had done of barges on the Thames.

These were the weeks of the phoney war, when we were both learning the meaning of fire-watching, and the intricacies and stealthy approach needed to deal with an explosive noise. (You slink into a room like a snake on your belly.) We were also taught to use a hatchet for destructive purposes when fire-fighting. It was a return to mere survival.

Some years before, my mother had let the Balfour Place house to Dorothy Paget (the Irish racehorse owner) and had moved into a flat in Grosvenor Square. Mama, a strong personality with an income to indulge it, was socially very active in London, and was disappointed that I had deserted her. When war was declared, my mother refused to go to America with Winifred and Hugh, who took their children there to avoid the bombing. (She claimed the Americans spent their time smoking, chewing and spitting – hardly the acme of civilisation.) Nor did she want to go back to the Argentine, where my eldest sister Dorothy had taken her children. However, Grosvenor Square no longer seemed a particularly healthy spot, so I was relieved when she moved into a self-contained flat in Lady Smiley's house at Wentworth, Sunningdale.

Pamela Travers, who was more of a friend of Winifred, but whom Joseph knew through Orage, lent us her cottage in Sussex, at Mayfield, near Midhurst, for a honeymoon. It was only a break of a week before we returned to the blackout in London, but it was still a welcome respite. I did a couple of portraits of Pamela about this time (there is a collage head dated 1939) and several drawings of her adopted son Camillus. Like so many other people, they too went to America for the duration of the war.

The dismal possibility of being called up depressed me enormously, for I am not a war-like creature, and I could see my efforts to turn myself into a better painter being blown to bits. Luckily I knew a singer who very soon became the boss of a canteen in Savile Row, serving hot meals to civil servants and Ministry of Information personnel. My singer friend was a Mrs Mott who used to perform regularly at the Wigmore Hall, and I met her through my sister Dorothy's husband, Colonel Quin-Smith. She enlisted me as a daily maid-of-all-work with about twenty others, peeling potatoes, scrubbing floors and washing up. We were all amateurs at the game of handing round hot plates during the scramble of luncheon rush-hour, and then pushing the tea-trolleys in the afternoon. But I thanked my stars that I had not been called up and sent to some remote part of England, Scotland or Wales, but could still live in my flat in London instead of battling with the elements or marching round a parade ground. For some reason, I felt I could take bombs in my stride.

In 1940, Joseph became an examiner for the Oxford and Cambridge Boards in French, German and Italian, moving around the country, dodging bombs, and visiting Haileybury, Stowe and many other public schools. Admiral Sir Charles Carpendale, long known to me as Chippy, was still friendly but he certainly stamped on the idea of Joseph having anything to do with the Admiralty. Some other friend had suggested that Joseph could do useful work for the navy, but Chippy looked with great suspicion on all artists and writers. Joseph was by now a naturalised Englishman as he had voluntarily relinquished Hungarian citizenship (in 1928), with all eagerness to become an English gentleman. There was no question of Joseph's loyalty to his adopted country (his pride at being awarded a certificate for Warden's Service in the Royal Borough of Kensington was enormous), but for some he would always be a foreigner. My sister Winifred published her second novel in 1940, called by the enchanting title of *Mermaids Sleep Alone*. As usual, she was on target. She made one of her characters say: 'Otto! Mentioning the soul! What's the matter with you, darling? Do please remember you're a naturalised Englishman.'

At home I tried to work, with almost no success. The war

overwhelmed me. I felt it impossible to concentrate on painting when you could turn to look out of the window and see, as I once did, a Messerschmidt flying low over the tree tops.

For a welcome distraction we used to go frequently in 1940 to concerts given by Admiral Cunningham's wife, herself a gifted pianist. She was the mother of Diana and Griselda Gould, later to marry, respectively, Yehudi Menuhin and Louis Kentner (another pianist). They were exciting Sunday afternoons with magnificent professional performances in her spacious flat. Otherwise London was heavy with foreboding and blackout. Diana was a ballet dancer at that time, and she was coached by a Russian friend of ours, Catherine de Villiers. Katusha (as she was called) used to urge Diana to be 'more indecent' when she was dancing the *Walpurgis Nacht* ballet in Mussorgsky's 'Sorochinsky Fair'.

For us, in May 1940, the *Walpurgis Nacht* blitzkrieg had begun and everyone watched horrified while the European continent was overrun. More friends fled to America, thinking, no doubt, that England would be the next country to fall to the Germans. Joseph lent his small flat to an artist friend and his wife, who arrived from Paris with only a handbag by way of luggage. John Buckland-Wright was a well-known engraver and painter of an Abstract-Surrealist flavour, and managed to get night work as a censor. He and his wife stayed about a year in Joseph's flat and we crowded into my small flat, bulldog, cat, books, paintings and all. We got used to diving under the table when the bombs dropped. We were both fire-watchers on night duty, in turn, and Joseph was an air-raid warden as well. It was impossible to sleep on account of the ack-ack guns. I had utilised the cork Picasso had given me, but I put it into an assemblage instead of between my teeth to stop them chattering as he had advised.

At that time we had a characterful Cockney charlady who used to say scornfully, 'the decorator's boys were over again last night,' the morning after a raid. She had heard that Hitler had once been a house painter, and she was not likely to forget it!

I remember Professor Denis Saurat (the head of the French Institute in Cromwell Road) telling us at the time about a tall Brigadier-General called de Gaulle who had just arrived in London to continue the fight for France. We used to go often to the Saurats' evening gatherings, and I met the French Professor who used to teach us at the Ozannes, and he asked me once again: 'Fâites-vous toujours de la peinture?' At one of those meetings Joseph introduced me to Rebecca West, who was on the point of leaving. She (a great friend of Dorothy Thompson) shook hands with me saying: 'How do you do? Goodbye,' and went. I also remember a suggestion of wife-swapping at the Saurats. I was not sure that I liked being swapped – like a cigarette card or a conker – and luckily it came to nothing.

In June 1940, there was an exhibition called 'Surrealism Today' at the Zwemmer Gallery. The window display excited a lot of comment, for it consisted of a rumpled bed, its sheets transfixed by a dagger, and a chair upholstered as a fat mammy. This extraordinary object had been sitting on the pavement outside a junk shop in Chelsea when I found it. I was told it was English and about three hundred years old. (Highly surreal.) It was in the shape of a large negro mammy, you sat in her lap, and her white-cuffed hands were the chair's arms. A grinning head surmounted the back. An unusual sitting experience indeed.

In order to get away from the bombs we went to stay for a while with our friends Catherine de Villiers and her inseparable companion Princess Dilkusha de Rohan. We were in their cottage high up in the Sussex woods when we heard over the radio the account of the Germans invading Katusha's beloved Russia. She had tears streaming down her cheeks as she listened aghast to the horrors and wickedness of the war. Before this, it had been a joy to see her dancing in the woods and singing to the birds. She called these woods the International Stores because they provided so many delicious mushrooms for the picking in a time of strict rationing. She had danced in the twenties in Picasso's 'Tricorne', and although no longer young, she taught ballet-dancing in

London. She was a tremendous character, very vivid in speech and movement.

Her girlfriend Dilkusha de Rohan was an American whose 'Standard Oil' father had been determined that she should marry into the European aristocracy. She told us how on her wedding night at the Ritz, she discovered that her bridegroom had on what she thought was a fur coat; it turned out to be his skin. The marriage did not last long, as one day her husband crashed through the windscreen of his car and was killed. Dilkusha lost most of her money in the 1929 economic crash, and she joined Schiaparelli (who used to dress her) to learn the art of fine feathers. She went to America after the war, and sticking to her title, was a success at dress-making. When last I heard, she was living in Switzerland, a country that has all the virtues that make life dull.

While I was working in the canteen in Savile Row, and when he was down in London from Oxford, Paul Nash came to see me there. We used to go to drink noodle juice together in a little tea-shop in Cork Street. We wondered what had happened to all our friends. The Nashes had given up the house they had in Eldon Grove, Hampstead, but we had a farewell luncheon party there before they left. Roland Penrose I knew was in a camouflage unit, and Lee Miller had returned to London to be near him. She was quite fearless, switching from a life of unlimited luxury with Aziz in Egypt, to that of photographic reporter in wartime. She was ready to go anywhere and do anything, as her arresting photographs show. A book entitled *Grim Glory* to which she contributed photos is a heart-rending record of the effect of the blitz on London. But of course, when France fell, everyone was worried about Picasso. Rumour abounded, but what had actually happened to him, nobody seemed to know.

In 1942 Joseph's ironic radio play *Nietszche* was broadcast on the BBC Home service. It was produced by our friend D. G. Bridson, who had persuaded Joseph to write it. As if Nietszche's thunder-claps were not enough, my mother's house in Balfour Place was bombed in May of that year. Luckily the house was empty at the time, but later a lot of the contents were looted, and as the front door disappeared, it was soon vandalised. My mother had little remaining of the large sum left her by my father. She had been quite happy with her old friend Lady Smiley at Heronsbrook, Wentworth, but when refugee children from London were billeted on the big house, Mama moved on to another friend, nearer Virginia Water. Joseph and I used to go down to stay for the weekend at the hotel nearby whenever we could, to be with Mama and console her. She was lamenting the loss of everything she had stood for and believed in; she was bereft of two of her children and all her grandchildren, her house had been bombed and the world was in chaos, but she refused to flee any further. We visited her ('Is Your Journey REALLY NECESSARY?', shouted the posters) and took a bottle of whisky as a gift when we could, not knowing that she had been addicted to whisky for some time. Evidently my father had suggested to her years ago when she complained of insomnia, that she take a spot of whisky at bedtime. Gradually it became more than a spot and then more still. My father was abstemious himself and would have been horrified to see what his suggestion had led to. For alas the whisky bottle changed Mama a lot: she became more tyrannical with the servants, and lost her temper more frequently, and the lovely figure she had had when she was a young girl was concealed beneath too much extra weight, though she ate very little. Mamie Agar watched bitterly as not only her own small kingdom, but also the wider world she had known, disintegrated around her. She died on 13 April 1943.

After her death, I went back to see the house I had walked out of twenty years before. 8 Balfour Place was a sad and sorry sight, looted and desolate. I still have a bit of ironwork I picked up that once belonged to the front door. So much had ended, and in those war years it seemed as if nothing new could begin to fill the empty spaces.

1942, however, was a good year for the work I had already done. I exhibited in several group shows in London and as far afield as Leicester ('New Movements in Art'), while the United Artists exhibition from the Royal Academy toured up to Stockport and Kettering. (Not quite as exotic as Tokyo or America, but better than nothing.) When I did lend some work abroad, for an exhibition in the inscrutable East, it took over two years to be returned from China! However, I was assured that gigantic crowds came to see that exhibition, so one must not complain.

The main event for me though, was a one-man show at the Redfern Gallery in Cork Street, arranged by one of the directors, Rex Nan Kivel. I exhibited twenty-four collages, and Paul Nash wrote a splendid foreword to the catalogue. He wrote of the paradox and enigma of my images, and certainly I intended that my work should be mysterious, not open to immediate or rational explanation. It must be felt; though the ambience of the war was by no means a sympathetic context for my kind of art. How does one communicate with any subtlety when the world is deafened by explosions?

I was not an official war artist like Paul Nash or Henry Moore, and had no inclination to be one, and I do not believe that many women were inspired to produce war paintings. Dame Laura Knight – one of nature's Valkyries – was a notable exception. The only painting I did of the war (apart from one entitled 'Cry Havoc' which is a composition of images of war as they appeared to me) was of a fire devouring a bombed house.

The bombs dropping on London were beginning to take a heavy toll. We very rarely went down to the basement which was cold and uncomfortable and draughty. While upstairs in our flat (when Joseph was not up on the roof as an air-raid warden) we were at least fairly warm if not so safe, though how a basement can be safe when the house comes down is beyond me. Anyhow, it was more exciting if a bit terrifying, to peer through the blackout curtains and watch the empty house opposite us go up in flames one night after an incendiary bomb had been dropped. It was a near miss; it so easily might have been our house that was hit. The blaze was terrific; the fire seemed like an all-devouring element of diabolic significance, invested with a peculiar mystery, a radiant and yet invisible demon of smoke and flames, which we were all drawn to. The fire engines were busy in the road among the burning debris, while very high up on a ladder, a lone figure luridly silhouetted against the blazing building fought the fire bravely with what seemed an inadequate jet of water. I did a painting soon after (in the time I had spare from canteen service), of that lone fire-fighting figure. But on the whole, the war did not inspire me, and I longed to get it over and done with.

By this time social life was virtually impossible, telephone lines were down and everyone was working (no unemployment) either driving ambulances or doing war work of some other kind. During the day buses usually plying the Earl's Court Road, passed our front door instead, as everywhere there were holes in the road. The fishmonger's wife, once dulled with stale routine, seemed almost cheerful as she remarked to Joseph: 'We *are* seeing a bit of life,' as he bought some fish after a particularly noisy night. The concerts at the National Gallery with Myra Hess at the piano were something of a tonic, but my mood was generally one of deep depression.

It was a Scot called Henry Simpson, a bank manager and one-time president of the Poets Club, who introduced Joseph to the Royal Society of Literature. During the early days the RSL used to meet in a small room in Bloomsbury, and according to Joseph, Lord Lytton, who was the president at the time, was the spit image of Bellini's 'Doge of Venice' in the National Gallery. Joseph became a fellow of the Society in 1942 and a member of the Council in 1944, when he gave a lecture on 'Tradition and Experiment'. Walter de la Mare, in his introduction to the collection of essays which included Joseph's, commented: 'This "experiment" may be compared to a pool of imaginative reverie, intermittently broken into ripples . . . its dreaming depths being those of its writer's mind and sensibilities.'

In 1943 we heard that Geoffrey Bridson was travelling over to New York on a placement for the BBC, and I asked him to take a set of gouaches in his luggage which I had promised to Peggy Guggenheim. Communications with the United

States were so hazardous that I felt that a special envoy was the only way to send them, and Geoffrey, as a tireless promoter of art he believed in, was generous enough to be the carrier. It was important for me since Peggy Guggenheim was holding an exhibition of Surrealist art in which I was keen to be represented. Geoffrey wrote an amusing piece on the trials and tribulations he underwent getting my gouaches past the American customs and excise men, who had evidently never seen anything quite like them before.

The same year, Joseph visited the United States in a quite different fashion – on the airwaves. In July he took part in a radio discussion programme between London and New York, called 'Answering You'. This was hosted by Alistair Cooke in America and Mary Adams in England. Joseph spoke about being an expatriate, and his words convey more directly than I could his reverence for his adopted country. 'The English way of life is characterised by giving freedom, and respecting the inner life of men. These are much more adequate conceptions of what is necessary for human beings to keep alive and feel happy, than any continental countries have.'

We still managed to see one or two people during these dark months. Horace Kesteven's daughter Mary used occasionally to visit, and it was at our flat that she met that versatile Frenchman Jacques Brunius. Brunius was a talented film director and Surrealist, and was fast becoming an effective broadcaster for the Free French. Mary fell in love with Jacques, and I got the blame: Horace Kesteven was convinced that I had led his daughter astray, immoral artist that I was. In that case, he should never have encouraged me to be a painter.

After waking up to the thunder of aircraft crossing to France on D Day, we planned to go up to the Lake District for the summer, but while waiting in the train at St Pancras, we heard the sinister noise of a V bomb approaching. We waited anxiously with the others in the compartment, ears alert, trying to guess whether the bomb was going to explode over our heads and blow us all to kingdom come, or pass us by on the way to other destruction. It was another close shave, for the bomb exploded not far off with a terrific detonation, while we, shaken, still waited for the train to move.

When we arrived in the country of the lakes, we found our friends and London neighbours Lindsay Drummond, the publisher, and his wife staying at the same crazy hotel. Actually, it was the proprietor who was crazy, as he firmly believed in a pagan world and had a large goat's head hanging in the hall to prove that neither Christianity nor the Romans had ever succeeded in penetrating the Valley of Buttermere, which in those days was effectively cut off by cliff and rock from the rest of the surrounding countryside. This proprietor used to approach the slightly reserved Mrs Drummond and ask her if she would sew on his trouser buttons. In the evenings he would regale us with stories of pagan feasts and ancient folklore. He had other unusual habits, such as tearing up telegrams from London asking for rooms, saying that he was only interested in notice of arrival times.

It was delightful to be away from falling bombs, and I was so relaxed that I did a number of small landscapes of our beautiful surroundings. Joseph and I almost decided to commission the architect Wells Coates (for our friend Rodney Thomas was designing houses for bombed-out families) to build a house for us in Buttermere. Luckily we thought better of it – the isolation would probably have driven us both mad – and we ended our holiday with a visit to Edinburgh.

Joseph met the explorer Tschiffely at the Savage Club, who was interested to hear that this Bard was married to an Agar, as he had been out in the Argentine himself as a schoolmaster before he made his famous ride through two continents. Tschiffely brought his wife, Violet Marquesita, to see us. She was a star actress of the period, particularly remembered for her performance in *The Beggar's Opera*, an extremely elegant and sophisticated woman. Tschiffely was a rough diamond, a gaucho of the pampas; there could not have been a greater contrast between two people. Tschiffely used to complain that there was never any room to put out his clothes in any of the hotels they stayed in while travelling together. Every chair, bed or bit of furniture was covered in fine dresses. He was more at home on a horse than in a hotel, and their flat in Chelsea was full of saddles, lassoes, stirrups, and mementoes of his famous ride to the North American continent.

Conrad Senat founded an ambitious new magazine in 1944 which he intended to deal with all branches of vital artistic activity going on in contemporary Britain. He called his periodical *Counterpoint*, subtitled it 'A Survey of Modern Art' and tried to keep it not only independent and broad-minded but also produced to the highest standards on good quality pre-war art paper. He was interested in my work and decided to run an illustrated article on my paintings in the first issue. He commissioned Terence Dennis to write the text, and reproduced four of my paintings to accompany it. Later on that year, I designed a cover for *Counterpoint 3* (Gerald Wilde had done the first, and Cecil Collins the second), but unfortunately it was never printed. Conrad Senat's high hopes were dashed when he was unable to get a paper licence for his magazine (essential in the days of shortages), and the project had to be abandoned early in 1945.

As the war came to a victorious and bloody end, slowly all the relations and friends trickled back from America, some before the swallow dared, and some astonished to find us shaken, like the daffodils, but still alive. After the initial rejoicing and greeting, my somewhat shamefaced relatives made the astonishing remark that we had not even had our windows blown out! We had had them blown out three times as a matter of fact. And so we settled down to a life of continuing austerity and rationing. I remember the flattening effect it had on me. I suppose it was partly a reaction to those years of living on one's nerves, and partly a sense of anti-climax; I felt that something new and marvellous ought to happen, but instead, I was exhausted and leading a humdrum life, just more tired and dispirited than usual. It seemed I had had no contact with artists for years, and I was suffering from a sort of spiritual famine which undermined my health.

Soon after the war, my sister Winifred turned up one day with a present for me, a painted beer bottle disguised as a nude woman, the neck of the bottle forming the face, the rest of it being the torso to the thighs, painted very realistically in Magritte's dead-pan manner. I naturally was more than delight with this surreal object. Winifred was not aware at the time she bought it that it was a Magritte, which showed perspicacity on her part. So I added this excellent object to my small collection (Joseph had lately bought me two small Magritte paintings from the Redfern Gallery for £15 each) and was cheered for a day or two.

With the end of the war we realised we had been physically and spiritually imprisoned for too long. A short holiday in 1945 to Cornwall and the Lizard did not seem to unlock the chains, so we planned a longer trip within the British Isles, since foreign travel was still restricted. It was the beginning of our wandering years, the first of many excursions, so in order to get our sea legs we set off in the summer of 1946 for Ireland.

After a very rough crossing (the Irish Sea is said to be second only to the Bay of Biscay for turbulence), we got into an extremely dilapidated, one-horse-and-carriage affair, wondering if it would get us as far as Dublin in one piece. We arrived at the hotel, and the cabby tried to charge us some monstrous amount for the journey. When Joseph remonstrated, he was told with scorn: 'You English Locusts can pay it!' Joseph was so taken aback at being called an English Locust that he paid it!

We had one or two days in Dublin before taking the long slow train to Waterville. We had never been in Ireland before. It was a beautiful if beclouded country which happened past our railway carriage window, with a priest or two (a copy of an Evelyn Waugh book under an arm) thumbing a lift. The Irish were not in a hurry in those days, so we did not arrive till ten at night. After the austerity of London with one egg a week and even clothes rationed, to see salmon strewn on the floor as you came into the hotel was a treat. It was plentiful at Waterville and reminded me of how the staff at any house in Scotland used to refuse to eat salmon more than once a week. They were sick of it, they said. Rather like servants in London who refused to eat oysters too often in the nineteenth century.

In the village, stern white-faced old women wrapped in

mournful black, stood in the doorways of their cottages, while rain ran down the damp walls. What with the poverty and the despair, it was not the most cheerful of holidays, but it was a delight to be on the move again. Some of the waitresses at the hotel had husbands who were tailors in the village, and Joseph, remembering rationing, was fired by the desire to have an Irish tweed overcoat made for him. We had heard rumours of a customs barrier, but took no notice until we came to board ship, when the Customs stopped us, recognising the very Irish overcoat. They told Joseph he could not take the coat back to England. After a lot of argument, the English Locust suddenly said: 'You wouldn't take the coat off the back of an old poet would you?' and they (perhaps thinking of Yeats) laughed and let him go.

Back in London, I was shocked and dismayed to hear of the death of Paul Nash. I was in a tiny paint shop on the Earl's Court Road, when the man serving behind the counter told me he had just heard the news over the radio. I had lost more than a good friend: such encounters as ours are indeed rare in life. He was a demanding demon, and at the same time patiently resigned to his ill-health and what he thought was his failure to put his work across. (He was worried that his art might not last; but if anything, his status has risen since his death.)

Throughout the war we snatched moments together, though Paul's wife Margaret tried to persuade him that I did not love him and was only after sex. (This still seems ridiculous when I think what a vigorous lover Joseph was, and how sadly reduced by asthma was Paul.) We had to be circumspect in our meetings, for Joseph was losing patience with the situation. He issued an ultimatum in April 1940 that I must stop seeing Paul, and he usually hung up every time Paul telephoned.

Paul wrote me a letter about 'Fortress Agar' and the impossibility of communication between us. He joked that he had heard a lot of clanking of chains and growling while Joseph decided whether or not to take the message on the one occasion when Paul had managed to get some response by phone. I hope it was Dandy the bulldog growling, though it might well have been Joseph, given his mood. 'Fortress Agar' was also a reference to Rodney Thomas' magnificent wardrobe, for Paul used to maintain that it was in there that I kept my other lovers; he was always absurdly jealous.

When I was not at work in the Savile Canteen, and Paul was in town (he taught at the Royal College), we met at Newmans paint shop in Kensington Church Street, or at the Café Royal, and sometimes in the Park as before. Paul rented a flat in a dark and glowering block near Euston Station, and we used occasionally to meet there in the earlier years. It must have been to his workroom-cum-bedroom in this flat that he referred when he wrote of his 'Magic room'. Later, when the flat had been given up, Paul stayed mostly at the Russell Hotel, and we met in less than intimate surroundings, but never at the hotel itself. He lamented that I had grown up when I married, though he also said that this had not diminished his feelings for me. He called me his chaffinch and his snow bunting and he asked for more letters in my 'chinese hand'.

It is strange that words are so inadequate; yet like an asthmatic struggling for breath, so a friend must struggle for words.

CHAPTER SEVEN

Colour Comes Back into My World

The war over, I returned to painting as if I were renewing a belief in life itself. I worked energetically, but I felt that somehow I was forcing the pace; I was losing naturalness and spontaneity even if I was gaining in technical expertise. By now the problems of picture construction were far less intimidating to me, and I was more than prepared to experiment with all kinds of materials, often within the same picture or object. In fact the rigorous dividing lines between 'collage', 'painting' and 'object' had begun to fade: I made images on stretched canvas which involved all three of these processes.

Since we first met, Joseph had been opening up the classical world to me – partly through his collection of ancient rings and engraved gems, and partly through his enthusiasm and knowledge of the subject. I found that classical motifs added a new time-dimension to my images, as well as a series of cultural cross-references. Joseph was a great reader, and since I read little in those days, his literary knowledge was a source of inspiration to me. One should be able, ideally, to make paintings which throw off imagery of different kinds at different times to different people, continually unfolding different aspects of themselves, ambiguous and paradoxical paintings with no main 'theme', but from which the spectator may, by participation, extract his own images. I used natural elements (the sea and sky, fish, birds, trees and leaves, landscape) to establish the context of nature, and then figures or technological artefacts (a bridge or an aeroplane) to bring out the dialogue. Mankind as a part of nature; the individual who pits himself or herself against our mass-media society;

mankind outside nature. Increasingly this was the underlying subject of my work.

I had a show at the Leger Gallery in Old Bond Street in January 1947, mostly small paintings, oils and gouaches. Ceri Richards came to see it, after he had seen his name in connection with mine in a review in the *Sunday Times*. I had not seen him since we used to meet at Roland Penrose's house in Downshire Hill in the thirties. Ceri was a short stocky Welshman, with a slightly rolling Welsh accent, a lot of black hair and big blue intense eyes which seemed to pierce. He had a lovely sense of humour and often told ribald Welsh jokes which Joseph particularly enjoyed. Ceri was a strong painter of erotic scenes, one of his favourite paintings being Rubens's 'The Rape of the Sabines'. There was something sympathetic about him which made you like him immediately you met him.

At the end of the Leger show I was presented with a cheque for £100 by the gallery for the work I had sold. I was overjoyed, but when my sister Winifred heard she grumbled at my success, saying half-jokingly that she was supposed to be the clever one, so what was I up to?

Later in the year we went with the International PEN Club to Stockholm, on a ship called the Saga. It was a breath of fresh air to be abroad again, and to see abundance. Ernest Raymond, the writer, and Lord Samuel and his son Edwin were on board as well as the Taboris and many other *écrivains* and *écrivasses*, and a good story-telling time was had by all. When we arrived in Stockholm, the women went wild with excitement at the sight of silk stockings and other luxuries for sale, for there was still great austerity in England. An immense banquet was given to PEN in the Golden Room of Stockholm Town Hall. Prince So-and-So of Sweden presided, and the food was brought in to the sound of trumpets. No one was tongue-tied among the five hundred-odd guests, and justice was done to the Tower of Babel. There were also lectures and visits to museums, vast restaurants, and a general feeling of euphoria. PEN was a very worthy cause to which Joseph was particularly sympathetic; in addition it provided the perfect excuse for a holiday in an unfamiliar part of the world.

Back in London, I was working for a show at the Hanover Gallery, which had recently opened. We had a surprise visit from Dorothy Thompson and her third husband, Maxim Kopf, who was a painter. Dorothy had become buxom, important and authoritative; no wonder, syndicated as she was to newspapers all over the United States. Dorothy was now the voice or conscience of America, but it had not done a lot for her modesty. She wanted to see how we lived, and as she had lately been addressing the Royal Navy we told her we were all lit up.

Maxim was interested in what was going on in my studio, and we talked enjoyable shop. He was a big hefty fellow, and Dorothy said that he was the only man she knew who had come out of the concentration camp smiling. Luckily he did not pick me up as Sinclair Lewis had done, saying jovially: 'Well Eileen, I'm going to marry you next!' Dorothy's marriage to Sinclair Lewis had had its moments but on the whole was a disaster, she confessed to us when we were lunching with her in her private sitting room at the Savoy. He had made her life hell, but she was a very spirited woman, and instead of drowning in despair, she married Maxim. She was still fond of Joseph and always anxious to know if we were happily married.

We visited the Gargoyle Club, of which I was a member. It was a very popular nightclub where one could dine and dance and enjoy a late-night cabaret. Afterwards, Dorothy said it was one of the happiest evenings of her life.

We continued to see a good deal of Professor Denis Saurat and his wife, and he took us one afternoon to visit Mrs Watts-Dunton at the Pines in Putney. Mrs Watts-Dunton was the widow of Swinburne's self-appointed keeper, a red-haired floozie who enjoyed giving tea-parties and sitting round the table talking with friends. After she had shown us the couch on which Swinburne lay, Joseph asked how she entertained the poet and her husband, Theodore, thinking that she would probably say that she read aloud to them. But not at all. First, 'the bride was stripped bare by her bachelors,' then she was delicately dusted all over with chocolate powder, and then two eager tongues (those ready symbols of language and literature) slowly licked it all off. So ended an imaginative evening performance by two poets and a willing woman. There followed an astonished gasp of good humoured delight from the small audience at such a tasty finish to a tea-party at the Pines.

1948 saw my introduction to television, though since most people did not have a TV set until the Coronation in 1953, I wonder how many watched my appearances. In August I was asked to appear on a programme called 'Eye of the Artist', which went out live from Alexandra Palace, and was intended to explore fantastic art by way of Surrealism. The narrator was Halam Fordham, and fellow-painter Ithell Colquhoun was also interviewed about her art and techniques. I was asked to make an object in front of the cameras from a variety of raw material provided by the production staff. I ended up with a raft of dreams, metamorphosed from a gourd, sponges, shells and branches; I called it 'Phantom of the Sea' and talked a little about my method of work. It was all slightly hair-raising, particularly as the show went out live, but nevertheless it put me on my mettle to be under the arc-lights. I remember I was paid 15 guineas for my cooperation.

I must have been bitten by the screen bug for I agreed to appear again on television only two months later. This time it was on a show compèred by the well-known costume historian and writer James Laver. He decided it would be amusing to devote a programme to hats – of all shapes and types. I had made a 'Ceremonial Hat for Eating Bouillabaisse' a few years before, and it was in this extravagant concoction that I appeared. It consisted of a cork basket picked up in St Tropez and painted blue, which I covered with fishnet, a lobster's tail, starfish and other marine objects. It was a sort of Arcimboldo headgear for the fashion-conscious, and received a lot of rather startled publicity.

Unfortunately, I was only given an afternoon to devise a hat, and after experimenting with gramophone records (which I could not make stay on my head) I had to wear the Ceremonial Hat I had already made. For my first TV appearance, I had practised at home a little before going in front of the cameras live. For the hat show, we were rehearsed by someone who kept shouting, 'smile, smile' until the joke almost froze on your face.

Also in 1948, Ezra Pound published his *Pisan Cantos* – those sections of his great work written in the Pisan detention camp when the poet was under threat of death for supposed treason. Both Joseph and I figure briefly in these verses, and we were immensely touched that in his extremity Ezra should have remembered us.

From Canto LXXVI:

But Eileen's trick sunlight softens London's November

And Canto LXXXI:

or as Jo Bard says: they never speak to each other,
if it is baker and concierge visibly
it is La Rochefoucauld and de Maintenon audibly.

Perhaps a word of explanation is useful here. Ezra referring to my trick sunlight obviously had some memory of visiting us (in 1938, I think, when he came over to England for the funeral of his friend and mother-in-law, Olivia Shakespear) and seeing what Joseph described as pillars of light I had put behind yellow curtains in my flat to cheer up the gloom of an English winter. And the reference to Joseph is based on his comment that even the poorer French spoke with a beauty of language inherited from a sophisticated literary past. One gets the feeling that Ezra missed very little.

My show at the Hanover Gallery in the spring of 1949 was a success from my point of view since it came as something of a release after the war years when I could hardly work at all. Geoffrey Grigson wrote it up at length for the *Listener*, saying: 'The paintings attack, they do not wait for an introduction, neither are they mean, timid or indecisive.' I accepted that as praise. Another critic said, 'Miss Agar is painting for the twenty-first century'; I was not so sure how to take that.

In September, we again joined the PEN Club, this time on its trip to Venice. It was an even more splendid gathering than at Stockholm, and the setting of course was superb. We found old friends there, like Alec Waugh and Eric Newton and his wife, Derek Patmore entertaining de Chirico, and my long-lost friend Nancy Cunard, they were all enjoying the PEN Club festivities and the fluid Venetian air. Stephen Spender, Cyril Connolly, Auden and Cecil Day Lewis were to be seen together in the Piazza San Marco. Pamela Travers was also in Venice, though not with PEN. She said she hated the narrow streets across which one could hold a conversation, from balcony to balcony. In fact friends seemed to pop up from the pavement; they certainly glided by in gondolas and waved from Venetian windows.

Then there was Peggy Guggenheim in her palazzo on the Grand Canal, surrounded by her magnificent collection of paintings. We went to have dinner with her in her curtailed palace (land had to be rationed in Venice), and after cocktails, as dusk fell over the lagoon, Peggy went to remove the gigantic prick from Marino Marini's sculptured horse on the terrace so that, with his adapted genitalia, he was incapacitated for any nightmare orgies, and effectively stabled. For Venice is a city of masks and revelry, where light and darkness are like changes of identity. It is the city of love and death. My parents went there on their honeymoon, while at any time affairs seem to be almost *de rigeur*. Meanwhile the gondolas glide by, only too often laden with coffins.

To crown the festivities, the Italians gave the congress a grand ball in the Ca' Rezzonico. We arrived at night by gondola, then climbing the immense stone staircase we found a room flooded with friends and acquaintances, as well as literary lights from all over the continent. Stella Newton, Eric's wife, had taken me to her dressmaker in Venice (Stella was an authority on costume from the fourteenth century onwards), so I had a beautiful dress of black Venetian silk striped diagonally with green, with a green chiffon scarf as a belt. With my dark red opera cloak, I felt I was able to sit languidly in a gondola, a fitting companion to my handsome husband in white tie and tails. The ball was a splendid mixture of the world and the intellect, the transitory and the lasting. Continued rationing and shortages in England made this continental indulgence all the more precious; for it was these life-enhancing trips abroad which made it possible for me to work back in grey London.

After the PEN Congress was over, we decided to make an Italian tour, and started out for Siena where we stayed for about ten days. We motored to dusty Arezzo to see the Piero della Francesca frescoes high up on the church wall, silent, dignified and timeless, beyond the reach of the grasping world. (We had already been with some PEN friends to Padua to gaze at Giotto's jewel-box, the Arena Chapel, that marvel of early Renaissance wall painting.) We motored on to Monte Oliveto, to the monastery of white-clad monks (some of them on motor-bikes), driving through country which made us think we were actually in a fourteenth-century painting, not in the everyday world. In the monastery there were intriguing cupboard doors covered in wood intarsia (a kind of inlay), depicting geometrical instruments, compasses, books, anything that was angular and interesting. Each was a work of art; like the cool white library with its slender columns and carved ceilings.

From Siena, where I was awestruck by the black-and-white striped cathedral, we moved to Rome for a short week. St Peter's, the Pincio, museums galore and art galleries, it was a whistle-stop tour. Watching the ruined Aurelian walls guarding the entrance to the Porta Pinciana from our balcony at night, Rome was the romantic artist's ideal. At sunset, as the sun settled in the white clouds behind St Peter's, turning them to flaming gold, man's works – the buildings, the created beauty – vied unsuccessfully with nature for mastery, but the darkness always won.

There is something ghost-like in walking through the streets of an ancient Italian town. Nobody knows you, you have no friends there, no function (except to spend) and even the official, who fingers your passport and peers at the text in an unknown language, half doubts the reality of your being, and seems more willing to think that you have just crawled out of the earth, or the walls of a neighbouring palace. Joseph reflected that many more children had expressive facial features than did adults whose physiognomies were rather lifeless arrangements of organs, not expressions of a mental quality. 'There are faces as keen as the driving board of a car, or the gadget of a hoover, but you seldom see the graceful and growing expression of a soul, so frequent before World War One,' he said. The people who move about the museums and galleries of Italy and glare at ancient sculpture or paintings had suffered this loss of face, and by no means all had gained an inner faith in compensation.

The deep blue waves of the Gulf of Naples and the sudden hump of rock, verdure and white houses which is known as Capri, was the next to greet us. 'There is more of God's work in Italy, and a poet will be like a fish or a bird living inside a miracle, not like Sherlock Holmes living in the thick of a cunning man-made world. The Creator is so manifestly superior, that in Italy one feels small,' said Joseph.

I wish I could still smell that delicious fragrance (compounded of jasmine, bougainvillea and crushed herbs) which greeted our nostrils each time we left the pensione Tragara and moved towards the view with the Arca Naturale hiding behind two chunks of the Faraglione cliffs. Capri out of season was a delight, and we refused to be seduced into seeing that tourist-trap the Blue Grotto, but had some splendid walks to the ruins of the Roman Palace of Tiberio.

We used to see Norman Douglas lunching at his favourite restaurant, but as he was usually in company, we did not like to interrupt. However, one day Douglas was alone, and I encouraged Joseph to greet him. They spoke mostly about rings and seals, for Douglas had some interest in these matters and was able to recommend to Joseph one or two dealers on Capri.

We saw fifty Capresi watching from the Piazza as vaporetti took off one stormy afternoon for Naples, on a sea that was *molto agitato*. As they watched the huge waves you knew these people were descendants of a race which saw living and often sinister powers in the forces of nature. No Anglo-Saxon could eye a sea with this mixture of scrutiny, foreboding and anguish. But Joseph also noticed a slightly bedevilled expression amongst the local people; their eyes seemed to be set in a satanic criss-cross fashion. They were friendly enough, but devils nonetheless. Joseph saw a deeper connection between the Capresi and the ancient Romans than with any other Italians he had met. The guard at the Villa Tiberio knew more than books could teach him, simply by living on the lonely heights in the ruined home of Caesar, and listening to the mysteries in the walls.

Our travels continued, an inspiration and release for us both. In the autumn of 1950, we took Winifred with us to Provence as she had not been well. We stayed for a week or two in Aix, that town of fountains, at an hotel with a swimming pool of spring water. We visited Cézanne's house in its overgrown garden several times. The painter would not allow any of the vegetation to be pruned, and we had to fight our way through thickets to get a view of the house. In the large studio, all the jugs, bottles and other still-life objects Cézanne had used were neatly in place. The painter alone was missing; although neither were there examples of his work (now spread worldwide) on the dusty and deserted walls.

In the train on the way to Arles, we heard two old women talking. Said one, between sobs: 'Mon fils a été mangé par les indigènes.' ('My son has been eaten by natives.') 'Ah madame,' sighed the other, 'on est très en retard en ce pays là.' ('Ah madam, they are very backward in that country.') In some ways, Arles was also 'en retard' in those days. I remember having to squat over the most horrifying stink-pot of a hole in the Hotel Diderot. I was glad to come out alive, only to be shown how all the rubbish was simply chucked out of the windows on to the street below.

But it was a delicious and fascinating town, a poet's town with the statue of Mistral in the square, a town where the inhabitants kept you awake until four o'clock in the morning, dancing to the same tune. For me it was a painter's town alive with the memory of van Gogh, for Joseph an archaeological dream town with its Roman arena where we watched the Provençal version of the Spanish bullfight. This more humane tradition featured energetic young boys in white trying to snatch the cockade from angry and spirited young bulls, without getting tossed or trampled on. We drove to the monumental Abbey of Montmajour, empty in the heart of Provence, and then on to Saint-Rémy where the ghost of van Gogh lingered in the quiet countryside.

In London, old friends came to visit, and Joseph, even more conversation-loving than myself, made new acquaintances, often through his clubs. Kokoschka we met again after twenty years, at a dinner given by the philosopher Lance Whyte. When we used to see him in Fitzroy Square, Oskar had been convinced that oil abounded below the sand of the Sahara desert. In those days not many were prepared to believe him, and we (rather good humouredly) lost the chance of making our fortunes.

Koko, as we called him, still resembled Hoa-Kaka-Nana-Ia, the Easter Island idol which used to stand before the entrance to the British Museum. He was full of warnings that the world had lost its stability and that we should take great care of our lives. After dinner, O.K. proceeded to do physical jerks on two upturned chairs in order to show how fit he was and that he could still perform life-saving deeds if in mortal danger.

Lance Whyte, the intellectual, watched his antics with amusement. Lance was much concerned with the next development of human nature, in the light of the split between love and aggression. I maintained that the true heirs of love are women, and that the more aggression there is, the more need there will be for the sustaining powers of women to uphold the unity and balance of the world.

For women's state of mind encompasses more the possibility of a mixed world – a survival and fortune world, not the male world of absolute values which cannot stand for long without strife and war. Women have the greater capacity for social integration although their deeper nature has been prevented until now by Western and Eastern habits from being released into any other channel than the traditional role of marriage. The opening-up of the instinctive self is also essential. It is possible that the universal purpose, if there is one, is negated by man's intelligence, which has turned him into a war god. The true poem is not the work of the individual artist, it is the universe itself, in which the artist is a sort of somnambulist.

One of Joseph's new acquaintances was Louis Wilkinson, the friend and biographer of the Powys brothers (John Cowper, Theodore and Llewelyn), whose spell he alternately admitted and fought. Joseph first met him on the council of the Royal Society of Literature and was struck both by his Rosicrucian cufflinks (a present from Aleister Crowley) and his unusual openness in admitting the mysterious and occult as parts of the natural order. Another of Joseph's encounters was with the Armenian novelist Michael Arlen (of *The Green Hat* fame) whom he met one day at the Savage Club, looking shrivelled and monkey-like. They exchanged memories of Orage who had helped Arlen at the age of nineteen when he was first beginning to write. Arlen said that he in turn had helped to found the *New English Weekly*. Joseph noticed a distinct coldness towards Arlen in the Savage, in marked contrast to the great popular esteem he once enjoyed. Such are the betrayals of fashion.

1951 was the year of the Festival of Britain, which has few lasting memories for me apart from Rodney Thomas's impressive building. The Festival was splendidly located on the South bank of the Thames, and for many it was their first opportunity to see very modern architecture. There was a general feeling of uplift, of hope, at the Festival, which was a great tonic after the war.

Rodney had gone into partnership with J. C. Squire's son Raglan, and they had together formed a larger firm called Arcon. Rodney was largely responsible for the Ministry of Transport's building at the Festival, and his design was greeted with much acclaim. I think this gave him the confidence and opportunity to establish a research unit which began to investigate how to build flexible houses from mass-produced parts. Later Rodney designed a sky-city based on plant and flower forms which was far too revolutionary to be taken up by anyone, but the maquette for it is impressive in itself – a modern sculpture of lateral blocks on a central stem.

In March we went to Julian and Mary Trevelyan's boat-race party, held at their riverside wharf-dwelling at Chiswick. It was an annual event, but this year the Oxford boat sank at the start. Nevertheless the party went swimmingly, with our tall host providing enough beer to launch a dreadnought, and Mary making everyone feel at home. Not that an invasion of at least a hundred people trampling the flower beds and stampeding the studio can be easy to cope with! We met as well as made friends among the duffle-coated writers and artists. Elias Canetti was a new face. Joseph identified him as a visionary of the darker side of life, not a maker and sustainer of happy civilised existence. Joseph himself was pleasantly and basically sensuous, with a great warm sense of happily belonging to this planet; he favoured the life-enhancing celebration as against the ever-deeper penetration of misery. The depression of the modern age would often send him back into archaeology. At this party, he talked learnedly about gems with Julian Huxley, who was wearing a winged victory intaglio, while Julian Trevelyan sported a large signet ring which he claimed was Babylonian.

Joseph still wrote to Ezra Pound to give him news of events and friends in London. There is a most amusing letter which Joseph wrote in August, about meeting T. S. Eliot, always known as Possum, at the Garrick Club.

> In the old days, I used to run into Possum during my underground travels. He was invariably attached to an umbrella with an enormous manilla handle, a half-circle spacious enough to go round the trunk of a randy male elephant, and he was constantly fumbling with that handle, trying to lodge his thin arm into its unresponsive

profundities, the living symbol of a misunderstood husband displaying his objective correlative!

But nowadays I only see him at the Club, he must have given up the tube. Some time ago, I saw him, emerging from the backroom dining place with Herbert Read, leaning on a stick.

They both wore a solemn countenance, specially recommended by undertakers for state funerals. I have seen similar expressions when Capuchin meets Capuchin and a silent look asks: 'Shall I pickle your bones brother . . . or will you pickle mine?' Anyhow, I said to Possum, teasingly: 'Now do not pretend you are suffering from rheumatism.' Whereupon Possum with an increasing posse listening: 'I am not pretending that I am suffering from rheumatism.' *Con fuoco*: 'I no longer pretend that I am learned'. *Molto con brio*: 'I no longer pretend that I am pretending!' Then he looked at me and asked: 'And what makes you so pleased with life?'

I said, truthfully and unashamed: 'The wonderful horseradish sauce of our club'. And Possum, with a voice in which charity and patience with the feeble in mind were marvellously mixed, said: 'So that is what it is.' But then in a whisper, he added: 'And what do you eat it with?' And I, also in a whisper: 'With smoked river trout.'

Some weeks later, Joseph saw Eliot eating smoked trout and horseradish sauce, which, as he said, showed that Eliot was 'not as barmy as he sounds'.

In the autumn of 1951 I had another exhibition of recent work at the Hanover Gallery. I was painting a lot, but I was still aware of a sense of despondency in those aftermath-of-the-war years, and I felt threatened with morbidity. One painting in this show was called 'The Lunatic, the Lover and the Poet'. Evidently I had become convinced that love and lunacy had much in common. On a five-foot canvas I combined three figures in one macabre shape. The lunatic was represented by two wild eyes, the lover by a caressing hand, the poet by a shadowy profile. The shooting flames which leapt and crackled around the combined figure indicated the forces of love, madness and inspiration. I collaged some ears of wheat on to the canvas when I read about the poisoned bread which had led to an epidemic that summer in some French village. A form of bacteria or mould had caused those who ate it to go mad. Shakespeare mixed with home baking: a dream became a midsummer nightmare.

Joseph's passionate interest in gems led him to visit all manner of junk shops in search of lucky finds, but he also studied his subject from the academic viewpoint. So in April 1952 we went up to Cambridge to visit the noted antiquarian A. E. Cook, a charming old savant wrapped in rugs. He gave Joseph a short lecture on gnostic gems and the more obscure and long-forgotten Greek legends. We also visited Dr Charles Seltman, another authority, who entertained us in the Erasmus Room at Queen's College, showing us many of his treasures which were later to go to the Metropolitan Museum in America.

These travelling years were a great relief to us. They may sound frenziedly energetic, but we were gradually and very enjoyably working out the reaction of being cooped up in London during the war. Not content with the continent, we went to Tenerife in the wicked winter of 1952–3, when smog was killing off so many people. We stayed with a charming and ebullient friend called Mollie Gordon in her lovely old house in Puerto de la Cruz. In fact it was so delectable that we went back every winter for four years running until we moved to Melbury Road.

Oh to be abroad again, not stuck in the mud of mundane daily life! Even the embarkation at Tilbury made me feel that we were moving into a new world of colour and excitement: the sound of foghorns, steamer whistles and the rustle of the dirty silk waters of the Thames, over which seagulls swooped and cawed. In a day or two, we would be in the warmth of a sub-tropical island, amidst all the sizzling colours of an unknown country. Even the idea of it seemed magical after a dank and dismal England which was taking so long to recover from that grisly war. I could not wait to see the sky again, the green of palm trees and the dazzling pinks and blues of the village houses as I imagined them.

In the ship's lounge one afternoon (for we were travelling this first time by Blue Star Liner), an elderly man approached Joseph and said: 'Do you know you are wearing a Garrick Tie?' 'Of course I do,' replied Joseph, 'I'm a member of the Club.' The stranger replied rather frostily: 'I'm on the committee and I've never seen you there.' When Joseph explained that he went once or twice a week and that he had been put up for membership by Sir Patrick Hastings in 1948, the man became more friendly. Indeed, he asked us to join him and his young wife for a drink, and we discovered that he was on his way to Buenos Aires where he had some property. His name was Max Trelawny Irving, and his great-grandfather was the Trelawny who saved Shelley's heart from the fire.

Before we disembarked at Santa Cruz, Trelawny Irving invited us to stay at his Elizabethan manor house near Wendover, which we duly did. We also discovered that he was joint owner of Champney's at Tring, the one-time home of a Rothschild, then run as an expensive health farm and known all over England; it was there that he had met his wife. We also planned a journey to Greece with them on the trail of Byron (to discover the cave he apparently lurked in), but alas, it never took place.

Tenerife was certainly a new visual experience for me: the first view of the island from the ship was unforgettable – the profile of sharp-pointed and massive blue-grey mountains towering over the calm sea, and the miraculous appearance of a radian rainbow linking together the small white city of Santa Cruz and the mountainous landscape, with its soft welcoming shaft of prismatic colour.

As Mollie Gordon drove us to Puerto, she explained that we would be staying in a rather decrepit summer house, in need of restoration, called Sitio Litre. We were enchanted to discover a lovely white-washed house, beautifully sited on the hillside, white doves around the large dovecote and tall palm trees completing the scene. On a nearby plantation about fifty workers made an Egyptian silhouette against a reddening sky, digging trenches in order that more bananas might thrive.

Mollie's great-great-grandfather had bought Sitio Litre in Napoleonic times when he had been told he had not long to live unless he moved to a warmer climate. He survived, despite being shipwrecked on the way, bought a small villa and started a cochineal farm. When the dye business began to fail, bananas were found to flourish; when we arrived there, some of the descendants of the original workers were still working on the farm, now tending the plantations.

We were given a large bedroom and a sitting-room overlooking the terrace at the front, with our bathroom looking seawards over banana trees and the village church, where a dwarf beggar squatted permanently at the door. We breakfasted on the verandah at the back of the house, sometimes in the company of Pico the small pet monkey, who had no table manners but kept us amused with his antics. This back verandah ran the length of the house and gave a superb view of the two-acre garden with its orange trees and papaya, its jacaranda, pomegranate and lemons, small croquet lawn and pergola. Amaryllis and roses and lilies abounded. Underneath the terrace at the front, the horses and carriage were kept, while outside the mounting block was still in position.

Just outside my window was one of the astonishing dragon trees of Tenerife with its strange bulbous branches topped by large star-shaped clusters of spikey leaves. These trees have long been famous, and one on the island was reputed to be three thousand years old. Roman ladies in Imperial times used the dried resin that oozed from the trunk (red in colour and inevitably known as dragon's blood) as a cosmetic to rouge their cheeks. In 'The Garden of Eden', the left panel of the famous triptych painting 'The Garden of Earthly Delights', Hieronymous Bosch painted a dragon tree, growing behind Adam who watches God creating Eve. It is often taken for the tree of good and evil; its grotesque and fleshy outlines seem ideally suited to Bosch's vision. The Spaniards fought the Guanches, the indigenous natives of Tenerife, in the fifteenth century, so my guess is that it was somehow or other from

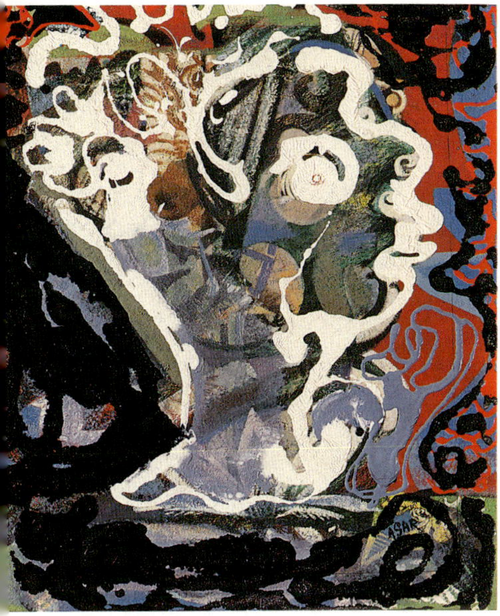

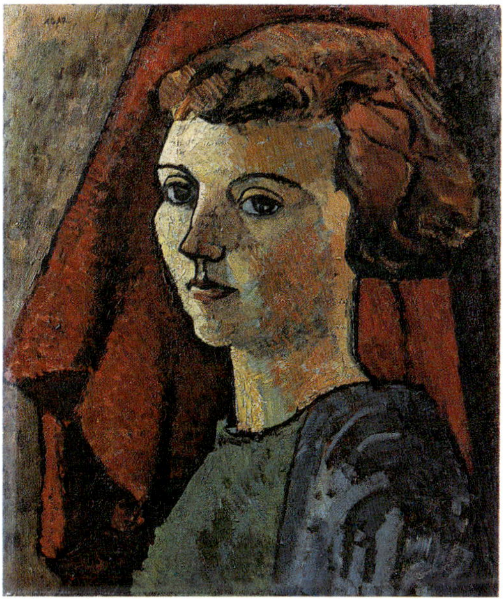

1a 'Head of Dylan Thomas',
1960; oil and acrylic on board
(Tate Gallery)

1b 'Self-portrait',
1927; oil on canvas
(National Portrait Gallery)

1c 'The Sleepwalkers',
1979-81; acrylic on canvas
(Artist's Collection)

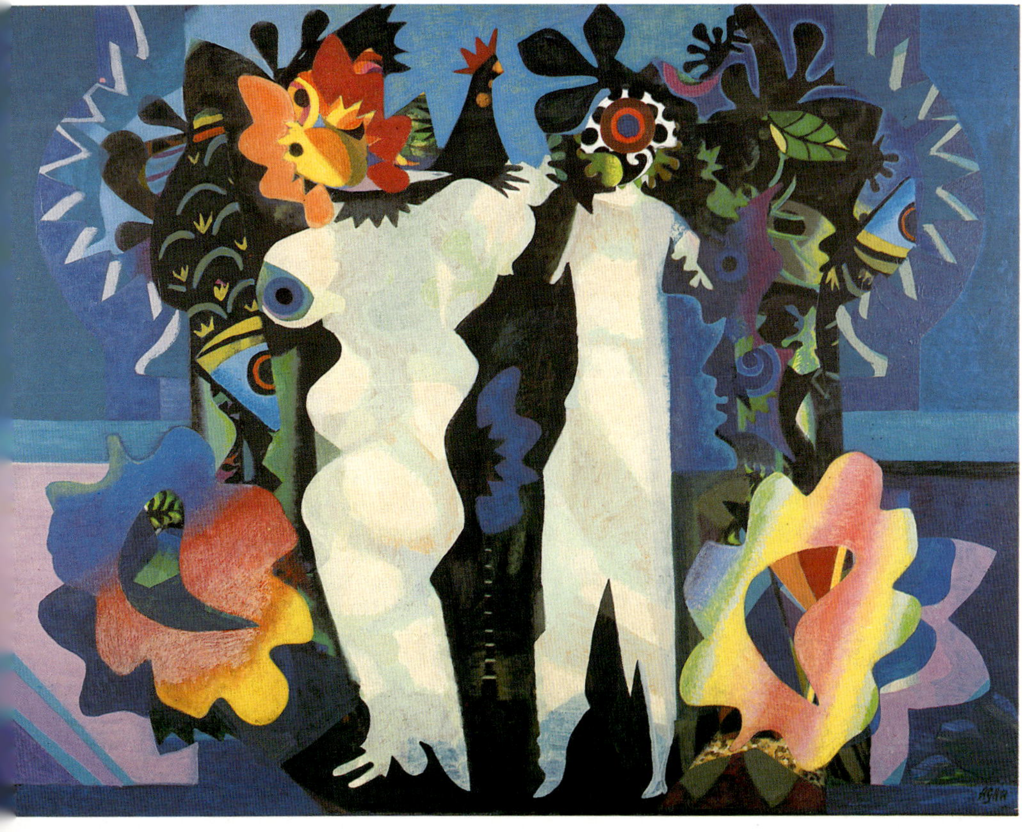

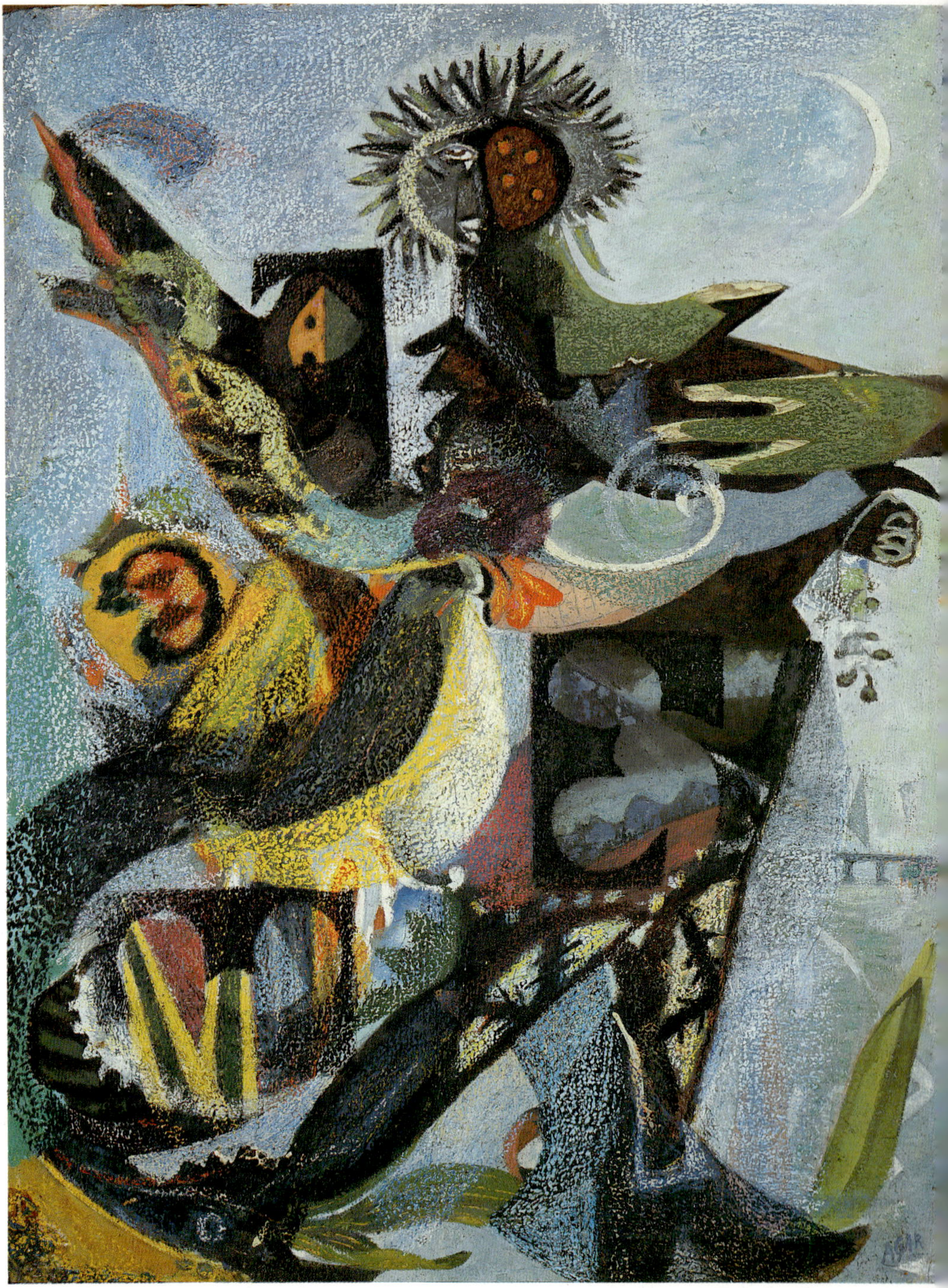

2 'Wandering Minstrel',
1932; oil on board
(Private Collection)

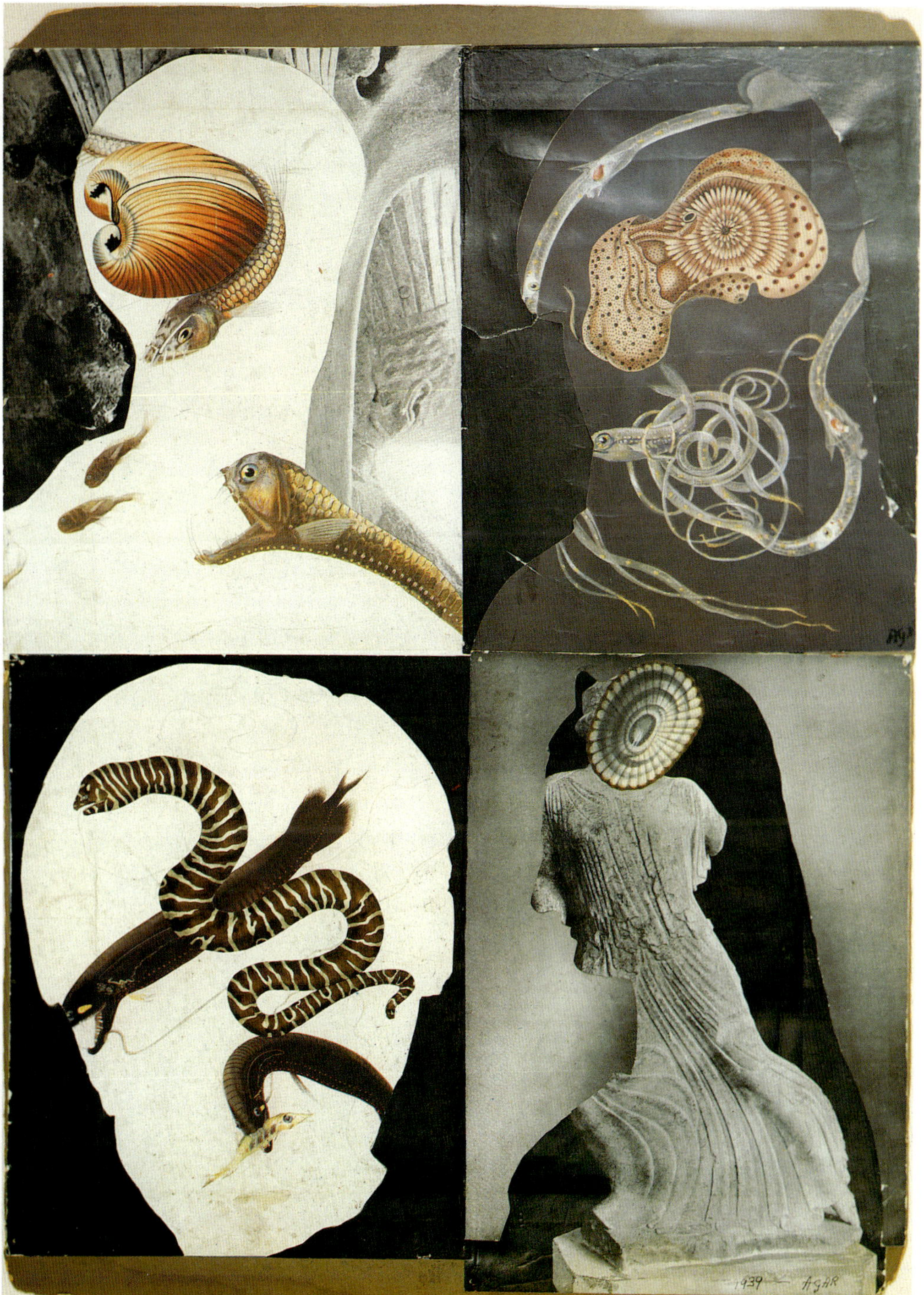

3 'Marine Collage',
1939; collage
(Whitford and Hughes)

4a 'Angel of Anarchy' (second version), 1940-3; object (Tate Gallery)

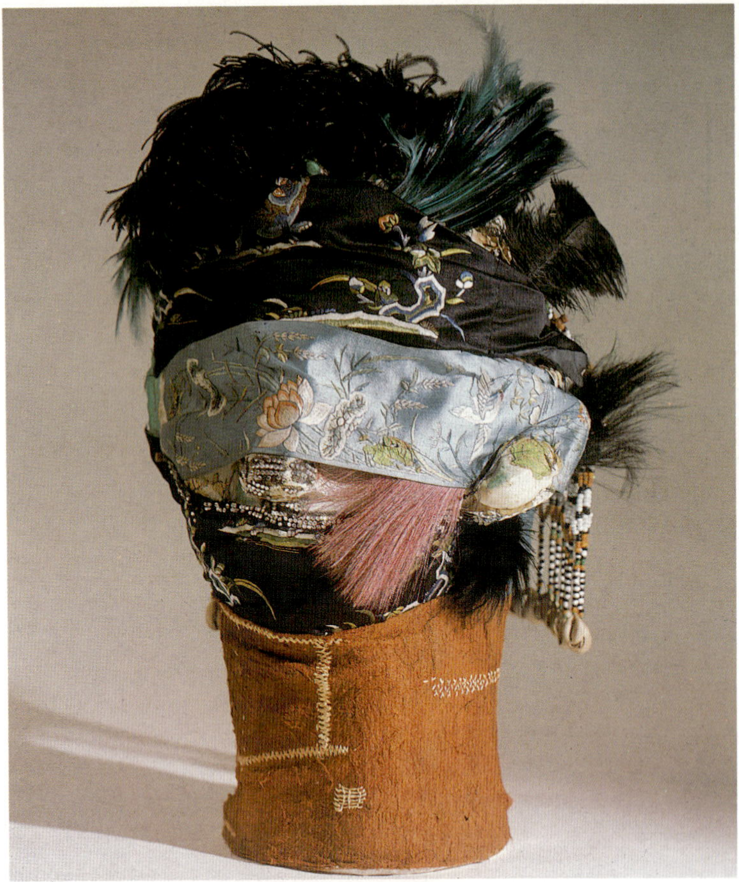

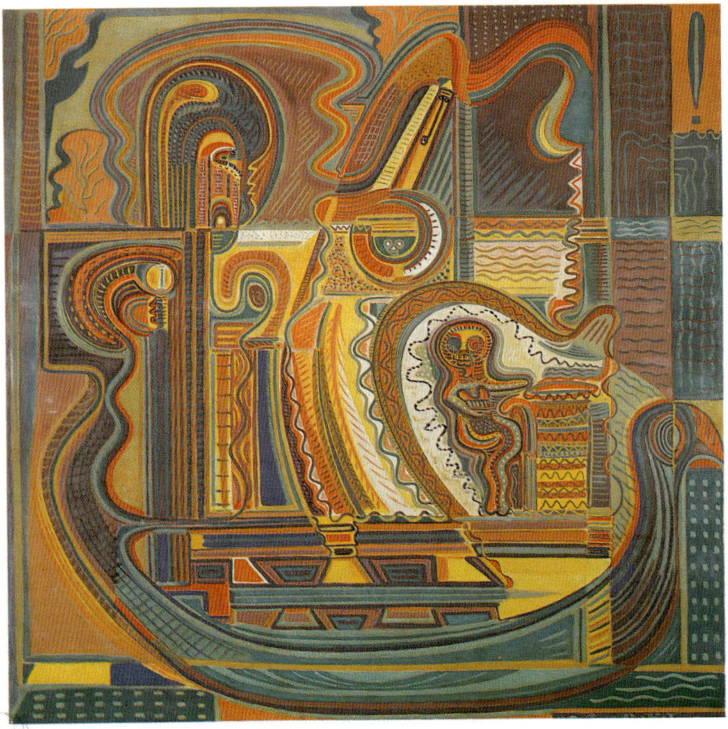

4b 'Egyptian Family', 1932; oil on canvas (Courtesy of Birch and Conran Fine Art, London)

Spain that Hieronymous Bosch gained his knowledge of dragon trees.

Sitio Litre was in an idyllic setting: sun, space and freshness without the cramp of time. The drowsy square in the village was planted with old trees and boasted a café-cum-bar with the inappropriate name of 'el Dynamico'. At the other end of the square lay the tiny harbour, fishing nets drying in the sun, and houses which the Romans might have built. One incident in particular underlined the timelessness of Tenerife. We had asked a *guardia civil* the right time of day. He put his hand into his pocket, pulled out a live lizard, and looking at his pet told us what we wanted to know. (To the nearest millenium.)

Mollie Gordon was a generous hostess and drove us all over the island. The successive landscapes were never the same: tropical valleys, naked mountains, land scorched by lava, dark fresh forests. To go from one landscape to another, to receive a surprise round every curve in the road, led us to discover that there are two different worlds in Tenerife. A mountain backbone divides them: the north where we lived, a riot of colour, green and sub-tropical with a basaltic solidity. The south is surreal in its hot empty expanses, its dry stones and tufa swept by arid winds and desert sands; where the prickly profile of black volcanic rock met the white waves, it looked as if Dali had been visiting, spreading his strange magic.

The Canary Islands are the islands of mystery and myth, the Fortunate Isles at the edge of the world, mentioned by Homer. It is said that they were the daughters of a love-match between sea and fire. Tenerife's intimacy with fire has continued as long as its dialogue with the sea. The colour of the soil, as it ranges from blue through red to yellow, from white to black and back again, is a startling testimony to the many volcanic eruptions. The exoticism of the islands has contributed to the idea that here was the Lost Atlantis. Over the island of Tenerife soars Teide, known as the column of the sky, once the highest volcano in the world, and still active. High winds about its summit must have smoothed its formation to its present shape of a solitary breast. From the sea it seems like a delicate watercolour printed on the sky. A single species of bird sings on this majestic mountain, and a single flower, a 'fleur mystique' flourishes there. The bird is grey, as if made of stone, and the violet of Teide is a pale blue, and they are the only living things to bear the sulphurous fumes. As Yeats wrote: 'In the condition of fire is all music and all rest.'

Our life at Sitio Litre was luxurious: we would perhaps eat lunch on the terrace with Domenica, the maid, in constant attendance, and a cook in the background as well as a washerwoman. They were all from the village and specially trained by Mollie. We were regaled with cocktail parties and dinner parties and picnics in Teide's crater. Mollie was a gregarious and happy hostess and knew practically everyone on the island.

There were a few assorted floating artists in Tenerife at the time, letting themselves go with the drift of the period, along with a few American writers, Swedish dress designers and the painter Ursula Tyrwhitt, an early flame of Augustus John. She had been a lifelong friend of Gwen John and was living with a charming old lady called Cookie, in a delicate bamboo-hung house in Puerto. It had an open patio, and the garden was filled with trees and flowers, birds, plants and vines, and seemed to have something of the flavour of a Somerset Maugham story.

Higher up the hill lived the Marquis de Casteja in a large house with superb views. He was looked after devotedly by his wife, who had been a nurse. She evidently won the race to be his third or fourth wife, for I understand there had been several beautiful women waiting in the wings for this aristocratic old Frenchman with the white moustache. We had many delicious meals at his house, and I shall not forget the tiny emerald frogs hopping from leaf to leaf in the lily-laden ponds. The Marquis had benevolent eyes but a sharp tongue, and amused himself and others by spreading scandal and gossip around the small town of Puerto amongst its harmless inhabitants.

The days were full of delight. We bathed in the swimming

pool near the house, or in the rough seas where the black volcanic sand covered us with uneatable caviare, and then lunched *al fresco* on fish freshly caught, bread and wine and fruit, under the shade of a thatched but open-sided hut, to the music of a guitar. Sometimes we played tennis. Or else we drove across the island to a white sandy deserted beach where we could bathe, passing fields and fields of almond trees in bloom.

Exploring the village of Puerto one day I wandered into a tiny art gallery and was amazed to find paintings by Miró, Oscar Dominguez, Ben Nicholson and others. I found out that this precious collection was the property of a bank manager, collector and art critic in Santa Cruz, called Eduardo Westerdahl. His wife Maud, had been married to Oscar Dominguez, himself born in Tacaronte, a nearby town. Antonio Ruiz, the head of the Spanish Institute and a kind of cultural attaché, arranged that I should meet Westerdahl, and a few days later, Eduardo and Maud turned up from Santa Cruz to lunch with us at Sitio Litre.

Eduardo, Swedish by birth, had lived all his life in Tenerife and was a devotee of modern painting, keeping up a correspondence with many artists. My name was not unknown to him (Maud had known Picasso and Eluard which was another link between us), and he was eager to meet us when he heard we were staying some time. We became good friends and Eduardo wrote a review in *La Tarde*, the island newspaper, of a small exhibition I put on in the Puerto gallery. I believe that Westerdahl is now a well-known art critic lecturing all over Europe, his days of banking past.

I was working a great deal, intoxicated by the colour and the light, which brought a new sense of joy to my painting – or so I was told by Joseph (always a helpful critic of my work). I responded directly to the landscape and was grateful to the terraces of stone on which the bananas were cultivated – for giving an architectural counterpoint to the otherwise too lush valley. They drew lines of force and direction across the country, complementing the symmetry of the strong mountain spine which ran down to the sea.

By the end of April 1953 we decided that we should make tracks for London, and in May we found two berths on a banana boat headed for Tilbury. It was a small Norwegian ship, belonging to the Olsen line, laden with green bananas and ripening tomatoes. Its decks were crowded with packing cases and fruit but there was room for about twelve passengers. As our ship only stopped at Lisbon, it was considerably quicker than a Blue Star Liner. The food was excellent: for lunch we had smorgasbord, where you helped yourself to colourful dishes and got to know everyone on ship. Dinner was at the Captain's table with excellent wine, then we repaired to small but comfortable cabins.

So we said goodbye to our enchanted land which now looked like a dew-drop in the ocean, as a slight mist enveloped the mountains. The haze gave the island a mysterious aura and yet paradoxically seemed to increase the luminosity of the terraces. A number of small water tanks scattered over the countryside (which the inhabitants called 'Ten-cent mirrors') gleamed and blinked at us in the setting sun, as if signalling farewell.

We had hardly returned to England before the Coronation with all its mugs was upon us. That June morning we were up at five o'clock, and breakfasting at the Savage Club in Carlton House Terrace, when we heard of the conquest of Everest. Of course it was raining, but to see the sad grey streets of London suddenly enlivened by the procession made our vigil worthwhile. It will indeed be a dire day for London when technical civilisation and the spirit of routine make everything anonymous, colourless and drab; when the gifts of imagination, intelligence and courage are drowned in a spirit of conformity.

The highlight of these years in the early 1950s was holidaying in Tenerife. Both Joseph and I stored up energy during our sunny winters in order to get through the rest of the year in England. We were not unhappy in London, but Tenerife was a sort of extended rest-cure-cum-inspiration after the war. In England we had old friends and made new ones, and I was working better than ever before. Joseph seemed to be more involved with his gems and his clubs, and in the Royal Society of Literature, than with actual writing. He relished friendship with writers like Charles Morgan, and went to some length in his notebooks to prove that Morgan was not a stiff academician as sometimes portrayed, but rather an uninhibited and observant storyteller. I remember that Morgan took us one evening to see his play *The River Line*, a wartime story with a mystical slant to it, but he was unhappy because the main critical response in England was always hostile to his theatrical writing.

In Tenerife one winter Joseph gave a lecture at the Spanish Institute (organized by Antonio Ruiz again) on Ezra Pound. It was a personal talk and seemed to surprise some of the audience of British subjects. Joseph sent a copy of the text to Ezra, who replied appreciatively that it was probably the best introduction yet, since it could claim the advantage of being by a truly literate person, rather than by the usual obfuscating and uncultured commentator.

Joseph and I enjoyed Tenerife so much that we toyed with the idea of buying a piece of land near Sitio Litre, nicknamed Joseph's Rock, and building a studio there as a permanent winter retreat. But the increasing cost of travel, together with such a definite commitment to one foreign place, were against this plan. And as it turned out, our travelling years were actually drawing to a close.

In 1956, the Russian tanks which ploughed into Budapest recalled to Joseph thoughts of his youth, for the girl he had loved in those days had remained in Hungary to bear his daughter. Events and Joseph's family had split them up, and Joseph had never seen his daughter, though he had provided financially for his girlfriend, Yolan. When the Russians came to Hungary nearly fifty years later, Joseph's daughter Valentine fled to America with her two sons (her mother having died in 1946), but not without difficulty and danger. Valentine's mother had married a major in the army, and the family had been comfortable, but a step-father can never be quite the same. Valentine ended up in Buffalo, learning to speak English and cope with American ways, and with a firm resolve to come to England in search of her father.

Joseph also had an older sister, Melanie, who had remained in Hungary with her daughter. Days of terror followed the arrival of the Russian tanks, but after a nightmare cross-country hike, mother and daughter escaped via Vienna to America, where Melanie's son had been practising as a doctor for several years. The daughter had been a psychiatrist in Budapest, and was soon able to practise successfully in New York, having passed the necessary examinations.

It was a time of upheaval and change. We were about to move from Bramham Gardens to Melbury Road, but the experiences of the last few years had been valuable ones, and I had a stock of ideas and memories to take with me. Tenerife was in fact a watershed in my life. For I had been suffering from a painter's dreaded middle period. I had been too long cut off from the world of nature, too cooped up in a tiny flat, too cribbed and confined in London during the war, unable to work well, if at all, and the relief of finding one's roots responding to the quickening pulse of vegetation, the vast mountain landscapes, the sea horizons, Joyce's 'heaven tree of stars' giving one a marvellous sense of liberation, with its 'humid nightblue fruit', brilliant, brilliant with an intensity unknown in England, all this made me fall in love with that mountainous dew-drop in the ocean and I revived and could work again; indeed, I have never stopped working since.

CHAPTER EIGHT

The New Studio

It was becoming evident that we would have to leave Bramham Gardens. The rent was going up in leaps and bounds and we could no longer afford our dual 'porcupine' residence. Once again, Joseph wanted to move to the country and we did look at one or two possible houses in Kent and Sussex, but the responsibilities of rural life still did not seem right for us, car-less and careless as we were. Both of us enjoyed the social possibilities of a London existence; as for me, I liked to escape to the country now and again to dip my roots in nature, but I was just as fond of the seaside. (If either of us had a cold or the flu, Joseph always said it was time to go to Brighton.) If there had to be a base somewhere, I voted for the city and its cultural amenities; in the end, Joseph agreed with me. After all, his beloved clubs were in London, and only an increasing restlessness drove him to think of moving to the countryside. For the truth of the matter was, that Joseph was not a little disappointed in his willingly adopted country.

He missed the warmth and conversation of the European cafés – the exchange of wit and ideas; the temperature of English emotions was just warm enough 'to give you a cold on the liver', he said. The land of liberty was not such a marvellous place: Joseph lamented the passionless philistinism of the British, the reserved behaviour, the lack of inspiration. As a writer he could not flourish in such a climate, and so he directed his energies elsewhere – but he was left with a sense of defeat, for he had not achieved many of his literary ambitions. He still wrote an article or two, and reviewed the occasional book, but for the most part he collected gems and literary friendships. His involvement with the RSL gave him ample opportunity for the latter, and together we made many interesting acquaintances.

In 1957 we had dinner with Angela Thirkell at her house in Chelsea (next to an undertakers), which was stuffed full of Pre-Raphaelite relics. She brought out a book of verse by Swinburne which was dedicated to her grandfather (Burne-Jones the painter) in the poet's childish handwriting. Angela was very opinionated and at one point insisted that gnostics and agnostics were the same; she was preoccupied with death, but agreed with Joseph that no one could explain sex, beyond the miracle of attraction which the English so often fight. Her son, the novelist Colin MacInnes, telephoned during our visit, and Angela was visibly unsettled. She complained of his behaviour, that he was only ever in the company of prostitutes and pimps, and that he only rang up for money. There was little we could say to comfort her, a sweet and intelligent woman, obviously distressed.

Joseph was always on the look-out for rings and seals, and went into any new shop he saw. One day, searching through a good-looking junk shop in Sidney Street, South Kensington, he began chatting to its owner and happened to mention that a pot he had just examined was undoubtedly a fake. Immediately the proprietor seized the pot and smashed it on the floor. Joseph (after he had got over the shock) was highly impressed at this un-English spontaneity.

Jimmy McMullen was an amusing Irishman, an art dealer who ran a gallery called The Obelisk in Crawford Street just off the Edgware Road. He was charming and loquacious and could wheedle your grandmother's lace cap off her head if he had a mind to. By a mixture of humorous talk and persistence, coupled with a real interest in and love of the object he was pursuing, you would find it gradually slipping out of your grasp into his. Between bouts of euphoria Jimmy would stick his head in the gas oven if one of his deals had not come off, but his friends or his common sense always rescued him in time. He was a slippery customer in many ways, but had an eye for the strange and avant garde. He had a soft spot for Surrealism (which was anathema to many people at that time, since abstract expressionism or kitchen sink realism were currently fashionable) and he came to look at my work in order to decide whether to show it.

It turned out to be disastrous to let Jimmy into the flat, especially since we were contemplating a move. He had his eye on the two small Magritte sketches Joseph had bought me, and also on Winifred's present of the Magritte bottle. His timing was perfect: he returned one day when we were in the middle of packing up, surrounded by a chaos of books and other impedimenta, some of which we actually wanted to sell. Jimmy would not rest nor give us peace until the Magrittes were his. Together with the Henry Moore sculpture and drawings Jimmy wheedled out of Joseph later, these are the possessions I most regret having sold.

So in April 1958 we moved to West House, in Melbury Road, Kensington, a road famous for its artists. Holman Hunt used to live round the corner (as did Lord Leighton, though Leighton House with its magnificent Arab hall is in Holland Park Road), and the academic sculptor Hamo Thorneycroft once used the studio opposite. At last, I had a proper studio to myself – the whole of the top floor of this large red-brick Victorian house. Underneath was a flat which suited us, particularly as all the furniture which Rodney Thomas had designed for Bramham Gardens could easily be fitted into our new rooms. Joseph was not so happy to leave the flat which had been his home for so many years, and he grumbled that human beings were merely travellers between two holes – the womb and the grave. Yes, I replied, but think how exciting and memorable is the journey in-between! And that is what matters, to be *échauffé par la vie*.

Isabel Wretham was a lean, upright, grey-haired spinster, the daughter of a policeman, who came to see us looking for a job. She took one look at Joseph and stayed to be our house-keeper for nearly fifteen years. She adored Joseph, and although he was slightly embarrassed by all this adulation, he enjoyed it also. If Joseph was ill, Isabel thought nothing of rushing down to Piccadilly Circus in the middle of the night to get something he needed, though she never lived particularly near to us. She only stopped working for us when she became too old to manage any more, and even then she still came to visit.

Jimmy McMullen, perhaps to make up for the Magrittes, gave me a show at the Obelisk Gallery later that year. As the *Evening News* reported, nearly everything was sold in the first two days, at prices which ranged from £70 to £300. The Tenerife years were certainly bearing fruit. It was also reported that next year I was to be given a large retrospective exhibition at the Whitechapel Art Gallery. This was rather premature, as the exhibition unfortunately never materialised; but the next few years were still to prove eventful as far as showing my work was concerned.

Carl Bode was cultural attaché at the American Embassy, and we used to see him and his wife Margaret frequently when they lived in London. Carl arranged for Joseph and the other RSL councillors to visit the home of the American ambassador in Regent's Park. Our hosts, Mr and Mrs Jock Witney, had a famous collection of Impressionist and Post-Impressionist paintings in their elegant and spacious house, and Mrs Witney took some of us round to see particular treasures. She told us how an American woman, seeing a self-portrait by Vincent van Gogh over the mantelpiece, had exclaimed: 'Oh I know that one – it's Kirk Douglas!'

Whenever we could, we would spend a few days with friends in the country. One memorable weekend was passed with Alan and Babette Sainsbury in their house in Essex, an old farmhouse with a magnificent barn and a long low living-room. On the Sunday we had a long argument over the relative merits of Englishmen and continentals as lovers. Alan Sainsbury stood up for the English with gusto and humour, but I maintained that nationality had less to do with it than zodiac sign. Joseph, for instance, was a Taurus; their constancy and dependability are supposed to make them superb lovers and attentive and devoted partners! We laughed a lot and came to no conclusion.

In 1959, Geoffrey Bridson produced Joseph's story 'The Game of Chess' to be broadcast on BBC Radio. It had been published in Woodrow Wyatt's First Series of 'English Story', and written in 1941; Joseph described himself then as a citizen of London and a vanished Europe. In the broadcast, the inimitable Patricia Hayes took the part of the small boy in Belgrade who plays chess with the colonel who is about to murder King Alexander and his Queen that night. The boy wins. In a voice of unfeigned simplicity, he comments that nobody who hates his King will ever make a good chess player.

The lack of imagination in England worried Joseph, as did the worship of 'horse-sense'. He was all for the articulacy of the sensitive, but also saw the necessity of putting on some of the armour of the cynic. He had a streak of Oscar Wilde's wit and a streak of Byron's vanity (he greatly admired the poet and could recite most of *Don Juan* with ease and enjoyment); Joseph was occasionally arrogant, but always endearing. When he first came to England, Dickens had a decisive hold on his mind. He imagined, I think, that London in the twenties and thirties would be peopled with Dickens's characters. Instead, even the age of P. G. Wodehouse (another love of his) was passing – if indeed it ever existed – to be replaced by the harsher realities of Evelyn Waugh.

We had been seeing quite a lot of Laurence Meynell, whom Joseph had met at the Savage Club, and his wife Joan. He was a writer of detective stories, and she acted occasionally for the BBC. In 1960 we decided to go to Venice together, for a holiday. We had virtually settled our plans when Laurence announced to us that his wife insisted on being at the seaside for at least a week or ten days in order to bathe. Would we mind joining them at Jesolo, a seaside resort near Venice? We were not very keen, but finally agreed. But we had hardly been in Jesolo two days when the Meynells broke it to us that they disliked the large hotel (which they had chosen), the food, their room and everything about the place. Jesolo was a typical Italian resort, alive with screaming children, bouncing beach balls, bats and buckets, miles of sand covered with ladies' li-los, gaily-coloured parasols and other paraphernalia. The Meynells told us that they were leaving the next day.

We were left kicking our heels in Jesolo in the pouring rain, for we could not get into our hotel in Venice sooner than arranged.

The holiday was not a success. Joseph was not well in Venice: he had a bad foot exacerbated by long walks in the soft sand at Jesolo, so we were glad to get back to London. But even at home, Joseph refused to see the doctor, and instead we went down to Cornwall soon after our return. Max Trelawny Irving lent us his white-washed cottage on the cliff-top of Gurnard's Head, a few miles from St Ives. It was an isolated spot, a white speck in the landscape of wind and water and rock, with a sheer drop to the ocean below. Gurnard's Head itself was on the left, a conglomeration of headland, heath and honeysuckle which tempted practising commandos to climb amongst the granite boulders, and Cornishmen to plunder the occasional ship which foundered on the rocks below. The cottage was a walk through fields (dodging cow-pats again), had two bedrooms and a stunning coastline view, and was lit by gas-burners. Mrs Pascoe, who looked after us, had never been further afield than Penzance. She was a true country woman, well over sixty, who lived in a cottage the other side of the fields and sang old Cornish songs, accompanying herself on the upright piano.

Babette Sainsbury came down from London to stay for a day or two, and we went into St Ives to show her the fishing village that had become Britain's seaside art colony. St Ives in the early sixties was already overburdened with sightseers and tourists, its narrow twisting cobbled streets clogged with people, and the picture postcard harbour sticky as a honey pot. It was a relief to get out of it, back to the wildness of cliff and sea. When Babette returned to London she was wearing bright red jeans and a coat bought at the fisherman's shop in St Ives. It was easy to imagine her walking in on Alan in the early morning, like a red devil with a jewel in her navel. . . .

That year the Arts Council bought a painting of mine called 'Poet and His Muse'. It was a good augury for my work in my new studio (it always takes a little time to settle down in a new milieu), for I was working now harder than ever. Over the years I must have destroyed many paintings and drawings that have not been up to the mark. Others I have simply put away in the attic and forgotten about. My studio at West House had two wonderfully huge attics, originally apple lofts I think, which gradually filled up with discarded frames and older work I no longer had the space to hang.

I must also have painted over many paintings in my time, no doubt including some good ones, but I suppose a destructive urge inhabits every painter who desires to do better. And if there is not a fresh canvas handy one leaps on a half-resolved or abandoned one, momentarily forgetting the injunction, 'le mieux est l'ennemi du bien' ('Leave well alone'). Sometimes the second attempt succeeds, sometimes one mourns the loss of the first version. But if not satisfied, I firmly believe in having a second try – whether in marriage, on the tennis court or on canvas.

In 1960 Joseph first met Edmund Fuller, the distinguished American author, who later wrote *Successful Calamity*, a comic and endearing tale of life on a farm in Vermont. A man with immense charm, a Shavian look, and a white-bearded Father Christmas benevolence in his twinkling blue eyes, Edmund is serious but not solemn, possessing a nice sense of humour. We used to meet him and his wife Ann intermittently when they were living in London, and we spent many enjoyable hours in spirited conversation. Edmund is an extremely versatile man, reviewing for a string of American magazines, a sometime colleague of the German theatre director Piscator, and a teacher of English literature. The long arm of coincidence brought us together again later, in a different way, when we discovered that David Fuller, their son, had taken a flat in Bramham Gardens. It turned out to be in the same corner house that we had inhabited so happily for so many years, picked by chance by David's New York office. Patterns were forming again.

As 1960 gave way to 1961 we celebrated with Robert Medley and Rupert Doone, an informal New Year's Eve party with a number of their other friends. Robert and Rupert were excellent hosts, vivacious and entertaining, and it was always a pleasure to see them. Surprisingly, Robert is always a bit secretive about his work, and I never feel I have seen very much of it, though what I have seen I have liked. There was a small group of artists whom we saw a lot of in those years: Robert and Rupert, F. E. McWilliam and his wife Beth, the Ceri Richards, Patrick Heron and one or two others. Joseph used to enjoy discussing art and literature, so that anyone who could talk well was always most welcome. In February he gave an address to the RSL entitled 'Ezra Pound, an Encounter', to which Robert and Rupert came; afterwards Robert was kind enough to say that Joseph's lecture had been like a poem, but Joseph was exhausted by the whole business. He was nervous and unsettled, and I racked my brains over how to cheer him up.

I knew Joseph felt the English had never taken to him in quite the same way as he had taken to them, and his disappointment at this doubtless helped to lower him. And then at the end of January we heard that Dorothy Thompson had died. We had not seen her for some time but her death was a blow to Joseph; he was nearly seventy and thoughts of age and mortality were painful to him. I think the fact that Dorothy died completely alone in Lisbon depressed him particularly. Slowly he was beginning to review his life and achievements, and like most people, he was not entirely satisfied with what he saw.

In an attempt to cheer us both up, we set off for Penzance again, to stay in the cottage at Gurnard's Head. We arrived there on a beautiful day in late June and had to search out Mrs Pascoe to unlock our cottage. This time we took Isabel, our daily help, with us as Joseph needed more care than before. After shopping one day we ran into Patrick and Delia Heron in St Ives, and spent the rest of that weekend eating in turn at each other's home, despite the fog at night.

They lived in a lovely old house called Eagle's Nest at nearby Zennor, with a garden full of large rocks which must have been there since the Stone Age. Henry Moore, who used to visit, was envious of all these granite boulders. 'Enough material for a lifetime,' he said. Patrick was also a considerable gardener, as was Delia, and it was a memorable experience walking with them amongst the lovely flowers, dodging the boulders. The turf was so productive that anything grew in no time at all. Pat took us over his immense studio which used to belong to Ben Nicholson (No. 5 on the harbour). I much admired Pat's paintings; he is a rigorous theorist, prepared to put ideas into practice in the most beautiful and startling combinations of colour.

We had several days of gorgeous weather to rejoice the senses, and we returned to London quite refreshed. But the main event which did more than anything else to lift Joseph out of his gloom was an invitation to a garden party at Buckingham Palace. We lunched first with the poet, Sir George Rostrevor Hamilton (a friend from the RSL) and his wife Marion, at his club in Pall Mall, and then walked in stately fashion down the Mall to join the hundreds of gaily-dressed crowds swarming on the splendid lawns of Buck House. It was a superb day, a colourful scene recalling the painters of the nineteenth century, with the twentieth-century addition of enormous black African chiefs in an astonishing array of cotton prints, holding aloft vast umbrellas covered in dazzling designs. Tents, top hats and parasols; strawberries and cream; at the bottom of the garden, flamingoes picking their delicate way through the reeds of the lakes. And six bishops, three tall and three short, who looked like the chorus of priests from Mozart's *Magic Flute*, as if three were about to kiss the navels of the other three. It was altogether a delightful afternoon.

In 1961 William Seitz, then of the Museum of Modern Art in New York, organised an exhibition called 'The Art of Assemblage', and since I was a contributor, I was sent a catalogue. To my dismay, there illustrated was my once-treasured Magritte bottle, complete with the stopper I had added to it. In a moment of light-heartedness I had inserted a small African wooden cork, carved in the shape of two buttocks, which fitted the bottle perfectly as a stopper. I had been careful to tell Jimmy McMullen that my cork did not belong originally to the bottle woman, but in the chaos of the moment of sale, I had not realised that he had made off with the stopper as well.

I felt that I had to write to William Seitz to explain. He replied saying that I had solved a mystery, as he had received a slightly piqued letter from Magritte warning that the exhibition catalogue might contain other mistakes, since he had never put a cork in his bottle. Later on I received a very pained letter from Magritte himself, explaining that what he conceived of as valuable in his work was that which set it apart from all style; by adding an African cork I had made it my work. I must admit that at the time, I thought so too; and that I had improved it!

In October we returned to Cornwall for another fortnight, but although the countryside was less overrun with tourists at that time of year, the weather was not so enjoyable. There was too much wind, which cat-like, I would rather avoid. Nor did the countryside seem to be having a particularly stimulating effect on my painting; evidently, I was not born to be a member of the St Ives School.

1961 was quite a good year for exhibiting however, with some early collages and gouaches being shown at the Brook Street Gallery in February, the Art of Assemblage exhibition, a portrait in the Contemporary Portrait Society's show at Wildenstein's, and then the news that the selection panel of the prestigious John Moores exhibition in Liverpool had chosen a painting. Public interest in my paintings and objects had been growing steadily since 1936, and I was now beginning to feel the need for a sizeable retrospective exhibition, so that I (as well as those who followed my work) could get what is now fashionably called 'an overview' of my career.

Bob Lewin, who was the director of the Brook Street Gallery, came in early January to the studio to select work for an exhibition of recent paintings to be held in March. I was very excited, but the divine forces which guide and rule us had no intention of letting me get too big-headed. On the night of 21 January, wind tore the lead from the roof of my studio and rain flooded in. Luckily the damage was not too great. But it was a timely reminder that Nature was still untamed, even if I had caught a spark in one or two of my paintings.

I listened to a programme that Geoffrey Bridson recorded for radio about the H-bomb. The world was poised on the brink of annihilation because mankind had perfected his arrogance. Men! I wished Joseph had strangled the Teller boy when they played together. By what right did man elect himself lord of destruction, able to melt the earth and put out the sun? Would no one listen to womb-sense? I went to see an exhibition of Spanish artists (Tapies was among them) who painted with a recognisably post-atom bomb awareness. The paintings were dark and earthy and grim. I felt that my own work was like an old-fashioned cocktail in comparison. But surely room must always be made for joy in this world? There have to be hope and celebration.

We take a step back and another forward: the cosmic dance goes on. In February, John Glenn orbited the earth three times in a space craft and landed safely. I was so involved in watching the TV transmission of this great event that our supper was spoilt in the kitchen. Burnt tongue – another warning symbol? I hoped not, for my exhibition was approaching and the catalogue was printed.

We went to have a drink that evening with Nick Bentley, the cartoonist, an old friend. He was anything but happy at what I regarded as an astonishing achievement. Nor did he admire the courage of a man travelling in space, since he was paid to do it like any other job. Nick was convinced it would lead to war in space and he was deeply pessimistic. However, in 1988, there seems at least a chance that mankind has come to its senses, and decided not to blow up this beautiful planet. We can only hope.

The day of the exhibition arrived, and it turned out to be one of the highlights of my life. A number of paintings were sold at the preview – to Roland Penrose and Lord Dufferin and Alva amongst others. At the Private View there was a lot more interest (though inevitably it was a bit of an anti-climax after the night before), and then a few days later, the Tate Gallery decided to buy the head of Dylan Thomas I had painted from one of those quick sketches of some years before. I was delighted – so much so that I once again let the cat out of the bag, and a small item was published in the *Evening Standard* mentioning the Tate's purchase. There was a great to-do, and I was in hot water again. Luckily, Sir John Rothenstein, who was then Director of the Tate, wrote me a charming and reassuring letter to say that no harm had been done, for which I was profoundly thankful.

We used to spend many happy weekends with our friends the Dears down in their large country house in Hampshire, where we watched their enchanting children grow up. In 1962, they had a villa for the summer in Alassio, northern Italy, on the other side of the Gulf of Genoa from Rapallo, at the foot of the Ligurian Alps. They asked us if we would like to join them there, but I was very uncertain about the idea, simply because Joseph was not well. At the same time, he wished to keep it a dark secret, and kept on refusing to see a doctor.

In June his foot was again very bad, and he had to lie up and rest it in bed. Meanwhile we had to make a decision about whether to go on holiday or not, so finally I persuaded Joseph to see a doctor. This man was very sympathetic, and reassured us that of course we could go to Alassio (he himself had spent his honeymoon there and it had done him good!). However, the doctor did suspect Joseph of suffering from diabetes, so immediately put him on a very strict diet and wanted to make a number of tests. We went to Alassio, but, alas, it did Joseph no good, and we had to fly him back to London with his foot in plaster of Paris. He ended up in a nursing home in Fitzroy Square; and back we were to square one, as he himself said.

It took Joseph at least six months to recover some of his strength; I spent a lot of time with him, trying to keep up his spirits. I continued to paint and make collages, and even though I had less time in the studio, I was working with increased vigour and belief, encouraged by the recognition my latest work had received. In 1963 I showed more paintings at the Brook Street Gallery in a mixed exhibition, and was approached by an Italian dealer to show in Rome. My one-man exhibition at 'Il Bilico' Gallery was only a modest success, but it was good to be showing in a new country.

Joseph was just beginning to feel more himself, and enjoying a renewed mobility, when another blow fell. He was leafing through the American magazine *Time* (the issue for 15 November 1963 was the offending one) when he came across a scurrilous attack on his reputation in a review of a book about Dorothy Thompson and Sinclair Lewis. An American journalist, Vincent Sheean, had written a book entitled *Dorothy and Red* ('Red' being a nickname of Sinclair Lewis), and early passages of it attacked Joseph for having left such a Pearl of the Press, and for having behaved dishonestly and dishonourably towards a woman who had become an American institution.

Joseph loathed publicity of this sort as much as Lewis Carroll, but he was advised that he must fight back, and though ill and still weak, he did so. It was a shocking and painful experience for Joseph to read *Dorothy and Red*; he felt that the book was a caricature of his relationship with Dorothy, malicious and stupid into the bargain. Joseph was deeply upset to find that he had been so seriously misrepresented, and that his character had been slandered. After all, he taught Dorothy how to be a journalist, he started her on the road that was to be so successful for her. She herself confessed to being an inveterate brain-picker, and Joseph always maintained that Dorothy stole the fire out of his *Mind of Europe* and made it pay. Now to be represented as a 'pathological half-wit' (as he put it) was to add gross insult to old injury.

Joseph asserted that Dorothy had a bad conscience about what she had done to him. He also used to say that her one real failing was her love of money and possessions. He always rather optimistically hoped Dorothy would behave differently, and that when they were parting, she would say something like:

> Look, we met empty-handed six years ago, I have picked your brains ever since, used you in my work without mercy, stolen your ideas which were then new

and potent – now I sit in a large flat full of exquisite things all bought by our common earnings and efforts, I am already rising to be a celebrity in international journalism, I am beginning to earn real money; you are still empty-handed, your book in fragments (much of it used in my articles without giving you credit for it), you have been moved away from your own circles by following my career and interests, you are a nervous wreck in a bloody country which is full of murderers and smells like a slaughter-house – Josef! How shall we share what we have acquired together?

Somehow this was too much to hope for, and instead Dorothy started to be indignant about infidelities and insincerities (which Joseph conveniently considered to be abstractions!). So Dorothy kept everything for herself and entertained the 'great writer', Sinclair Lewis, in a sumptuous flat built by the combined efforts of Joseph and herself. Sheean's book was ridiculously biased, so Joseph tried to put the record straight.

Our dear friend and solicitor, Anthony Rubinstein, was of immense help at this difficult time as Joseph fought the Time-Life machine, and insisted on the English version of *Dorothy and Red* being properly edited. Towards the end of January 1964, Joseph received an anonymous telephone call at ten o'clock at night, threatening: 'You had better drop the case, or else.' However, Joseph's perseverence was rewarded. Heinemann agreed to cut the offending passages from the English edition of Sheean's book, and Joseph won a substantial amount in compensation for the damage done by the *Time* article. But the whole episode had exhausted and depressed him; it was a desolate winter indeed.

1964 improved as it got older, like some smelly cheeses, but not all the news was good. Agar Cross finally closed down, having been failing slowly since 1940. The Argentines had grown increasingly nationalistic and refused to buy from British or foreign companies; by 1948 the country was sliding into anarchy. Herbert Read, visiting there in 1962, was shocked by the incredible disorganisation. The only memorials to the firm which had built my parents' fortune were the windmills; and like the fortunes of Argentina itself, the windmills continue to turn.

The main event of the year for me was the long-awaited retrospective exhibition of my work at the Brook Street Gallery. Herbert Read had written a warm and enthusiastic piece for my show in 1962 but we had decided to save it for the catalogue of this exhibition. I had been approached by the Redfern Gallery (where I had exhibited in the war) to show with them again, but I was happy with Bob and Rena Lewin at the Brook Street Gallery, and my retrospective in October/November turned out well. Again the Tate Gallery bought a painting, this time the early oil from 1930 which I called 'The Flying Pillar'. It was renamed 'Three Symbols' which is a more prosaic title, but which underlines my intentions in the imagery. It was an important early painting for me, and I was glad that the Tate purchased it.

In the same year I took part in the London Group Jubilee exhibition. There was certainly an atmosphere of assessment about, but I had had enough of looking back. I had seen how I had progressed, but I did not feel the need now for consolidation. Once again I was restless, in search of new inspiration. In 1965 I found it in a new medium – acrylics. I saw an exhibition of a painter called Robert van Eyck, a very individual Surrealist-type painter, who used a lot of *décalcomanie*, a technique usually attributed to Oscar Dominguez. (*Décalcomanie* is the process of slapping on to paper random paint strokes, then applying another sheet on top, and gently moving the two sheets together. Peel apart for the results of a supposedly 'automatic' technique.) While talking to the artist, I was surprised to learn that he used acrylic paints instead of oils as I had thought. He suggested I try this new wonder medium, and I have never gone back to oils since. (As the Flemish van Eyck brothers were traditionally credited with inventing oil paint at the beginning of the fifteenth century, it seemed more than appropriate that another van Eyck should introduce me to acrylics.)

Acrylic is a water-based polymer emulsion paint which had lately come on the market after extensive tests. It is easy to handle, quick drying, and does not have many of the disadvantages of oil, though it has a slightly unpleasant skin unless used with discretion. It will not crack when rolled up, and after four hundred years of oil painting, I felt artists should move on to something else. Acrylic is very versatile, it can be used as impasto, with palette knife, or a thin wash gives wonderful glazes. The only thing you cannot do is scrape it off when dry, but of course while still wet it can be removed. I usually do a very small drawing of the main forms or outlines I intend to create on the canvas, the seed of what I hope is to come. Then, as I dislike squaring up, I start straight ahead on the canvas, not in charcoal, but in pencil or light paint, altering as I go along, sometimes changing drastically. But the real equipment of the artist is in his or her attitude of mind, in one's vision, not in what one finds in art shops.

The next year or two I exhibited mainly outside London, at the Harlow Arts Festival, and down in Surrey. It was a period of constant experiment, of testing the effects of new pigments, new colour combinations. I was very interested to discover that people can very seldom tell the difference between acrylic and oil, which is the sort of sleight of hand the Surrealists would have appreciated. In acrylics, I had found what I considered to be an ideal medium, and I wanted both to master it and to stretch it.

CHAPTER NINE

Looking Back

As one grows older it becomes more and more difficult to avoid living in the past. The adventures of youth seem brighter and more poignant than the infirmities of the present, and one is filled with that nostalgic yearning which leads too often to profound melancholy. Joseph was not well, and though he battled bravely against age, he was lame and found difficulty in walking. His was turning into an old man's world; 'a dark and difficult landscape dotted with graves,' he called it, remembering all the friends he had lost.

Joseph was a splendid raconteur whose conversation sparkled with anecdote and wit. Several friends tried to persuade him to write his memoirs, notably the poet and critic and fellow member of the RSL, John Press. It would have been an extraordinary book if Joseph had written it, but although he continued to reassure everyone he was making good progress, the book did not get beyond pages of scattered notes; for the most part, nearly illegible jottings. *This* book is the story of my life, but it has also been written in tribute to Joseph, and I have tried to introduce him accurately to the reader. I hope I do him justice.

In 1967 Joseph read Claud Cockburn's autobiography *I Claud*, and wrote to him on the strength of an incident linking them forty years before. Joseph had left Dorothy Thompson when Claud met her, and Sinclair Lewis had 'inherited' Joseph's pedigree Airedale. This dog, which went by the name of Rolfe van der Eichenberg was a great character, much cherished by Joseph; he said that when he absconded from Berlin, Rolfe was the thing nearest to his heart.

Rolfe had a unique personality and, like Joseph, had not enjoyed the move from Vienna to Berlin which Dorothy's work had made necessary. Once when taking a long walk, Joseph and Rolfe had happened to pass the Hindenburg residence. Rolfe proceeded to lift his leg against the front steps and Joseph had a very heated argument with the guard who approached with murder in his heart and bayonet fixed and lowered. . . . Joseph however, was very proud of his dog. The American writer Ludwig Lewisohn used to describe them both as 'two creatures of inimitable elegance'.

Anyhow, Claud Cockburn was asked to take charge of Rolfe while Dorothy and Sinclair were absent from Berlin on their travels. Writer and dog spent a miserable poverty-stricken Christmas, with Cockburn reduced to eating half of the scraps donated by a generous butcher for Rolfe's Christmas dinner. Joseph wanted to thank Claud for his care, and also for the amusing description of the whole episode, with Rolfe dogging Sinclair Lewis's footsteps, occasionally biting the famous writer he must have regarded as a home-breaker, or attacking his friends.

Living so near Holland Park, we used to spend warm sunny afternoons lazing in deck-chairs, and on Saturdays watching the cricket. To me, Holland Park is the most intimate of London's parks, as well as the most interesting. On summer evenings, there are often open-air concerts, and sometimes theatre. Peacocks, emus, pheasants and ducks dwell in a small enclosure, and children come especially to watch their antics and learn their names. When there was no other special entertainment, we would bring a rug and lie on the grass, looking up at the sky to enjoy the passing clouds, hearing the shouts of children playing nearby. Holland Park was altogether an oasis for us in the desert of London, and I often brought souvenirs of bark or leaves back to the studio for use in collage or frottage.

Strangely enough, I never had the slightest desire to have children of my own for I was positive that at least one of my nieces would provide me with sufficient great-nieces and nephews to satisfy any curiosity about how they grew up, married or made themselves careers. And so it has turned out. Isabel, our faithful daily help, used to lament that no one had ever asked her to get married. It was the unbegotten children that she regretted more than the lack of a husband. I felt sorry for her though I could not share her regret.

At this time there was a renewal of interest in Surrealism, with one exhibition in particular taking the lead. Conroy Maddox was instrumental in this revival, and I got to know this energetic painter much better during the arrangements for 'The Enchanted Domain' show at Exeter. He knew more about Surrealism and its beginnings than most people, and had collected virtually every Surrealist catalogue and hand-out that was published. A most vital and dedicated artist, he still travels around the world on behalf of Surrealism.

The next year, 1968, besides showing in Manchester, I met with Donald Bowen, the director of the Commonwealth Institute in Kensington, who was keen to mount a major retrospective of my work. The gallery at the Commonwealth Institute is spacious and well-lit and I was at first intimidated by the size of it. The idea of the exhibition had been Joseph's, not mine, and I spent several sleepless nights wondering if I should be able to fill the gallery with satisfactory work.

If Joseph was looking back over his life, I also had to look back over mine, deciding which paintings and collages to borrow from friends and collectors to represent the different periods of my work. The problem was, that being a professional painter who earns her living from her work, I had sold most of my best things, and could not always remember where they had gone. And then, a collector or dealer who comes to the studio very often sells the work sooner or later to someone else, and so the chain goes on, making it more and more difficult to track paintings down. But that was not my only problem. I was asked to do ten or more large new canvases for the exhibition, and since the gallery needs striking paintings if they are not to be lost in it, I had quite a task before me. However, the next couple of years were fully booked for the gallery, so we arranged a date in October 1971, and I began my preparations.

There were other exhibitions in those years – for instance, I was selected again for the John Moores in 1969, and I continued to show with The London Group – but they appeared to be happening at a tangent to my main activity. Joseph scribbled out his past, I moved into the future. He took over the front room at West House, turning it into a study, while I spent much time in my attic studio, pausing now and again for an inspirational nap on the divan in one corner.

The seventies opened in dramatic fashion with a letter from Joseph's daughter Valentine. At last she was coming over from America with her scientist son Stephen and his wife, to seek out the father she had never met. Joseph took the news philosophically if not with amazed delight; I think he felt a certain amount of detached embarrassment, remarking that it was Nietzsche who said that one's past always catches up. For my part, I was curious to meet this woman who had shown such remarkable strength of character, and brought up two small sons in a strange land.

Joseph's sister Melanie, who had also settled in America, had come to London for a few days in 1968 with her daughter and stayed at the Grosvenor House Hotel on her way to the continent. Melanie had told us about her own meeting with Valentine, and how struck she had been by her personality, how upright and capable she was. Nevertheless it was a strange meeting between unknown father and middle-aged daughter. Valentine was a dark-haired, resolute woman, slim and erect, younger in looks than I had expected. I could see no resemblance to Joseph, but this was my step-daughter and I welcomed her with warmth.

Joseph took her to a lecture at the RSL, introducing her as 'my daughter', which hardly raised an eyebrow. (I think Joseph was slightly taken aback at this seeming decline in English morality; why was no one outraged? Again in this case he was more English than the English themselves.) Valentine stayed in London only for ten days, then like a phantom from the past, she was gone, her vow to meet her father fulfilled. Joseph tried to match her gaiety and pleasure, but he was inwardly *distrait* and sad, partly through ill-health, partly through age and memory beating at the door.

1971 was a hard year for Joseph. Pressure for me was building up as the Commonwealth Institute exhibition loomed larger and larger on the Kensington horizon, and I was able to give Joseph less care and consideration than I might have wished. For his part, depression grabbed him by the throat, and he slid into a dark despair brought on by age and illness, which made him convinced of his own failure in life. In fact, he had a minor nervous breakdown, and was under medication to suppress the symptoms. We were lucky in having a very capable lady doctor to whom Joseph was able to unburden himself – to some extent at least for so private a man. But for many months he wore what he later called a 'vinegar aspect,' and it was as if the light of his intellectual balance was suffering random cuts.

Joseph was distrustful of psychiatric therapy, and had argued the case often enough in the past with the likes of Ezra Pound. As he wrote to his doctor: 'Freud, to me at least, is a permanent warning light not to err into emotional falsettoes. . . .' But as he himself had helped others in the past by listening to their troubles, so now he was thankful that a sympathetic ear was open to him. By nature, Joseph was something of a worrier, and his concern about money had grown out of all proportion, until the Income Tax people had become horrific bogeys, and he was terrified of the future. With help, Joseph was gradually able to control his fears and recover his equilibrium, and thankfully his spirits began to rise again.

Meanwhile, I was working frantically for my big retrospective, both painting and dealing with the administrative side of things. Roland Penrose kindly agreed to write an introduction to the catalogue, and he traced our friendship back to 1936, and the early days of my career. Apart from that, there were photographs to have taken, insurance to arrange, framing to be done, and guest lists to compile. Also, since Surrealism was beginning to be reassessed at last, there were other exhibitions

I was asked to contribute to. The Hamet Gallery staged a show called 'Britain's Contribution to Surrealism', which contained work by a lot of old friends, many of whom I did not often see these days.

Roland helped Donald Bowen to hang the paintings in the Commonwealth Institute Gallery, and there on the walls – by the time of the Private View – was a cross-section of a lifetime's work, from 1927 to 1971. But the gallery, though full of paintings, looked more empty of people than it should have done, and we wondered why. It was only when a collector who had lent work rang up to apologise for his absence that we discovered one reason. The day we had chosen all unwittingly turned out to be Yom Kippur, the Jewish Day of Atonement. However, more than three thousand people came to see the show eventually, though my euphoria was short-lived. In ten days' time, Joseph had to go into hospital where he stayed for three weeks before he was allowed home. Then there was a protracted period of convalescence until he was able to get out for dinner at the Garrick, and go occasionally to the theatre.

With abundant white hair, Joseph kept his good looks despite all these troubles. In hospital he had been sunk in deep gloom and despondency, mental horrors crowding in on him in an hallucinatory way, with the dangerous added phenomenon of imagined events. But care and attention brought his will to be alive back again, and a certain inner gaiety and calm possessed him after he got home. It gave him great satisfaction and helped his recovery to know that he had been made a vice-president of the RSL at Cecil Day Lewis' instigation; for a transplanted European faces life in England with one arm metaphorically tied behind his back. The hapless continental has to find his way in the dark, and in the process of getting acclimatised, his inspiration and creative drive may suffer. This, I am told, happens to a lot of talents. I think this is one reason why Joseph wrote so little in England. A writer is always 'becoming' whereas Joseph was very essentially 'being'. What he could have kept for his books, he gave away in conversation, laughter and jokes; ideas floated out of him in response to human beings, but a typewriter left him cold.

The RSL had played a large part in Joseph's life since he became a Fellow in 1942. In 1946 he had been elected a member of the council, and through regular attendance at the meetings, Joseph formed many lasting friendships and attachments. He swapped anecdotes and added to his own collection of stories. He would recount how Lord Wavell, then President of the RSL, gave him a lift home in 1950, just a few months before he died. His impression of Wavell was of a taciturn but likeable man, evidently dutiful but sad and disillusioned, a man behind bars. Joseph went to the great soldier's funeral service at Westminster Abbey, shocked as he was by Wavell's death.

The friend who had introduced Joseph to the RSL, Henry Simpson, accompanied him on this trip to pay their last respects. Henry Simpson was made and moulded before the First World War. In his youth a new volume of Tennyson meant a thrill and a revelation. He told us that when he worked in a bank as a young man earning £1 a week, he usually gave the entire amount to his mother as a contribution towards the household expenses. One week he kept 1s. 6d. (7½p) back, and was immediately asked by his father, in all seriousness: 'Are you by any chance keeping a mistress?'

Simpson inherited the Poets Club from the philosopher-poet T. E. Hulme, and he presided over it for fifty years. Denis Saurat, Dylan Thomas, Joseph and Edith Sitwell all gave addresses at the Sesame Club where this poets' convention usually met. Henry Simpson watched Swinburne's ecstatic dance in Putney Vale, and naturally he was a champion of the poetic tradition. He resisted the values of the modern world, yet he tried to understand them. He was certainly a good friend and guide to Joseph – if somewhat old-fashioned and traditional in his thinking.

I had sent a catalogue of the Commonwealth Institute Retrospective with some photographs to Ezra Pound in 1971. Over the years I had continued to dip into his valuable book on Gaudier-Brzeska, so that, remembering the long road a painter travels, I was particularly pleased to get a card from him in response, congratulating me. But the next year we heard that Ezra had died, and we were much saddened by the news. It was another death to haunt Joseph, and he spent a lot of time with his notes of meetings with his old friend. I quote from Joseph's manuscripts:

> Once, in Firenze, I bribed one of those peddlers who sell miniature bronze busts of famous Italians and, lunching in the open with Pound, I watched his face when my peddler began to cry out: 'Buy gentlemen, buy – busts of Aristotle, Tasso, Dante and Mr Ezra Pound. . . .' I watched Pound's face: he was neither amused nor surprised. He was convinced of his immortality; the cask of time, in which reputations have to mature and survive, had no relevance for him.

Joseph was very mixed in his opinion of Ezra. He thought Ezra set himself enormous goals that could not be achieved by one man – rebuilding poetry, remaking language, remodelling politics and economics. In 1930 he recalled that he thought Ezra too earnest, too self-conscious in his efforts to revive the dead art of poetry. But at the same time, Pound was prepared to listen. For instance, it was Joseph who introduced him to the writings of Leo Frobenius, the German anthropologist, who was to provide important factual confirmation of Pound's theories. Then, EP was always ready with help and advice; suggestions of what you should read or what you should write; introductions to people who might be able to help you. Joseph used to speak of magnetic literary poles which fool your own internal needle. I think Ez may have been just such for Joseph, for the influence he wielded seemed to prevent Joseph from writing rather than encouraging him. Perhaps Joseph's dilemma may be finally expressed thus (a sentence from his notebooks): 'Ezra P. will go to Heaven as an angel, with blue eyes, apricot-coloured wings, a long white night-shirt, and with galoshes on his feet.'

1973 and 1974 were quieter years for Joseph, and I tried to

spend as much time with him as possible. Our social life was curtailed by his increasing immobility, but there were other pleasures to brighten Joseph's life. His enjoyment of literature was undimmed and he continued to read tirelessly. Then his collection of ancient gems gave him great satisfaction. Around 1932 I had given Joseph his first intaglio which initiated this collecting mania. He had admired a green gemstone supposedly carved with the head of Augustus, but after owning it some time, and learning more about this recondite subject, he came to the conclusion that the stone was eighteenth-century, not Roman, so back it went to the well-known dealer, who exchanged it for something more authentic.

Joseph was hooked, and so, after buying several fakes and making other mistakes, he embarked on a hobby which was to interest and excite him for the rest of his life. During the war especially he had the opportunity to wander the streets of London (when not fire-watching or acting as air-raid warden) in search of gems; good exercise, and doubly good for his health, as he gave up smoking in order to collect. Often he would come back with a prized possession, an engraved agate or other stone found in a shop window full of junk and false teeth. Indeed, one very beautiful Egyptian gem with Horus sitting on a lotus leaf was found amongst just such a conglomeration of objects, in an East End pawnbroker's shop. Someone had turned it into a tie-pin.

As there were no foreign dealers, due to the war, the coast for acquiring such treasures was clear, and Joseph's acumen enabled him to pick up many bargains for just a few pounds. Hardly anyone knew anything about gems, but it is obvious from their work that both Picasso and Braque must have looked at them. For Joseph, collecting became an obsession: finding a new (old) gem was rather better than a new love, and so ancient artefacts turned a philanderer into a faithful husband. I often wonder whether Joseph knew that an agate was also a person small in stature; would that have been why he was so fond of those banded variegated chalcedonies?

There was much history to be learnt and amusing stories to

tell about the sharp practice of past gem dealers. Long before heroin smugglers swallowed packets of drugs, collectors and dealers and workmen swallowed stones they wished to appropriate. The famous collector, Baron Storsch, swallowed the Michelangelo ring in the Bibliothèque Nationale in Paris, but was promptly given an emetic when the ring was missed. There was a long-established and substantial trade in fakes, and these counterfeit gems were often given to turkeys to swallow when they looked too new, so that the bird's gizzard would scratch marks of age on the stone.

Joseph's collection was formed from a literary point of view, besides being inevitably influenced by what was available at the time. If ever he was called to justify his collecting mania, he would first of all say it was like studying art history through a keyhole, and then go on to compare himself favourably with a man his fellow Hungarian George Mikes knew, who collected old hats. Joseph used to say that gems were the only illustrations left to us of those myths and legends now lost, and that these engraved images also included well-known statues and paintings which had subsequently disappeared. Some of his gems were quite extraordinary, especially one or two of the gryllus type (comic grotesques) which were highly surreal. (One I recall depicted four flies in a carriage drawn by a flea.) Joseph said that nothing – or almost nothing – would part him from his really good intaglios.

Interest in Surrealism was reaching new peaks, and in 1973, a young researcher from the University of Nancy in France came to interview us. Michel Remy has since written with Gallic intellectual rigour about the English Surrealists, and made this subject his own particular stamping ground. But, although I was more than prepared to be included in any survey of British Surrealism I was still unwilling to be categorised simply as a Surrealist artist. After all, my origins had been equally in abstraction, so it was fitting that I should be represented in a 1974 exhibition called 'Aspects of Abstract Painting'. I preferred to be seen as a contemporary imagina-

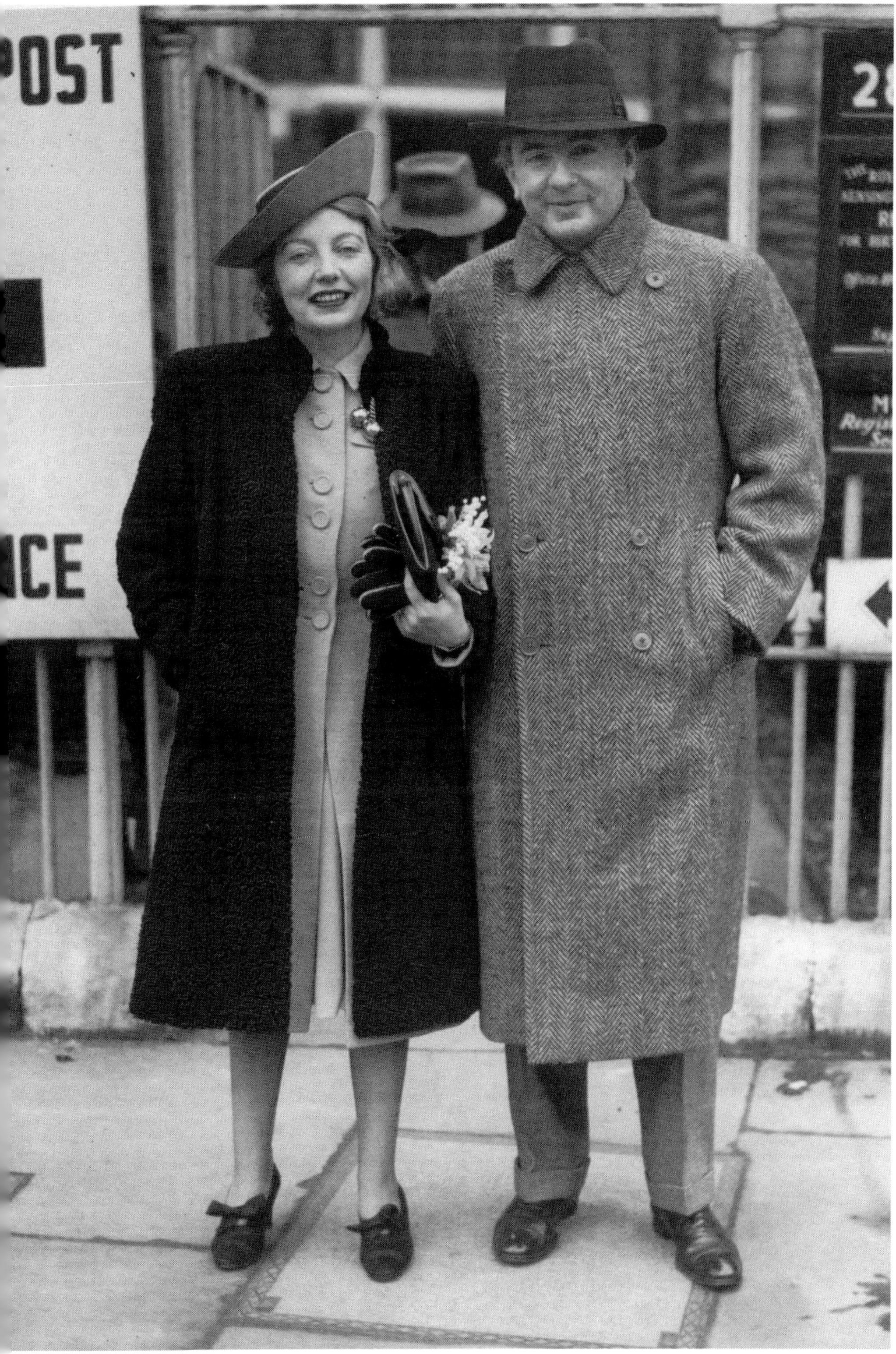

17 Just Married! 29 February 1940. Outside the Registry Office, Gloucester Road. (We put on weight to keep out the cold.)

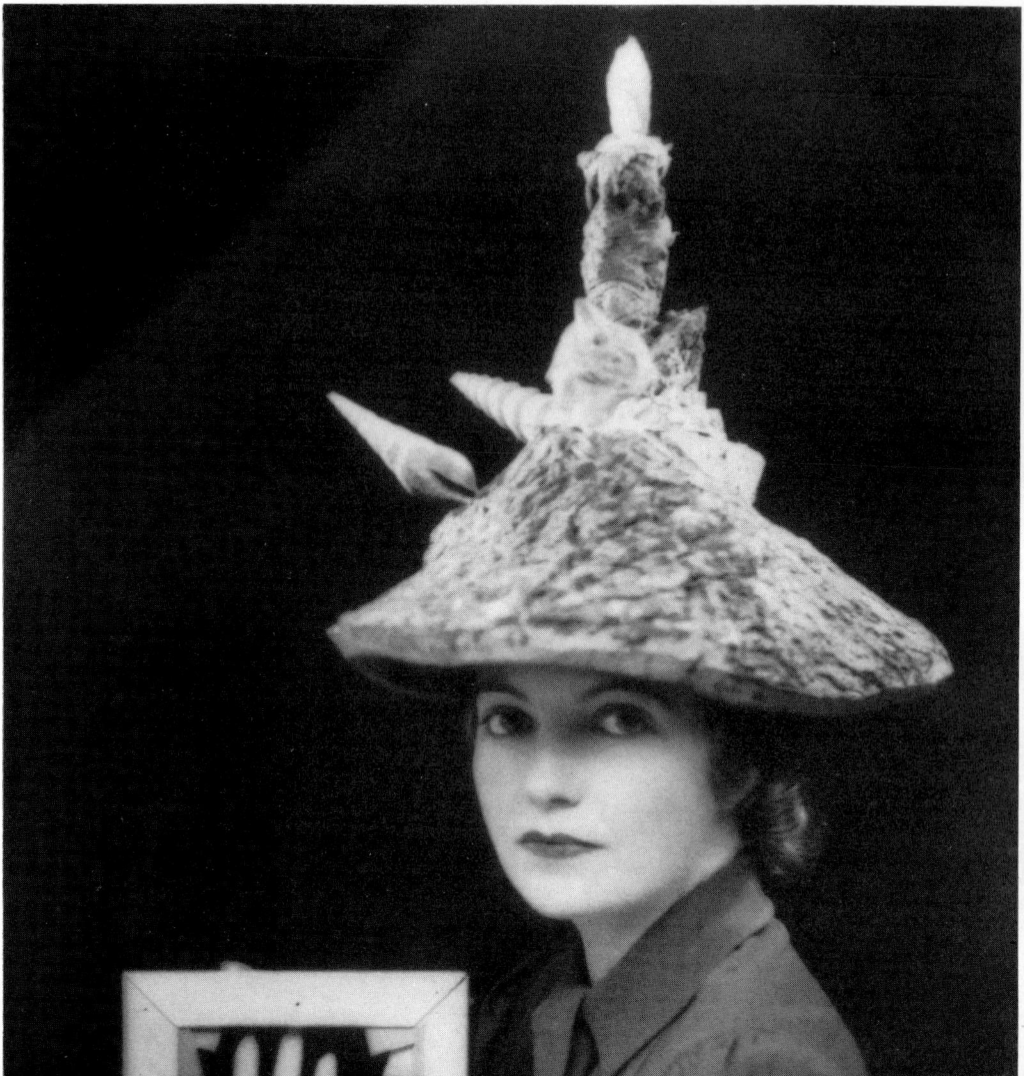

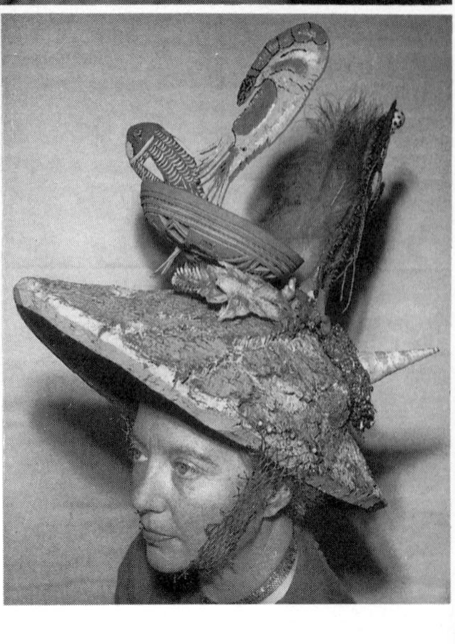

18a Self wearing 'Ceremonial Hat for Eating Bouillabaisse', seen here with the 'Hand of Fate', *c.* 1936.

18b Self in another version of 'Ceremonial Hat' – as seen on TV in 1948.

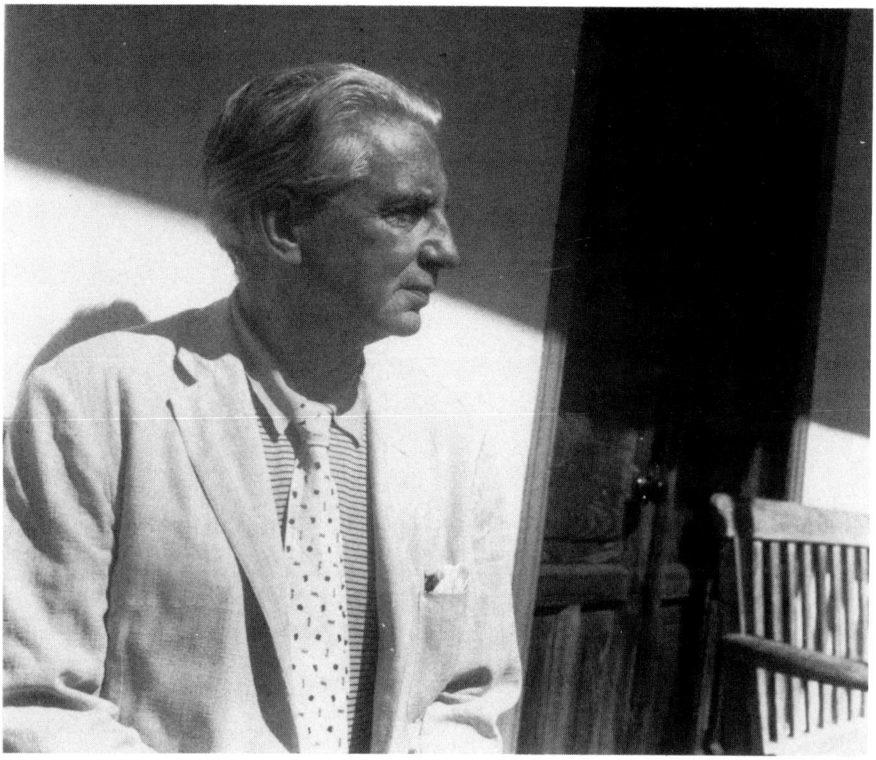

19a Joseph at Sitio Litre, Tenerife, in 1956. I chose the tie!

19b Sitio Litre, rear garden view.

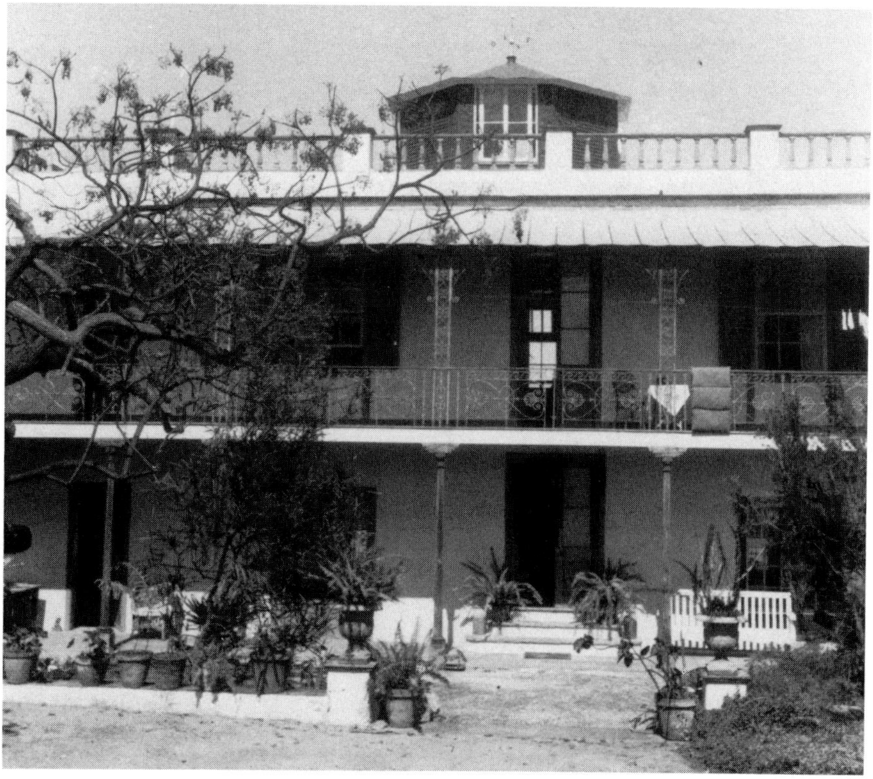

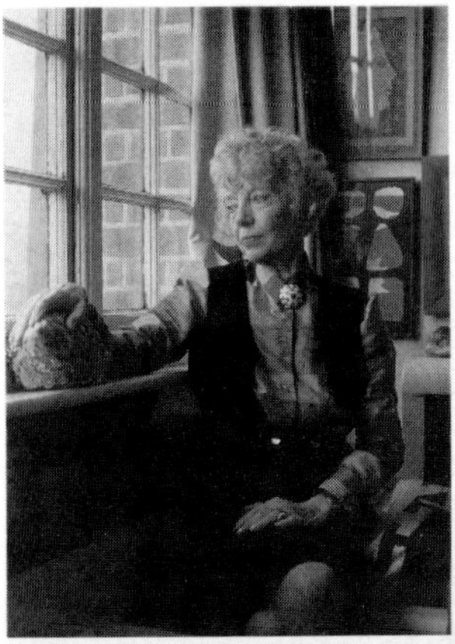

20a Self in the studio at West House
in 1975, after Joseph's death.

20b Snowdon's photograph of me modelling clothes
by Issey Miyake, in 1986.

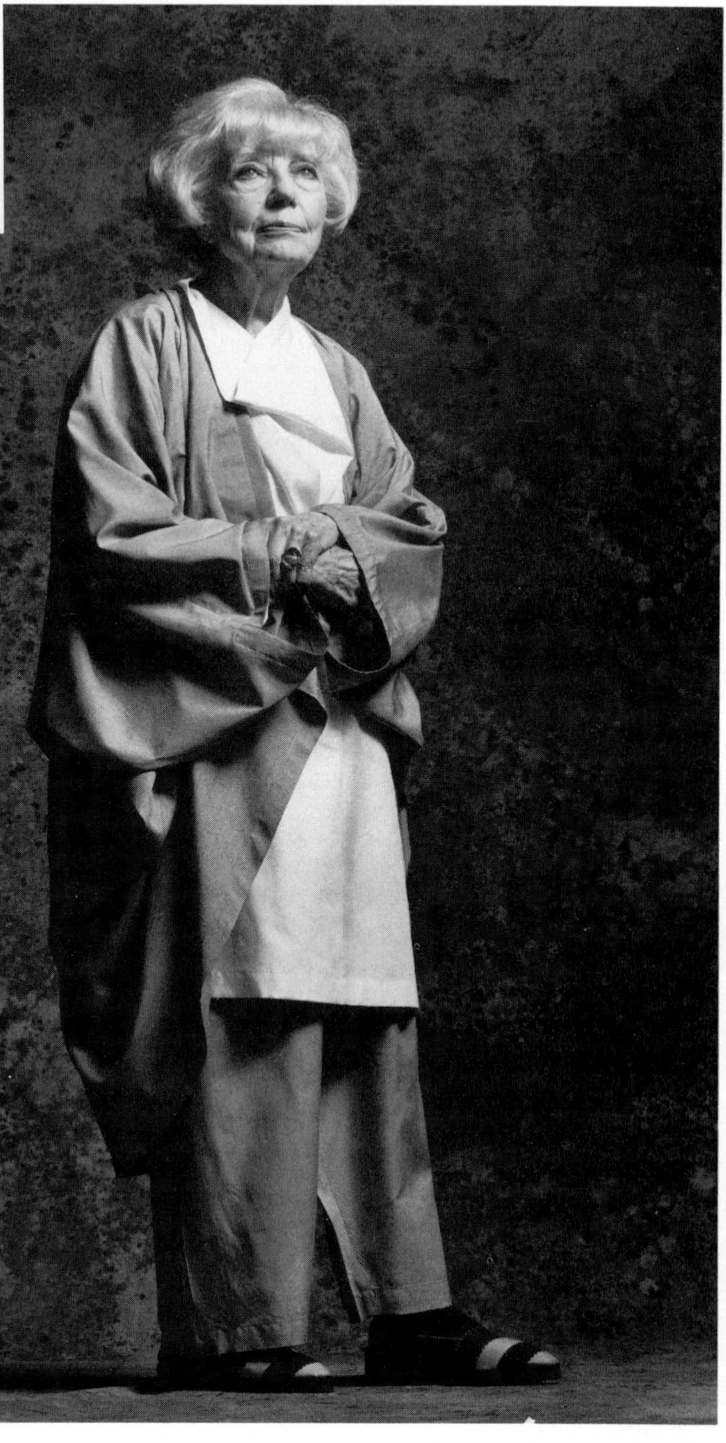

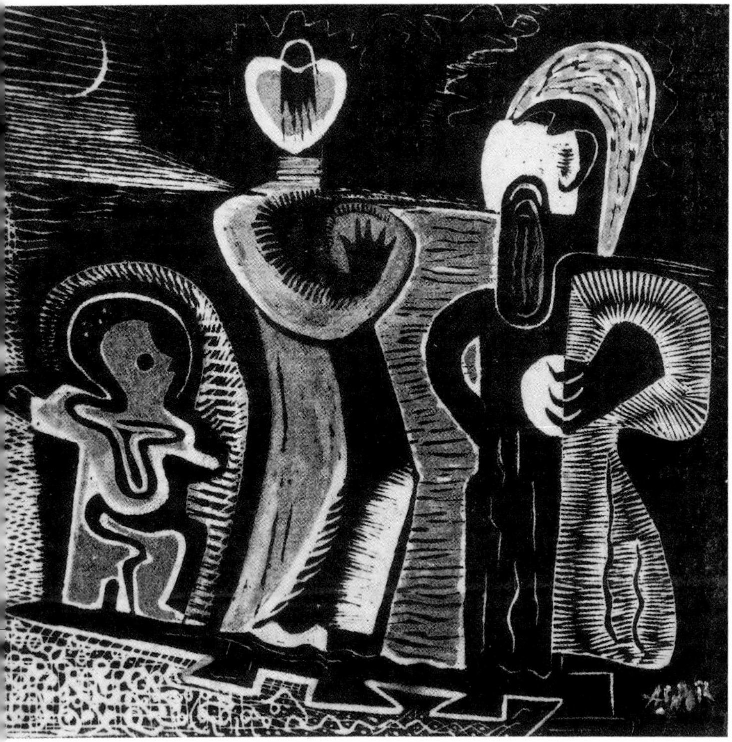

21a 'Family Trio', 1931; wood engraving (Artist's Collection).

21b 'Movement in Space', 1931; oil on canvas (Private Collection).

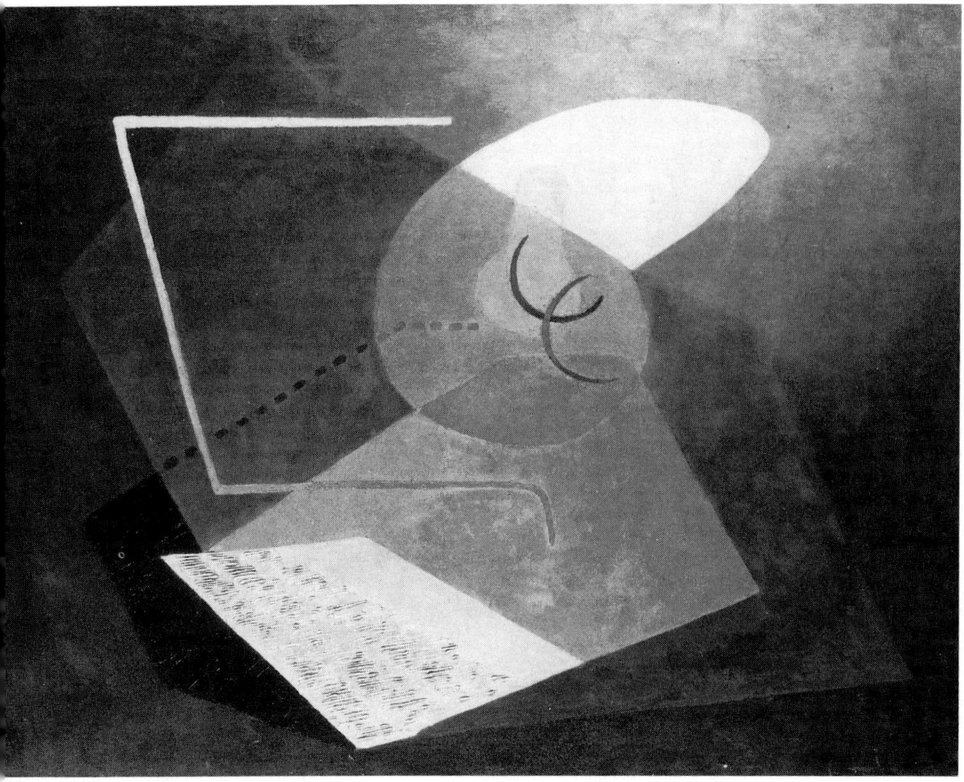

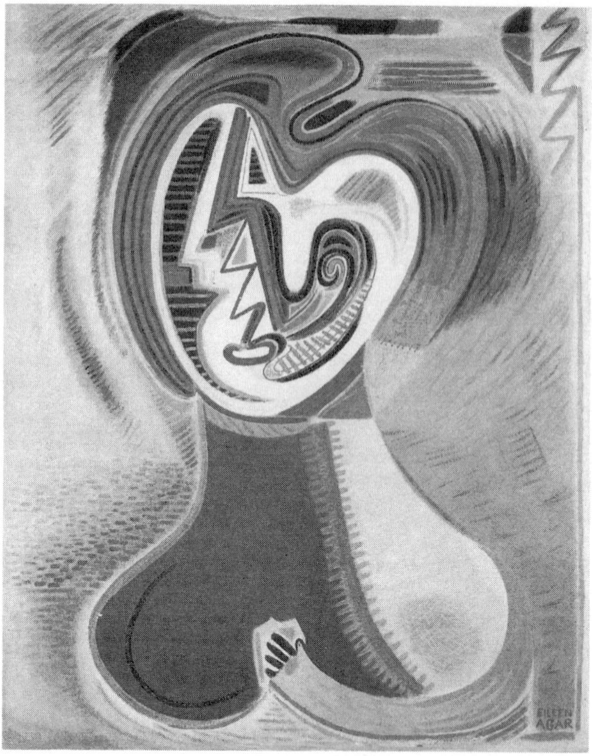

22a 'The Modern Muse',
1931; oil on canvas
(Private Collection).

22b 'Quadriga',
1935; oil on canvas
(Private Collection).

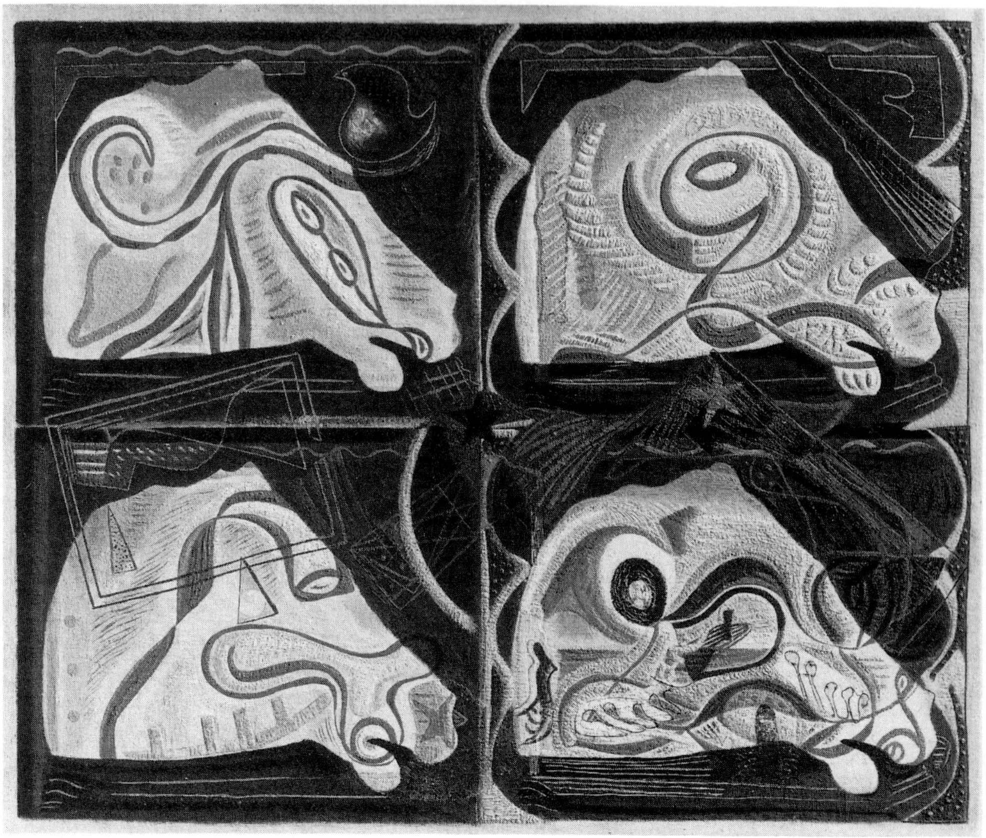

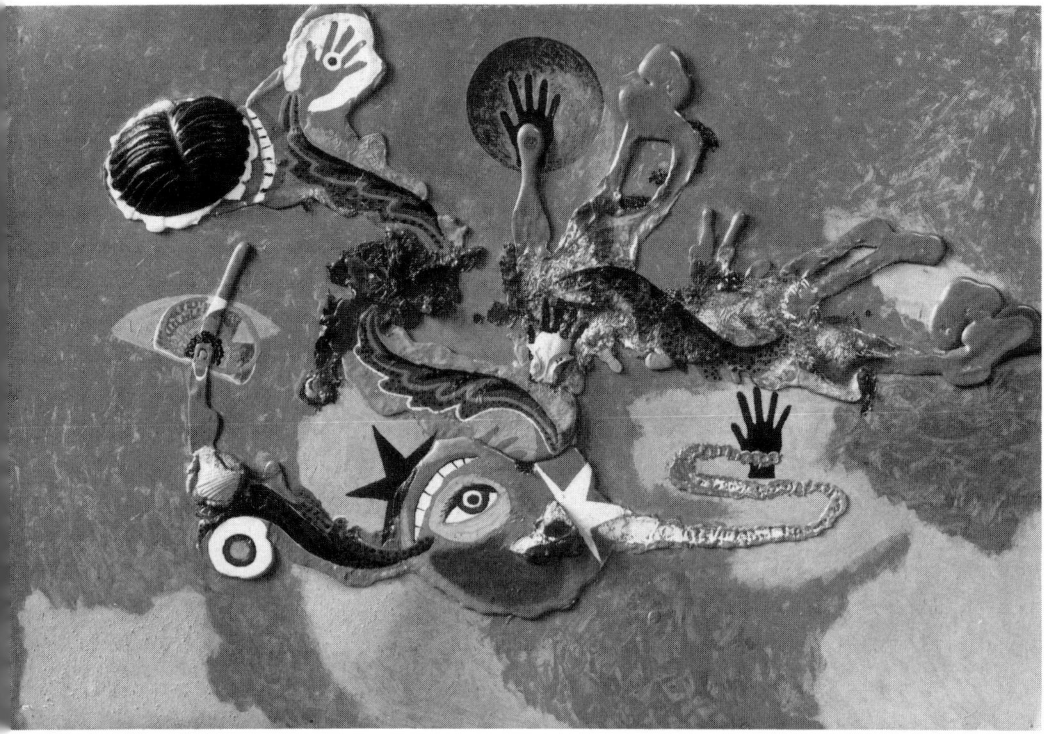

23a 'The Battle Cry' ('Bullet-proof painting'), 1938; lead, paint and plaster on metal (Collection: Gordon Onslow Ford).

23b 'Fish Circus', *c.* 1938; collage (Collection: Gabrielle Keiller).

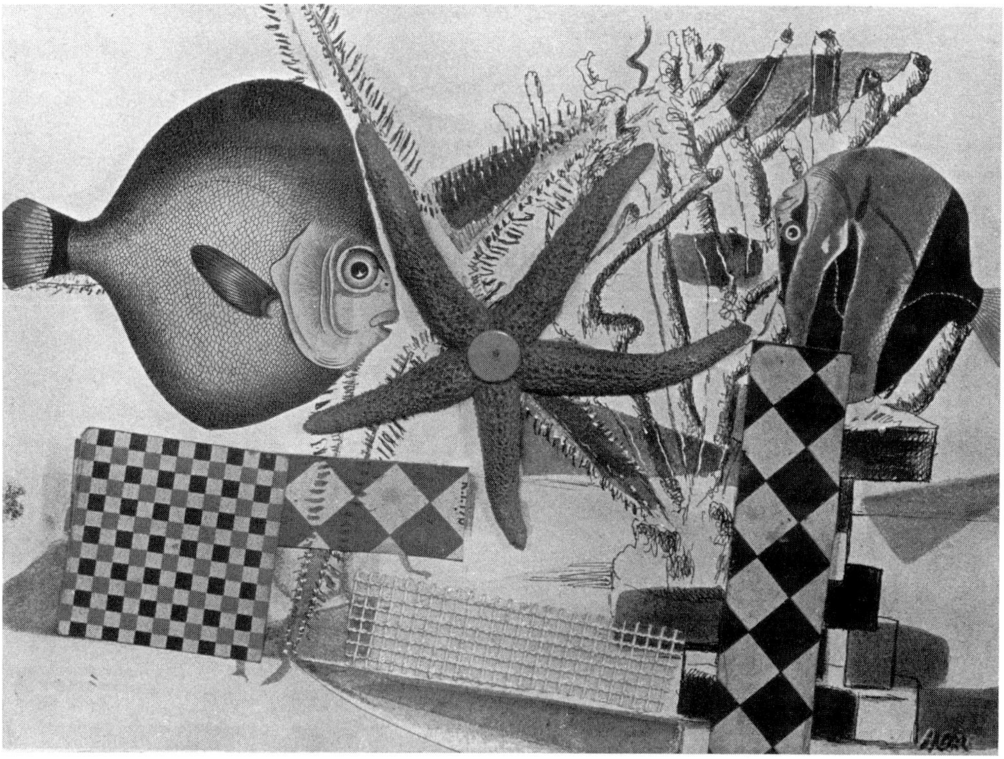

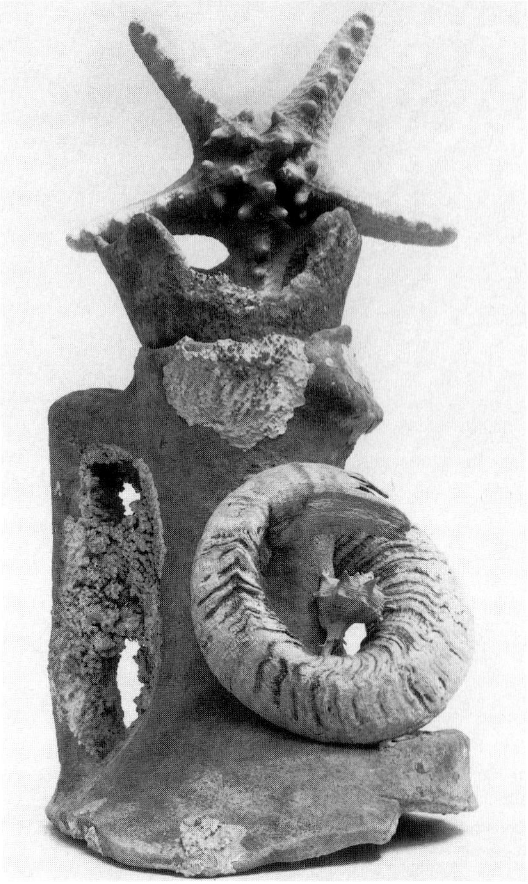

24a 'Marine Object', 1939 (Artist's Collection).

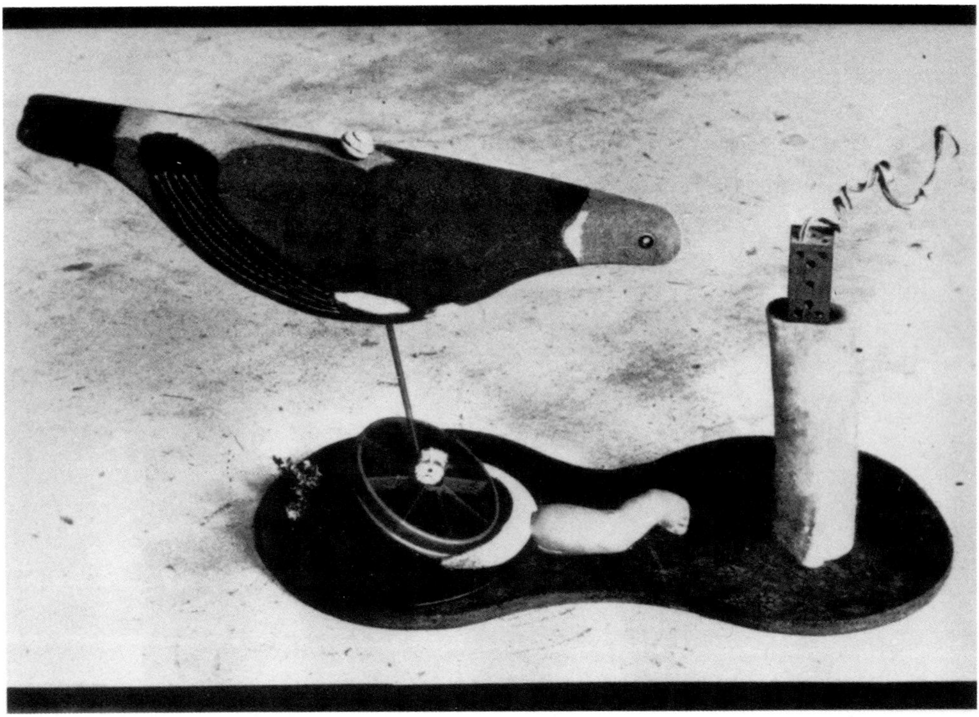

24b 'David and Jonathan', 1939; object.

tive painter rather than as some historical phenomenon, so I was pleased to be asked to contribute to 'British Painting '74' at the Hayward Gallery.

Joseph suffered a slight stroke on 19 June 1974, and was sent to hospital once more to recuperate. He spent ten days in St Stephen's and made another good recovery, but he was becoming less and less able to get around. However, we celebrated his recovery by going to the Garrick for dinner, little realising that it would be the last time for both of us. One evening in the following July, Joseph overtaxed his strength trying to remember some lines of Goethe which he wished to quote to a friend who had called. He got over-excited, drank another small glass of wine, and alas, in the night of 26 July 1975, he died. The silk thread of his life had spun itself out.

To give a true picture of such a rich personality as Joseph is an impossible task. There were so many sides to him, all equally important, that perhaps all I can do is hint at the man who was my lover, husband and lifelong companion.

Joseph was pleasure-loving, fond of touching, tasting, feeling. He loved silks and stuffs, and would spend hours at the tailor choosing the right material. He lamented the fact that men had lost their independence in matters of clothing, allowing themselves to be stereotyped into sombre grey suits. A friend, incidentally, once asked Joseph why he called his dog Dandy, when he was the dandy himself. Joseph was always being reproached for wearing his hair too long. I remember one excitable and chatty chemise in the early thirties, rushing up to me at a cocktail party and gasping: 'Who is that man with the extravagant hair?' She retired in confusion when I said he was my lover – did she want me to introduce her?

Good conversation in cafés and restaurants invigorated him, for he was a magnetic speaker. He was fond of patisseries and financial speculation, ice-cream and the stock-market. Life in England for Joseph was squandered on 'doing things'. This dissipated his mind and led him into a whirlwind of impressions, before he could catch hold of a thought and make it his own. In the end, he found the intellectual atmosphere witheringly restrictive in London, despite the solace of the RSL. He felt there was great difficulty in preserving any expansiveness in this grey land. For ideas must circulate in order to flourish, and social generosity is so much greater in Paris and on the continent generally, where people mix more freely and renew their vitality in an almost magical way. There was nothing like this in London. And as Joseph so succinctly put it in 1949: 'I'm only alive when I'm talking.'

For Joseph, it was clear that the great difficulty of our time was to carry our cultural luggage through the decades without cracking up under the weight. There has been such an accumulation of books and works of art and poetry in so many languages in our age. For many hundreds of years, the writers and artists of a dozen European countries have kept pouring out material and to this is added the material gathered from distant lands, now made comprehensible and therefore available. A young mind can be filled with so much cultural baggage that its owner can hardly turn round let alone sit down. This was one reason that Joseph was in no hurry to write himself: he saw every justification for not adding unthinkingly to this already suffocating *embarras de richesses*.

He was also fundamentally out of sympathy with the prevailing literary fashions. He felt that a cult of misery had taken over, and that too many writers were displaying their sick and tortured selves to the public's horrified gaze. Too much bad and unhealthy nature on show, all of which he regarded as a superior and patronising form of concealed sadism. As he wrote:

> If a country would declare that its highest ideals were the heightening of man's power, the broadening of his life's meaning and dignity, then great achievements in art, science and letters would follow, and the welfare of the common man would be included as well-earned increment. But the welfare of the common man as the

highest ideal in itself will level everything, the common man included.

Joseph had been in love with the idea of England, but that soon gave way to disillusionment, though he never lost his affection for English institutions and a paradoxical respect for English ideals. As he wrote in a letter to John Press:

> When I arrived in London, circa 1926, I had two serious handicaps – a strong anti-American bias, and a colossal euphoria, which was needed to survive the lost war in Mittel-Europa. The first made me hostile to Eliot, the second to the despondent spirit I found in England, the delayed shock-effect of the First War. I believed in Walter Bagehot's *obiter dicta*, that only buoyant poetry survives, and distrusted morbid sensibilities, such as the sentimental widower using black French letters in his amorous activities . . .

And again from his notebooks:

> Ask yourself how many were the warm friendly places in Europe, how many the kindly intelligent people? How many valuable experiences, people doing things worth doing, thirty years ago – and how many are left now? All our pleasures have grown cold and industrialised, impersonal and insignificant, warming your skin and not your heart, burning your liver, agitating your bladder, but not stimulating your mind.

Joseph added that luckily the human mind can never entirely clarify itself. It may have a few ordered and well-lit rooms, but it must also have an untidy lumber room, where things can be taken for granted without being exactly placed or seen. For T. S. Eliot, Joseph thought this room was Christianity; for himself, it was uncritical love and gratitude, which allowed him to behave in a way essential to his mental balance and endurance.

'Languages have to be cast away and new ones found, when, like bandages, they become soaked with blood, and no more clean linen is available for the banquet of the young.' I wish Joseph had written more like that, and perhaps found his own language and developed it, but deep down he was a lazy fellow. And it is surely revealing that the 'three big events in my pride', as he called them, had little to do with literature. The first was Henry Moore mending his wall at Wittersham, the second was Picasso wiping the lavatory seat for him at Mougins, and the third was being given a lift home by Lord Wavell.

Joseph was drawn to the warmth and sympathy of Spain, and especially towards the end of his life, experienced a certain urge to accept the consolations of religion, and Catholicism in particular. He relished the cosmopolitan society of Tenerife: in that warm and friendly climate one felt that laughter was a life force, that those 'pills of depression' which made up much of the twentieth-century European culture, could be laughed away or ignored. Curiously enough, the clergyman of the English Church in Puerto de la Cruz turned out to be a Fellow of the RSL. He reminded us, and told our friends, how Joseph had kept the heart in everyone during the darkest days of the war by his resilient spirit, even though bombs were dropping all over the country.

If it can be said to be a failing, then Joseph's great fault was to be always more prepared to live than to work. People came before writing, and conversation before composition. But how life-enhancing that was! He was aware of his bias, and to begin with, seemed to welcome his advancing years. Sixty he said, was a good age for a man whose appetites had been rather loud and exacting; perhaps he hoped and intended to devote more time to writing. But the leopard could not suddenly put on a tiger skin.

Joseph used to tell a poignant story from the war years which shows his knowledge of his own character:

> Once, when a large Danish blue cheese arrived in a food parcel, I took it to the grocer's for cutting and storing.

The manager asked for a piece rather shamefacedly and his second-in-command, flustered, whispered: 'You know he has a weakness for green cheese.' If such an iron character, riding the waves of austerity with as little apparent concern as a battleship, should fall into temptation because of a weakness for green cheese, how often have we fallen for green holidays? pink girls? golden rings? precious intaglios? How often have we wasted the substance of divine reason (or ordinary grey matter) through a weakness in delight?

Joseph was the warmth of my life for nearly sixty years, a man I loved and argued with; a man who made me laugh till I cried, who enthralled me with his serious talk and his uproarious stories. When he died in 1975, his protective concern for me and his love of life were no longer beside me to encourage and inspire, and I felt forlorn and dismayed at the loss of his vibrant and distinguished presence. I would never have chosen a different husband.

CHAPTER TEN

Looking Forward

The years since Joseph's death have been lonely ones, but I have tried to fill the gap he left with work and friendships. Now I have grown used to solitariness and can enjoy it for what it offers, but I have deliberately kept my life busy, for I miss Joseph sorely. New Year's Eve 1975 was one of the worst moments, for it was the first time since 1926 that we had not shared a New Year. One way of easing my memory of its burden was to write the book that Joseph himself should have written. I felt that I had little knowledge of how to write, but I knew instinctively that writing it all down would make my loss somehow more bearable. So I began to order my memories and hunt through old notebooks; soon I was ready to begin *Journal to Joseph*.

1976 was heralded by a great storm which brought a chimney crashing down through the attic roof. My lovely studio at West House was the hub of my work for many years, a lifelong box of dreams I once called it, but there was always trouble with the roof. Because there was so much glass in the way of skylights, the studio was beautifully lit but difficult to make watertight. Inevitably in winter it was terribly cold and I would be confined to working in the mornings only.

I struggled against the elements to keep working for I had become involved with a new gallery which wanted to put on an exhibition in the summer. The New Art Centre in Sloane Street represented my work for a number of years, and I enjoyed the friendship of the gallery staff – in particular Madeleine Ponsonby and Michael Servaes. It was through the New Art Centre that I also met Annette Armstrong, widow of the painter John Armstrong, who has become a great friend.

Meanwhile I was working on the manuscript of *Journal to Joseph*, and receiving guidance from friends like Geoffrey Bridson, an eminent writer himself. Annette Armstrong advised me to put myself more in the foreground, but I did not yet feel ready to do that – the first idea of the book was to make a record of Joseph's sayings and doings. But my own past was also forcing itself into the present. In March, a lunch party was given at the New Art Centre for the surviving students from Leon Underwood's school at Girdler's Road, as a sort of dry run for an exhibition of their work – and his – in December. Henry Moore did not come, but Rodney Thomas came with his wife Joan, as did Mary Underwood, Gertrude Hermes, Marion Mitchell, Lawrence Joseph and Vivian Pitchforth. Memories of fifty years before were exchanged, and forgotten incidents revived. Almost in spite of myself, I was reviewing my own past. In this kind of retrospective mood, I found it considerably easier to write *Journal to Joseph* and soon felt confident enough to invite a professional opinion.

However, the book did not prove as easy to get published as it did to write, and initially I was discouraged. But Annette would not let me give up all hope, and I continued to try to improve my writing style, to rearrange and edit Joseph's story whilst writing more about my own experiences. Joseph was still very much a presence in my daily life, and as simple an action as walking across Holland Park was made poignant; even the grass seemed saturated with memories of us together.

All too quickly my Private View at the New Art Centre was upon me. I went to the opening wearing scarlet trousers and a 1936 ivory blouse, and exhausted myself greeting over a hundred guests. Norman Reid, then director of the Tate Gallery, bought a collage for the Tate, and the Felton Bequest bought work for the Melbourne Art Gallery in Australia. It was exciting of course, but all the celebrations lacked something because Joseph was not there; no dinner party was ever quite the same, no conversation ever quite as lively.

When I finally managed to get back to work it was with a burst of renewed energy, and I immediately planned three or four new paintings. The people at the New Art Centre decided that my work should be properly catalogued at last, and they spent the better part of a week making lists of paintings and objects. But the security I had enjoyed in West House was to be uninterrupted no longer, for the agents or owners already had plans to redevelop the whole building. Although I did not have to move for several years, I was never to be free of the threat of expulsion until I settled into my new flat.

Isabel had proved herself more than a faithful friend to Joseph and myself. She visited his grave and put flowers there, and in November she came to see me with a jar of wild cherries she had collected. The cherry trees which blossomed so beautifully earlier in the year had now dropped their fruit abundantly over Joseph's tomb.

I had lent an object for exhibition to Sheffield City Art Gallery, and a part of it was the cork which Picasso had given me at Mougins. I called the piece 'Object Lesson', and it consisted of a beautifully carved lay figure I bought in Toulon in 1939, which I attached to a cane background (originally a platter for handing cheese or bread around) with a painting behind the cane, and the cork stuck onto the end of the brush that the lay figure held between its fingers. Unfortunately the cork was mislaid (I always suspected that someone stole it because it had been Picasso's) and so there was the whole problem of insurance and compensation to be sorted out. I was delighted when Southampton Museum and Art Gallery decided to buy 'Object Lesson' in April 1977, for it is among the few objects which have survived the course of time at least partially intact.

I was even more pleased that a new painting of mine, called 'Entombment', was accepted for the Tolly Cobbold exhibition and shown in Cambridge. I believe that amongst my new paintings were some of the best I had done. However, the title did not strike the right note, so I renamed it 'Satanic Mills'. The social dance continued as actively as ever; I saw a lot of Roland, whose company was as stimulating as always. His London flat was just up the road from me, and we met there or at restaurants or at West House, talking over the past and making plans for the future.

My sister Dorothy wrote saying that she wanted Winifred and myself to lunch with her on her birthday. Dorothy had spent much of her married life out of England, following the army career of her husband, but there had never been the closeness between us that there is in some families. (I had always tried to avoid being flooded by relations.) But now Dorothy had settled back in England, near Salisbury, and remarked that as we were all getting old, we should make up and be friendly. Unfortunately, what she wrote was all too true – we were getting old. My niece Miranda, one of Winifred's daughters, had recently taken some photographs of me, and although flashlights are notorious for making one look like Verdun after the battle, I could not believe that I looked like that. But I also felt myself growing tired more easily, and resolved to husband my energies (I who no longer had a husband to do it for me) and take life more carefully.

Surrealism was receiving more and more critical attention, and one day Conroy Maddox arrived at the flat armed with a tape recorder to interview me about the early 1930s. It feels curious to be part of history, but the great thing about Surrealism is that it is now appealing to new generations of young people. Michel Remy tends to drop in to see me whenever he is in London, and he keeps me informed about the latest publications and the exhibitions of young artists. Surrealist groups are being formed all the time throughout the world (in more countries than one would think possible) and new Surrealist poems, paintings and objects are constantly being produced. One can only salute this unquenchable spirit of creativity!

It was through Conroy that I met Michael Bullock, a big burly bearded man from Canada, a Surrealist writer who paints, speaks German, French and Italian, and is knowledgeable about books. A sympathetic fellow full of energy, and always a pleasure to see on his trips to England.

A friend had been cataloguing Joseph's gems for me, and the Ashmolean Museum was so impressed with the range of Joseph's collection that they came to photograph them all. I decided to sell the lot, and they were divided between the big auction houses, Sotheby's and Christie's, and attracted considerable interest and spirited bidding. I had not realised until that moment quite what unerring judgement for acquiring choice gems Joseph had developed, despite his limited financial means. The proceeds of these sales were Joseph's last gift to me, and I endowed a memorial lecture at the RSL in his name.

In July 1977, I heard that Lee Miller had died. Although we never got on very well together, I admired her complete lack of inhibition and her courage. In 1944 she had been one of the small group of uniformed Allies who formally liberated Picasso's studio in Paris. This was ironic, for Lee subsequently had to share her husband with Picasso, to whose artistic cause Roland was supremely devoted. That cannot have been easy for a woman of such a demanding nature. Roland had a painting of Lee by Picasso which caught her essence without being a likeness, a witty evocation of a remarkable woman, completely unsentimental and sometimes ruthless.

Right at the end of the year I was invited to appear on television again, this time at a reunion of Surrealists at the Barcelona Restaurant in Beak Street, one of our pre-war haunts. George Melly was ring-master, and the others numbered Robert Melville, a Turkish poet, Conroy Maddox and Roland. We six Surrealists each sat at separate tables with a glass of drink in hand trying to look intelligent but silent while the camera whirled. (Now I know why Marilyn Monroe committed suicide.) Then we got together on one table and talked until George Melly recited a poem and threw spoons and forks in the air. After that we drew one or two exquisite corpses very badly, and then it was all over. Decidedly tame for a Surrealist reunion.

Age was making its presence known. It was Miró's eighty-fifth birthday and I was asked to contribute something to a presentation book the Surrealists were putting together for him. It was also Dorothy's eightieth birthday when we visited her in Salisbury. It was so long since I had seen my older sister that if I had not known it was her, I doubt I would have recognised her, she seemed such a totally different personality, as if belonging to a different family. Then in June it was Alec Waugh's eightieth birthday, and my niece Miranda gave him a big party since he was her godfather. We spoke of old times together, and Alec reminded me how Evelyn had once pursued me. Two months later, Roland's first wife, the poet Valentine, died. She had been bed-ridden at his farm in Sussex and no longer able to recognise him. My old friends were indeed thinning out.

The best defence against age is work. New ventures have always appealed to me, and I have a special sympathy for small magazines which start up against hopeless odds to carry the gospel of the arts to the largely uninterested public. (I still had fond memories of *The Island*.) Some day perhaps one will succeed. So when Abdullah al-Udhari came to my studio to interview me for his magazine *TR*, I was happy to give him the time and allow him to reproduce some paintings. The title *TR* stands for *Translation*, and the magazine's aim is to present Arabic poetry to the British and British poetry and paintings to the Arabs. With other contributions from the likes of Ralph Steadman, John Heath-Stubbs and Samuel Beckett, I felt I was in good company.

The interest in work from the 1930s increased. The Victoria and Albert Museum mounted a large exhibition at the Hayward Gallery simply called 'The Thirties', and William Feaver, the *Observer*'s art critic, came to select work for it. (When I saw the show later, the paintings seemed a weakly-mixed bunch, except for Paul Nash, that is, who stood out strongly.) At the same time Richard Calvocoressi, the Kokoschka expert, came to choose something by me from the thirties for the Scottish National Gallery to buy. There was more interest in the woodcuts of mine and Henry Moore's which appeared in

The Island, and the V & A decided to purchase Rodney Thomas's spectacular clock which he designed for my Bramham Gardens studio so many years before.

But I refused to be neatly pigeon-holed as a museum piece. I started a series of new drawings for another, smaller, show at the New Art Centre. These drawings were dark on the front and light on the back and could be seen to equal effect from either side. I called them back-to-front images, and they had something in common with my own nature which is half pessimistic and rather gloomy and the other half gay and light-hearted. I felt these new works were a breakthrough.

It was marvellous to be able to get out of London now and again and breathe in wide-open spaces. Annette Armstrong would often pick me up in her car and we would go off for the day, perhaps for a picnic in one of the large parks. Before the war, Joseph and I used to motor out to Richmond and dine with Jock and Mary Oliver in Pembroke Lodge. It was a shock to me to find the lodge turned into a cafeteria when I visited Richmond Park on one of these excursions with Annette. From time to time I would get away for a whole weekend to Somerset, and one bank holiday was spent touring the West Country with Annette. Another excursion was to Avebury, which I was fascinated to see. The spirit of the place is so overpoweringly strong there that one feels a sense of displacement, and it is not wise to linger. That is something I have against archaeology – it tries to explode the mystery. It is literally fatal to reduce a thing to a fact alone, for the imagination must have room to stretch. That is what I aim for in my paintings; as Lord Halifax said, 'the enquiry into a dream is another dream.' And dreams reveal more of reality than science ever could.

Recent history is not real history for there is no perspective in which to see the lights and the shadows properly; there is none of the balance which distance brings. In the same way, looking back over the last twelve or so years, I cannot make much sense out of a jumble of memories and impressions. In many ways I looked forward, trying not to think too closely or too long about Joseph, content to distract myself with the present and with plans for future paintings and exhibitions. Yet I had to look back to write my book about Joseph. Perhaps there is no single direction to any period of a life; one is always glancing both ways, taking stock and preparing to jump onward, a Janus-faced image of existence.

All at once, the world seemed to be full of friends and acquaintances reaching eighty. At the end of 1979, it was my own eightieth birthday. Ridiculous! I felt more like fifty, and I had no desire to celebrate the event. There were more important things to do. When I look back through my diaries, I am more than satisfied by the blank pages; for when there is no written entry, it means I have been too busy working in the studio to bother with a diary.

In July 1980, Miranda, Winifred and I set out by train for St Mawes. It was pouring with rain at Paddington, but we were all joyful at the prospect of a holiday, and by the time we arrived in Cornwall the sun was shining. St Mawes had not really been spoilt by tourism but there were many more hotels; happily the bay was as glad as ever with boats and coloured sails. The sky was a moving panorama of comfortable clouds and blue depths – a vast canvas which made London seem a prison. It was a true release of the spirit. (That seems to be a living example of the Mexican saying that there should always be a little sky in a landscape composition, just enough to let the spirit out.)

We went over to St Ives on this trip and visited the Barbara Hepworth Museum which was enchanting, white and simple as her sculptures, which looked completely at home. The small garden with its tropical air was a splendid foil to Hepworth's pure and sometimes rigid art. St Ives bay was crowded and looked like a Dufy painting suddenly come alive. The shops there were more commercialised than before, but Cornwall was as delightful as it ever had been and we stayed on several days more than planned.

It was in October 1980 that I heard that my dear friend Geoffrey Bridson had died. He had been a great support and adviser to Joseph and me, an innovative writer and broadcaster, a compulsive traveller and a sympathetic and stimulating conversationalist. He loved art, collected what he could afford and kept an enormous filed and bound collection of reproductions which he had cut from books and magazines. (I think it was partly his example which made me less concerned about cutting up books – which might have been valuable – for collage.) He was a friend I would miss greatly. Geoffrey once said that if he was ever reincarnated he would like to appear in San Francisco. I hope his wish has been granted.

In November 1980, quite out of the blue, I met Joan McKecknie, who first introduced me to Robin Bartlett in 1921. I had not seen her since then. Odd that we should meet nearly sixty years later. It was as if I was not allowed to forget my past, for in 1977 a friend told me that he had met Robin's third wife at a party, where she told him how Robin had always followed my career with the greatest interest. According to her, Robin had still been in love with me when he came to see my retrospective exhibition at the Commonwealth Institute a year or two before his death.

Gertrude Hermes was eighty (another one) in 1981 and was given a retrospective exhibition of her engravings and sculpture at the Royal Academy that year. Some of the woodcuts and linocuts were technical marvels, very powerful as well as being lovely designs. Gerts worked consistently throughout her life, and I was glad to see her receiving this accolade, which was the least she deserved. I remembered her as a young woman, her clothes kept together with safety pins, heaving huge blocks of stone and wood around.

My own 1981 exhibition at the New Art Centre was a great event. I was showing only work from the last three years, and amongst the paintings exhibited were two that I felt conveyed the different nightmares which haunt us in the late twentieth century. These paintings, called 'The Bomber' and 'The Sleepwalkers', show our fears in the face of the unknown. 'The Bomber' was based on a memory of Tenerife, and depicted a menacing machine-cum-head flying over a bright landscape. While I was playing tennis one day at Sitio Litre, years before, the ball-girl had run screaming from the court when a jet aircraft passed overhead. 'The Sleepwalkers' recalls the moment when all conscious control is gone, but when we are also rich with fantasy and unrestricted imagination. This too can be terrifying, yet imagination is also our greatest strength. Perhaps we try to control it too much.

Occasionally, I used to go with Annette Armstrong to Kew Gardens to picnic. We visited the Marianne North house which is covered from floor to ceiling with the paintings and drawings this intrepid traveller made of the world's exotic flora. She was a courageous woman to be travelling at the end of the nineteenth century, and apparently stayed several winters in Tenerife, and even painted the famous dragon tree I had seen whilst at Sitio Litre. Is it age which makes coincidence crowd in upon one? We also visited the Palm House, where the French painter Douanier Rousseau would have gone mad with delight. I was scarcely less enthusiastic, for Kew Gardens is my idea of paradise.

In 1982 it was Rodney Thomas's turn to celebrate his eightieth birthday. He is one of my oldest and earliest friends, and he still has the same delicious sense of humour. I remember how he first explained to me that he lived in a Moravian cemetery. This is a cross between a well-kept field and an overgrown garden, with no headstones visible as the Moravians lay their tombstones flat on the ground. Along one side of this peaceful oasis in Chelsea are three or four studios. Apparently they were once Sir Thomas More's stable-block before a nineteenth-century conversion by a sculptor. The original roof-beams are still in place and look magnificent. Rodney lives there with his wife Joan, still painting a little. As he has grown older, he has become even more distinguished-looking, and now he resembles more than ever some Stone Age El Greco figure.

Along with the celebrations there were too many departures, even if new friends did appear in my life. My sister Dorothy died in 1982, and two years later Winifred was also gone. Roland Penrose died in 1984: a special friend and champion of Surrealism, no one could replace him, though the huge party at the ICA was some tribute to his dedication. One begins to feel like the sole survivor of a generation, and the obituary columns in newspapers have an insidious fascination.

But if life seemed at times to be closing in, other areas opened up. I went to the theatre more than I had done for years, and with Annette Armstrong rediscovered the delights of the ballet. Amongst the scintillating performers we saw were the exuberant Lindsay Kemp and a splendid benefit evening for Margot Fonteyn that has stayed in my mind ever since. Perhaps I love ballet because it comes nearest to flying, and I have always desired wings. The imagination can continually take wing, but in body we are sadly earthbound. Better by far to live in and with the imagination.

Books were another rediscovery. I began to read more when I wanted to become a writer myself, and the habit has grown to be a great pleasure. I read quantities of modern fiction and biography nowadays, but I have found little contemporary writing to be as memorable as Dickens. I think I have read nearly everything by him, which is ironic, since I loathed him as a girl. Perhaps it takes time to see his merits, though I still find his female characters often unbearable and much of the writing over-sentimental. His strength is as a descriptive writer; in passages like the great storm in *David Copperfield*, Dickens seems to me unrivalled.

My 1983 exhibition at the New Art Centre coincided with an Omnibus film featuring my career being shown on television. A young man called Kevin Lygo came to see me from the BBC to plan four or five days' filming in West House. The studio was invaded by a crew of cameramen and sound technicians, but it was worth it. Two days after the programme was broadcast, the Tate Gallery contacted me to say that they had decided to buy my large sculpture from 1943, the second 'Angel of Anarchy'. So often publicity gives you the pep to go on.

If anything, I would like to call myself a humanist. Whatever you are going to do, you should do it here, on this planet, now. You must listen to your spiritual side and develop it.

Listen to the things that whisper to you. They try to get through, but you get up and do something mundane like cutting the bread or answering the phone.

Art invokes the unconscious world to counterbalance the conscious results of materialism, and in the ideally perceptive sensibility there is contained the image of the whole world, infinitely susceptible to new shapes, because (like my wax Aladdin's Lamp which changes with the heat) no shape can be regarded as final. According to Hegel, when art becomes pure, it ceases to be serious. The work of art is a work of limitation, of concentration. On the other hand, it poses the questions of informality, infinity, the conscious need to give to the feelings 'a species of escape' from finite objects; the necessity of expressing internal perception visually. There is a continual conflict between the love of space and simplicity, or producing a feast for the eyes; between a desire to make holes in the walls of reality, and a desire for impact and intensity.

I had spent 1985 mostly working for an exhibition of paintings of the monumental rocks at Ploumanach. This exhibition was shown at the New Art Centre from December 1985 into January 1986, so the new year started well. Some critics thought these hallucinatory rock paintings were the best work that I had yet done. At the time, this was a major project for me, but now I am not so sure that the idea was particularly successful. I have found myself recently moving away from painting and concentrating more on the enlightening juxtaposition of images in collage and interpreted objects.

Early in 1986, Bill McAllister, director of the Institute of Contemporary Arts, came to see me to ask if I would model some new clothes by the Japanese designer Issey Miyake. Of course I accepted, so a cold Friday morning in late February found me en route for Lord Snowdon's studio in Earl's Court to be photographed. I was shown into a vast studio to meet Snowdon before being taken away to be made up and clothed. We chatted, and I told him I had known his uncle, Oliver Messel, at the Slade.

I was led into a cupboard of a room where the transformation was to take place, and sat down on a high stool before a large mirror with strong lights either side. A young American started to give me a new face. He worked for an hour, picking and choosing carefully from among the many pots and pans of colour that lay on his work table. He had almost finished when he exclaimed: 'Joan Collins had better watch out . . .' which made me laugh so much that my newly applied false eyelashes came unstuck! Luckily the make-up man decided I could do without them and, mirror, mirror, I found myself looking at a pale ivory face with large dark eyes and a slight blush on each cheek.

Once my hair had been re-styled, I was ready for the clothes. Looking at myself fully dressed, I realised that I had been freed from my own flesh, for these Issey Miyake designs were like new masks which released the wearer from him or herself. Back in the studio, I was loudly complimented and then left free to wander around for a while so that Snowdon had time to compose his thoughts and decide on which approach he would take. Snowdon took a number of shots of me sitting cross-legged on the floor against an all-purpose tachist backcloth (browny-grey cotton duck with little dashes, blobs and spots of yellow, pink, blue and green), and then sat me on an upturned waste-paper basket for a different series of photographs. After another coffee-break, Snowdon photographed me standing as well, and then the session was at an end. So I took off the beautiful clothes (later kindly made a present to me), and stepped back into daily life, though still disguised by the hair-style and make-up. It had been an absorbing experience.

On a May morning later that year, I got up at five o'clock in order to catch a plane from Gatwick, bound for Amsterdam. I had planned to spend five nights there with my niece Miranda and Annette Armstrong, looking at the museums and art collections during the day. We arrived safely, but on our first night, disaster nearly overwhelmed us.

We were walking quietly along one of the main streets looking in shop windows, when suddenly I felt my canvas handbag being grabbed from under my arm. I held on to it as tightly as I could, but the man shook me from side to side, and I lost my balance and fell against a parking meter. We all shouted for help, but the thief easily got away with my bag. The trouble was that I had put everything into it – money, cheque card, keys, passport – thinking that the hotel room would not be a safe place to leave my valuables.

As I fell I had broken my spectacles and picked up a black eye. Luckily I had a pair of dark glasses in my luggage which hid the worst of the damage. The hotel staff were amazed that we should decide to go out to dinner that night, but I had no intention of staying in. All I wanted was a glass of water and a rest, and then we headed for a Thai restaurant to celebrate. We were still alive, after all.

We visited the museums I had been longing to see, and in particular the van Gogh museum fulfilled all my hopes, and was even worth being mugged for! Van Gogh is indeed a great painter whose work must be seen in all its original freshness for his full impact to be felt. Unfortunately, since cash was now so short, we could not buy everything we might have wished, but at the Rijksmuseum, my black eye came in rather useful. When I told the museum attendants of the robbery, and then took off my dark glasses to prove it, they were most upset. They were so apologetic (and concerned that I might judge their city on this unlucky incident), that they let me into the museum free.

Back in London, life was becoming increasingly hectic. Not only did more people want to see and buy my work, but journalists wanted to interview me about it, film-makers wanted to put me on television, and historians wanted to fit me into any number of niches. I was a woman artist, a Surrealist, an avant-garde painter; my work was shown in relation to fashion; I was interviewed about the people I had known. So much was being crammed into each week that I hardly had time to think, let alone do my own work. Most of the time, all this was exciting, if rather exhausting. Now and again it became too much.

Some mornings I am besieged by wakefulness before it is

time to get up. Then, when one is at a low ebb, thoughts of old age crowd cruelly in. It is as if I am seized by lethargy and left limp and gasping on the shores of boredom. Age eating away at the structure of skin and bone that is myself. Flesh and femur, fingernails and fantasy dry up and crack; doom and gloom await me in my crumpled bed, but still I rise and swear to keep abreast of the incoming tide of devouring waves which throw phantom figures of the past along the curtains of my memory.

Death is an ever-present evil which I ignore. Life is what enchants me with its opening doors to new acquaintances and old; to strangers lost in time, deceived by Fate or rescued from oblivion. Creative lethargy is what I long for, and memory which gives resonance to some things and blots others out.

For some people age is a profession, but for me it is a disease that I fight with all my strength.

I have spent my life in revolt against convention, trying to bring colour and light and a sense of the mysterious to daily existence. But the English urge towards philistinism is impossible to avoid, though one may fight it root and branch. I remember H. G. Wells coming to a London Group exhibition to see my work over fifty years ago. Joseph and I found him sitting on a couch with Baroness Budberg. Wells criticised the title of one of my paintings, called 'Aurora', saying he saw no reason, except affectation of culture, not to call it 'Morning'. The accumulated associations of a word rolling through two millennia gathering past and present meanings, had no appeal for him. Finally he took us to stand in front of a still life, a very realistic painting of a clay pipe on a table, a chair and some other bits and pieces. That, he declared, was the best picture in the show, in his opinion.

Yet one must have a hunger for new colour, new shapes and new possibilities of discovery. The twentieth century has begun to realise that most of life's meaning is lost without the spirit of play. In play, all that is lovely and soaring in the human spirit strives to find expression. To play is to yield oneself to a kind of magic, and to give the lie to the inconvenient world of fact, and the hideous edifice of unrelieved utility. In play the mind is prepared to accept the unimagined and incredible, to enter a world where different laws apply, to be free, unfettered, and approach the divine.

Remembering Wells, I recall another story which seems to have a relevance to my own life. Bernard Shaw once told Wells that anyone of a certain stature could be amply characterised by two or three anecdotes. The earliest anecdote told of me, at the age of four (when my stature was of little account), was of me looking up at the ornate ceiling lavishly painted with naked ladies and flying cupids in the large restaurant where my parents were lunching. I said: 'I see something but I mustn't tell.' Was this a shocked awareness of what went on in the clouds? The second anecdote is of my constant and pressing request to all and sundry to buy me a balloon. I was obviously intent on exploring those clouds for myself.

Ever since I started sticking tram tickets together as a child, I have known instinctively how to make a collage. My nurse had persuaded me to collect the tickets so that we could send them to a children's hospital (some kind of donation and appeal system), but I pulled out the big box from under the bed and started to make a collage with some of them instead.

Much of the last two years has been taken up with writing my memoirs. I had not realised quite how all-absorbing a task writing is – not just the actual scribbling on bits of paper, but the constant thought and effort to recollect. Since my book was taking up so much of my energy, I felt unable to embark on a new series of paintings with all the demands on body and mind that that would entail, so I turned more to collage. It was a way of shrugging off logic and moving directly back into the heart of my visual work, at once both feeding and releasing the imagination.

I find that collage has become my chief preoccupation since, and my only concern is that I might run out of raw material! By now, my friends are used to requests for old magazines and posters, but there can never be too much to sift and ponder. I find the spark is often struck from the most unlikely things. There also seems to be some kind of justice about transforming posters – which one might judge to be examples of street or popular culture, precisely the area in which Surrealism has been most obviously influential – and bringing them back, via a Surrealist juxtaposition, to collage.

People are suspicious of collage because it seems too easy, but then, for the English, nothing is valued unless the toil involved is literally backbreaking. My mother, when I described the collage process to her, said: 'But that's cheating!' Had she never heard of inspiration?

Musing about my life in the late 1980s, I wonder at my own energy. I see myself hailing innumerable taxis and being driven to Soho or the East End, to galleries or dinner parties. Yet I have also learnt to live with my old age, and like it – especially as I have to put up with it. And then there is always something to be learnt about what Wilde called 'the pleasures of doing absolutely nothing'.

In the summer of 1987 I moved house finally. I had not wanted to leave my beautiful studio in West House, but the house was becoming increasingly leaky and dilapidated. I was offered a bright new first-floor flat, just round the corner, as an inducement to move. It certainly seemed more practical, and the discoveries I made in the process of packing up were an added bonus. In the attics were a number of rolled up canvases and other paintings, together with papers and old photographs and a couple of chairs from the 1930s designed by Mies van der Rohe – things I had somehow forgotten about, easily enough done perhaps when the latest painting or collage occupies one's mind.

One of the paintings I rediscovered in the attic was the seven-foot-long 'Autobiography of an Embryo' from 1933. I had been threatening to saw it in half when I moved (for I thought there would be no room for it in my new flat) but luckily the directors of the new Birch and Conran Gallery in Dean Street, Soho, encouraged me to put it in their exhibition instead. In fact, it turned out to be the centrepiece of the Birch and Conran retrospective of my work, and the Tate Gallery decided to buy it. I was delighted, for it will be the largest and probably the best piece of my work in the Tate's collection.

In September, I revisited Swanage and was filmed walking along the beach there as part of a documentary being made about my life. I was sad to see the way the town was changing, particularly as the Grosvenor Hotel – on whose lawn I had first met Paul Nash – was being demolished. The two Greek columns had gone from the drive, and I saw no love-swan in the bay.

Looking around my new living room, amongst the bric-à-brac of a lifetime's collecting, and in between my own paintings, I catch sight of Joseph in a drawing by Kokoschka. Unfortunately, it is only a photograph of the original (which was done in April 1926), since Dorothy Thompson kept the drawing for herself. As a likeness I do not think it is good. It makes Joseph too heavy-featured and the nose is more Kokoschka than Bard.

I hardly need to be reminded in order to see Joseph clearly in so many different moods and situations, for my life is soaked with memories of him. A characteristic gesture was to pluck at his forehead, as if trying to get a recalcitrant thought.

The starting point of conversation is contradiction, but nowadays by confining conversation to facts or the exchange of bland opinions, trouble is avoided, but the intellect weakened. For true sociability, being agreeable is not enough. Joseph was a master of true sociability.

I am a secret painter; painting for me is a very private occupation and I hardly like to talk about it. Too much limelight is bad for the brain – it makes it shrivel or overblow. One should put one's paintings to sleep for a time.

One has always to spoil a picture a little bit in order to finish it.

I hope to die in a sparkling moment.

Index

Abstract expressionism, 149, 189
Abstraction, 85, 90, 92, 93, 102, 121, 129, 130, 153, 212
Adams, Mary, 159
Adler, Alfred, 60
Ady, 135–6, 140
Agamemnon, 92
Agar, Cross (family firm), 4–5, 27–8, 39, 200
Agar, Dorothy (EA's sister), 9, 12–13, 22, 23, 24, 25, 26, 32, 33, 34
Agar, Eileen
  work: Rock paintings 1, 229
  early work: 47–8, 50, 72–3
  early portraits ('Mouma' etc): 84, 102
  drawings of Dylan Thomas: 108
  watercolour of seashore monster: 112
  makes aerial sculpture: 128
  barge painting: 151
  portraits of PL Travers: 151
  war painting: 157–8
  Tenerife work: 183
  back-to-front images: 224
  recent collages: 233–4
  'Ceremonial Hat for Eating Bouillabaisse', 19, 168–9
  'Self-Portrait': 73
  'Movement in Space': 92
  'Three Symbols' ('The Flying Pillar'): 93, 201
  'Quadriga': 121–2, 124
  'The Battle Years': 126
  'Angel of Anarchy' (1st version): 127–8
  'Angel of Anarchy' (2nd version): 128, 228
  'Marine Object': 144
  'Cry Havoc': 157
  'Phantom of the Sea': 168
  'The Lunatic, the Lover and the Poet': 177–8
  'Poet and His Muse': 192
  'Head of Dylan Thomas': 197–8
  'Object Lesson': 220
  'Entombment' ('Satanic Mills'): 220–1
  'The Bomber': 226–7
  'The Sleepwalkers': 226–7
  'Aurora': 232
  'Autobiography of an Embryo', 234–5
  early life: 3–31
  education: 23–31
  photographs: 30, 124, 136, 137–8
  art schools: 31, 37–8, 41–4
  meets Robin Bartlett: 42–3
  leaves home: 45–8
  moves to Chelsea: 47
  marries Robin Bartlett: 50
  meets Joseph Bard: 54–5, 64–5
  leaves Robin Bartlett: 68
  moves to Fitzroy Square: 69–70
  meets Dorothy Thompson: 70–1
  life in Fitzroy Square: 72–4
  moves to Portofino: 75
  meets Ezra Pound: 75–6
  renamed Allegra: 79
  leaves Portofino: 83
  moves to Paris: 84
  meets Foltyn: 85
  divorces Robin Bartlett: 88
  moves to Cap Martin: 91
  returns to settle in London: 93
  on womb-magic: 99
  contributes to *The Island*: 99, 101
  creates décor of Bramham Gardens flat: 101
  first exhibits work: 102
  in Swanage: 108–12
  relationship with Paul Nash: 109, 110–13, 133–4, 163–4
  discovers 'seashore monster': 112
  contributes to *Poems and Narrations*: 114
  identified as a Surrealist: 115
  work methods: 121, 125–6, 148, 165–6, 228–9, 232–3, 235
  visits Ploumanach and its rocks: 124
  on automatism: 125–6
  on dreams: 125
  holidays with Picasso: 135–43
  on techniques: 147, 201–2, 233
  marries Joseph Bard: 150
  in Savile Row canteen: 152, 155
  contributes to *Counterpoint*: 161
  and post-war malaise: 161
  in Ireland: 162–3
  on TV: 168–9, 222, 228
  on women: 174–5
  escapes to Tenerife: 178
  moves to West House: 189
  starts using acrylics: 201–2
  retrospectives: 201, 208, 235
  begins *Journal to Joseph*: 218
  holidays in St Mawes: 225
  moves house: 234
Agar family, 5, 7–8
Agar, James (EA's father), 4–10, 11, 13–14, 15, 19–23, 27–8, 32, 34, 37, 39, 40, 41, 43, 45, 46–7, 49, 50–1, 156
Agar, Mamie (née Bagley, EA's mother), 5–10, 11, 13–14, 15, 19–24, 25, 26, 28, 29, 30, 31–2, 33, 34, 35, 36, 37, 38–9, 40, 41, 43, 45, 46, 47, 49, 50, 51, 53, 88, 97–8, 104, 123–4, 150, 151, 155–6, 234
Agar, Winifred (EA's sister), 10, 12–13, 22, 23, 26, 29, 32, 33, 34, 39, 49

Index

Agate, James, 132
Aix-en-Provence, 173
A la recherche du temps perdu, 59
Alassio, 198
Alexandra Palace, 168
Alexandria, 135
Alexandrian, 141
Altenberg, Peter, 90
Al-Udhari, Abdullah, 223
Amiel's Journal, 34
Amsterdam, 128, 230–1
Anrep, Boris, 1, 84
Aragon, Louis, 123
Arcimboldo, Giuseppe, 168
Arcon, 175–6
Arena Chapel, 171
Arezzo, 171
Argentina, 3–19, 20, 21, 23, 27, 33, 39, 40, 46–7, 151, 200–1
Aristotle, 210
Arlen, Michael, 175
Arles, 173
Armstrong, Annette, 218–9, 224, 227, 228, 230
Armstrong, John, 219
Art of Assemblage Exhibition, 196
Arts Council, 192
Ascot, 24, 25
Ashmolean Museum, 222
'Aspects of Abstract Painting', 212
Asquith family, 31
Asquith, Herbert, 31–2
Asquith, Margot, 31–2
Associated Press of America, 60
Athlumney, Lord, 25–6, 47
Auden, W. H., 92, 170
Auger, Helen, 54–5
Augustus Caesar, 211
'Aurea-Mediocritas', 78
Austro-Hungarian Empire, 60
Avebury, 224
Aziz, 135, 155

Bagehot, Walter, 215
Bagley family, 5, 7
Balaton, Lake, 57
Balenciaga, 143
Bandol, 89
Banting, John, 115–6, 123, 146
Barbara Hepworth Museum, 225
Barcelona, 123
Bard, Joseph, 1, 3, 22, 38, 52–3, 54 et seq.
  admiration for England: 55, 74–5, 95, 152, 159, 187, 191, 194, 215
  as teacher: 56
  early life: 56–9
  in World War One: 60–1
  'Hungary: 1 May 1919': 61–2
  meets and marries Dorothy Thompson: 62
  love affair with Yolan: 64–5
  as conversationalist: 66
  'Why Europe Dislikes the Jew': 68, 83
  leaves Dorothy Thompson: 68–9
  painting: 70
  relationship with Dorothy Thompson: 71–2, 199–200
  in Torrington Square: 72
  friendship with Ezra Pound: 76–9, 210
  poems: 78, 83, 89–90
  on Sinclair Lewis: 82
  jealous of Pound: 82–3
  on Pound's parents: 88–9
  edits *The Island*: 97–100, 101
  reacts to Paul Nash: 110, 113, 163–4
  with Paul Eluard: 130–1, 133
  and Picasso: 137, 139
  on Mediterranean: 142–3
  as examiner: 152
  'Tradition and Experiment': 158
  influence on Eileen Agar: 165
  in Ireland: 162–3
  on Italy: 172–3
  character: 176, 187–8, 207, 208–9, 211, 213–17
  passion for gems: 165, 178, 187, 211–12, 222
  his daughter, Valentine: 185–6, 206–7
  his sister, Melanie: 186, 206
  unwell: 192, 198, 203, 207, 208, 213
  starts memoirs: 203
  dies: 213
Barney, Natalie, 87–8
Bartlett, Robin, 42–5, 48–54, 65, 66, 67, 68, 88, 93–4, 96, 226
Baudelaire, Charles, 131
BBC, 155, 158, 190, 191, 228
'Beachcomber', 102, 103
Beaton, Cecil, 44, 70
Beckett, Samuel, 223
Beerbohm, Max, 76
Belgrade, 191
Bellini, Giovanni, 111, 158
  'Doge of Venice': 158
Belloc, Hilaire, 103
Bennett, Arnold, 39
Bentley, Nicolas, 102, 197
Bergson, Henri, 59
Berlin, 55, 64, 68, 69, 74, 88, 203, 204
Berners, Lord, 119
Bernhardt, Sarah, 90–1
Berwick, North (Scotland), 31, 47
Biarritz, 88
Bibliothèque Nationale (Paris), 212
Birch and Conran Gallery, 234
Biriatou (Spain), 88
Birling Gap, 84
Blackbirds, 70
Blackpool, 40
Blake, William, 114
Bloomsbury Gallery, 102
Bode, Carl, 190
Bode, Margaret, 190
Boetia, 121–2
Boissevain, Eugen, 89–90
Bonnard, Pierre, 37
Book of Nonsense, 134
Borsas, Comte Guy de Bourg de, 36
Bosanquet, B. J. T., 17
Bosch, Hieronymous, 180–1
  'The Garden of Earthly Delights', 180
  'The Garden of Eden', 180
Bottome, Phyllis, 9
Boué, Valentine, 114
Bournemouth, 15
Bowen, Donald, 205, 208
Brancusi, Constantin, 86–7, 117
Braque, Georges, 46, 140, 141, 211
Bray (near Maidenhead), 25
Bremond, Abbé, 131
Brest, 124
Breton, André, 87, 114, 115, 117, 119, 120–1, 125, 128, 129–30, 149
Breton, Jacqueline, 120–1
Breuer, Marcel, 145, 146
Brides-les-Bains, 36

Bridport, 108
Bridson, D. G. (Geoffrey), 83, 155, 158, 190, 197, 219, 225–6
Brighton, 19, 187
'Britain's Contribution to Surrealism', 208
British Museum, 174
'British Painting '74', 213
Bronson, Mrs de Kay, 24
Brook Street Gallery, 196, 198, 201
Bruges, 143
Brunius, Jacques, 159
Buckland-Wright, John, 153
Budapest, 56, 58, 60, 62, 89, 185, 186
Budberg, Baroness, 232
'Buddha', 20
Buenos Aires, 3, 4, 5, 6, 7, 13, 15, 17, 20, 22, 23, 39, 140, 179
Buffalo (USA), 185
Bullock, Michael, 221–2
Bunting, Basil, 76
Burleigh, Lord, 35
Burne-Jones, Edward, 188
Burnham Beeches, 30
Burra, Edward, 115
Butler, Samuel, 34
Buttermere, 160
Byam Shaw School of Art, 31
Byron, Lord, 141, 179, 191

Cadogan family, 24
Calder, Alexander, 107
Calvocoressi, Richard, 223
Cambridge, 178, 220
Campbell, Mrs Patrick, 22
Canetti, Elias, 176
Canford Cliffs, 23, 26
Cannes, 135, 136, 139, 141
Cap d'Antibes, 36
Cap Martin, 91–3
Capek, Karel, 88
Carpendale, Admiral Sir Charles, 152
Capri, 172
Carquieranne, 144
Carroll, Lewis, 114, 199
Carswell, Catherine, 97
Caruso, Enrico, 4
Casteja, Marquis de, 182
Causey, Colonel, 62
Cavalcanti, Guido, 77
Cave of Harmony, 48
Cézanne, Paul, 173
Chamberlain, Houston Stuart, 64
Chaplin, Charlie, 18
Chartreuse de Parme, 28
Chavannes, Puvis de, 37
Chesterton, G. K., 20, 103
Chirico, Giorgio de, 11, 101, 111, 117, 170
Christie's, 222
Clerk, Sir George, 37
Clerk, Lady, 37
Clovelly (Devon), 27
Coates, Wells, 160
Coats, Ernest, 33
Cockburn, Claud, 203–4
Cocteau, Jean, 47, 98, 134
Cole, Rex Vicat, 31
Coliseum, 70
College of Arms, 110
Collins, Cecil, 161
Collins, Joan, 230
Colquhoun, Ithell, 168
Commonwealth Institute, 205–6, 207–8, 209, 226
Connolly, Cyril, 170
Conrad, Joseph, 103
Contemporary Portrait Society, 196
Cook, A. E., 178
Cooke, Alistair, 159
Cordoba (Argentina), 40
Corfe Castle, 15, 108
Counterpoint, 161
Country Life, 32
Cowles, Clement, 39
Cox, David, 32
Crawford, Sir William, 109–10
Crowley, Aleister, 175
Cubism, 85, 90, 92, 93, 147, 148
Cunard, Nancy, 31, 116, 170
Cunningham, Admiral, 153
Curzon, Lord, 22

Daily Express, 102, 103
Dali, Gala, 119, 132
Dali, Salvador, 117, 119, 120, 122, 123, 132, 148, 181
D'Annunzio, Gabriele, 87
Dante Alighieri, 77, 210
Danube, 57, 58, 60
Darwin, Charles, 63
David Copperfield, 228
David, Jacques-Louis, 110
Davidson, Jo, 99
Davies, Hugh Sykes, 122
Dear family, 198
Decline of the West, 67
De Gaulle, Brigadier-General, 154
De Gourmont, Rémy, 87
De la Mare, Walter, 158
Dennis, Terence, 161
Derain, André, 106
Diaghilev ballet, 92
Dickens, Charles, 34, 191, 228
Die Fackel, 60
Dodsworth, 80
Dominguez, Oscar, 183, 201
Don Juan, 191
Doone, Rupert, 92, 193–4
Dorn, Marion, 84
Dorothy and Red, 199, 200
Dostoyevsky, Fyodor, 34
Doucet, 143
Douglas Credit Scheme, 100
Douglas, Kirk, 190
Douglas, Norman, 172
Drummond, Lindsay, 160
Drummond, Mrs, 160
Drysdale and Dunn, 13
Drysdale, Joseph (Old Joe), 13–14, 15, 16, 17, 40
Dublin, 162
Duchamp, Marcel, 117
Du côté de chez Swann, 59
Dufferin and Alva, Lord, 197
Dufy, Raoul, 225
Duggan, Gracie, 22
Dulac, Edmund, 23
Duncan, Isadora, 92

Eastbourne, 84
Easter Island, 174
Edinburgh, 160
Eiffel, Alexandre, 93
Elective Affinities, 133

Index

El Greco, 41, 227
'Burial of Count Orgaz': 49
Eliot, T. S., 81, 92, 97, 117, 176–7, 215
Elizabethville (Hungary), 56
Elsie, Lily, 22
Eluard, Nusch, 123, 130, 132, 133, 140, 141, 142
Eluard, Paul, 1–2, 87, 114, 115, 117, 118, 119, 120, 122, 128, 130–1, 132–4, 135, 137, 139, 140, 141–2, 183
Emerson, Ralph Waldo, 32
Engelberg (Switzerland), 24
'English Story' (1st Series), 191
Enthoven, 143
Epstein, Jacob, 107
Ernst, Max, 114, 118–9, 120, 148
'The Elephant Celebes', 118–9
Eton, 41
Evening News, 190
Evening Standard, 198
Everest, 184
Exeter, 205
Exeter, Marquis of, 35
Eyck, brothers van, 201
Eyck, Robert van, 201

Falkland Islands, 4
Falmouth, 46
'Fantastic Art Dada Surrealism', 124
Feaver, William, 223
Feldkirch, 66
Felixstowe, 19
Felton Bequest, 219
Festival of Britain, 175
First Honved Regiment, 60
First World War, 26, 27–8, 29–30, 31, 34, 35, 36, 48, 60–1, 85, 172, 209
Firth of the Forth, 35
FitzGerald, Scott, 87
Fletcher, John Gould, 97
Flores (Buenos Aires), 3, 13
Foltyn, 85–6, 90, 91, 92, 93, 102
Fontainebleau, 100
Fonteyn, Margot, 228
Ford, Gordon Onslow, 147
Fordham, Halam, 168
Fordred, Dorice, 150–1
France, Anatole, 59
Franco, General, 123, 124
Fraser, Jenny, 73
Free French, 159
French Institute, 154
Frere-Reeves, A. S., 81
Freud, Sigmund, 60, 63, 207
Frobenius, Leo, 210
Fry, Roger, 114
Fuji, Mount, 23
Fuller, David, 193
Fuller, Edmund, 193

Gabo, Naum, 129, 130
Gallimard, 83
Galsworthy, John, 32
Gandhi, Mahatma, 99
Gargoyle Club, 167
Garrick Club, 74, 176–7, 179, 208, 213
Gascoyne, David, 107–8, 114–5, 123
Gate Theatre, 54
Gaudier-Brzeska, Henri, 87, 209
Gautier, Théophile, 49
Geneva, 70–1
Genoa, 80
Ghosts, 28
Giacometti, Alberto, 117
Gibbons, Floyd, 69
Gibraltar, 49
Gilbert, Stuart, 100
Giotto di Bondone, 171
Glenn, John, 197
Goethe, Johann Wolfgang von, 133, 213
Gogh, Vincent van, 174, 190, 231
Gordon, Mollie, 178, 179, 180, 181, 182
Gould, Diana, 153
Gould, Griselda, 153
Goya, Francisco de, 49
'The Family of Charles IV': 49
Granada, 49
Greene, Baby, 22–3
Greuze, Jean-Baptiste, 25
'La Cruche Cassée', 25
Grigson, Geoffrey, 144–5, 169
Grim Glory, 155
Gris, Juan, 93
Gropius, Walter, 145, 146
Group Theatre, 92
Guadalquivir, river, 49
Guadeloupe, 135
Guernsey, 96
Guggenheim, Peggy, 158–9, 170
Gulbenkian, Calouste, 24
Gulbenkian, Rita, 24
Gulf of Genoa, 75, 198
Gulf of Naples, 172
Gunther, Frances, 74
Gunther, John, 74, 83
Gurdjieff, Georgei Ivanovitch, 100

Haileybury, 152
Halifax, Lord, 224
Hamet Gallery, 208
Hamilton, Sir George Rostrevor, 195
Hamilton, Hamish, 74
Hamilton, Marion, 195
Hanover Gallery, 167, 169, 177–8
Harlow Arts Festival, 202
Harper and Brothers, 83, 99
Harpers Magazine, 68, 83
Haskell, Arnold, 100
Hastings, Sir Patrick, 179
Hatvany, Baron, 63
Hatzfeldt, Princess, 29–30
Havinden, Ashley, 109, 110
Havinden, Margaret (née Sangster), 109, 110
Hawke, Lord, 17
Hayes, Patricia, 191
Hayter, S. W. (Bill), 115
Hayward Gallery, 223
Heathfield, Ascot, 24–6, 27, 28, 30, 51
Heath-Stubbs, John, 223
Hegel, Georg Wilhelm Friedrich, 229
Helpmann, Robert, 150
Hemingway, Ernest, 87
Hendaye, 88
Hepworth, Barbara, 130, 225
Hermes, Gertrude, 38, 42, 97, 219, 226
Heron, Delia, 194–5
Heron, Patrick, 194–5
Hess, Myra, 158
Hitler, Adolf, 64, 140, 153
Hoa-Kaka-Nana-Ia, 174
Holland Park, 204, 219
Homer, 181
Horthy de Nagybanya, Miklos, 60

Houseman, John, 40–1
How to Behave in a Country House, 110
Howard, Charles, 123
Hughes-Stanton, Blair, 28, 42, 97
Hulme, T. E., 209
Hungarian Law Society, 59
Hunt, William Holman, 189
Hurlingham Club (Buenos Aires), 39
Hurlingham Club (Putney), 107
Huxley, Aldous, 48, 86
Huxley, Julian, 176
Huysmans, Joris-Karl, 145
Hyères, 144

Ibsen, Henrik, 28
I Claud, 203
Igls, 67–9
Il Bilico Gallery, 198–9
Iliad, 101
Illustrated London News, 32
Imagism, 97
Indigo Days, 101
Ingram, Bruce, 32
Innsbruck, 67
Institute of Contemporary Arts, 228, 229
International Conference of Suffragettes, 62
International PEN Club, 166, 170–1
International Surrealist Exhibition (1936), 87, 115, 117–20, 122–3, 124, 126, 145,
Irving, Max Trelawny, 179, 192
Isherwood, Christopher, 92
Isle of Wight, 45, 110
Israeli Museum, 107

James, Edward, 119
James, Henry, 25, 58, 76
Japan, 16, 23
Jardin des Plantes, 84
Jardin du Luxembourg, 59, 86
Jennings, Humphrey, 146
Jesolo, 191–2
John, Augustus, 44, 107, 118, 182
John, Gwen, 182
John Moores Exhibition, 196, 206
Joseph, Lawqrence, 219
Journal to Joseph, 218, 219
Journal to Stella, 100
Joyce, James, 86
Juan les Pins, 137
Jung, Carl, 108
Just So Stories, 17, 24

Kafka, Franz, 58
Kant, Immanuel, 120
Kay, Elizabeth de, 24
Kay, de, family, 46
Kemp, Lindsay, 228
Kemp-Welch, Lucy, 25
Kensington Gardens, 113, 164
Kentner, Louis, 153
Kepler, Johann, 63
Kesteven, Horace, 28, 29, 36, 39, 54, 93, 159
Kesteven, Mary, 159
Kesthely (Hungary), 57, 58
Kettering, 157
Kew Gardens, 227
Kipling, Rudyard, 17, 24, 32
Kitchen Sink Realism, 189
Kivel, Rex Nan, 157
Klee, Paul, 117
Knight, Dame Laura, 157
Knize, 86
Knokke, 143
Kokoschka, Oskar, 63, 86, 90, 143, 174, 223, 235
Konigsberg, 120
Kopf, Maxim, 167
Krabbe, Hilda, 22
Kraus, Karl, 60, 63
Kun, Bela, 60
Kyoto (Japan), 23

Lamb Creek, 132
Lamb, Henry, 28
Lanchester, Elsa, 48
Lanvin, 22
Laski, Harold, 88
La Tarde, 183
Laver, James, 168
Lawrence, D. H., 84, 88
Lawrence, Frieda, 38, 88
Leader, Benjamin, 32
Lear, Edward, 114, 134
Le Corbusier, 41
Lee, Diana Brinton, 122–3
Lee, Rupert, 122
Leger Gallery, 166
Legge, Sheila, 123
Leicester, 156
Leighton, Lord, 189
Lenin, Vladimir Ilyich, 60–1
Le Sang d'un Poète, 134
Les Fleurs du Mal, 131
Lewin, Bob, 196, 201
Lewin, Rena, 201
Lewis, Cecil Day, 170, 208
Lewis, Sinclair, 64, 72, 80–2, 87, 167, 199, 200, 203, 204
Lewis, Wyndham, 77
Lewisohn, Ludwig, 88, 204
Lewisohn, Thelma, 88
Leyland, Angela, 24
Liechtenstein, 66
Lisbon, 14, 184, 194
Listener, 169
Liverpool, 196
Living Aloud, 12
London Gallery, 126, 127
London Group, 102, 109, 206, 232
London Group Jubilee Exhibition, 201
Loos, Adolf, 63, 85, 86, 90
Lubbock family, 31
Lubbock, Geoffrey, 31
Lucille, 22, 39
Lulworth Cove, 111–112
Luyten, Meredith, 1
Lygo, Kevin, 228
Lytton, Lord, 158

Maar, Dora, 140, 141, 142
MacInnes, Colin, 188
Mackintosh, Hugh, 52, 91, 96, 102, 103, 144, 150, 151
Mackintosh, Miranda, 103, 221, 223, 225, 230
Mackintosh, Winifred (née Agar), 52, 67, 96, 102, 103, 105, 118, 144, 152, 161–2, 166, 173, 189, 221, 225, 227
Machiavelli, Niccolo, 77
Maddox, Conroy, 123, 146, 205, 221, 222
Madeira, 14
Madrid, 49
Magic Flute, 195
Magritte, René, 101, 116, 126, 148, 161–2, 189,

190, 195, 196
Mahabharata, 101
Mahler, Gustav, 60
Mainstreet, 82
Malthus, Thomas Robert, 34
Manchester, 205
Manet, Edouard, 70
'Olympia': 70
Mann Act, the, 88
Marcoussis, Louis, 87
Mar del Plata (Argentina), 17, 19, 21, 40
Marie Antoinette, 110
Marini, Marino, 170
Marjoriebanks, Sir George and Lady, 44
Marquesita, Violet, 160
Martineau, Henry, 34
Mary Poppins, 100
Masson, André, 118
Maugham, Somerset, 182
Mayfield, 151
McAllister, Bill, 229
MCC, 17
McKecknie, Joan, 226
McMullen, Jimmy, 188–9, 190, 195–6
McWilliam, Beth, 194
McWilliam, F. E., 194
Mecca, 140
Medley, Robert, 193–4
Megroz, R. L., 97
Melbourne Art Gallery, 219
Melly, George, 222
Melville, Robert, 222
Menton, 90
Menuhin, Yehudi, 153
Mermaids Sleep Alone, 12, 152
Mesens, E. L. T., 122, 126–7, 131, 133, 146–7
Mesopotamia, 106
Messel, Oliver, 44, 229
Metropolitan Museum (America), 178
Meudon, 37
Meynell, Joan, 191
Meynell, Laurence, 191
Michelangelo Buonarroti, 212
Midhurst, 151
Mies van der Rohe, Ludwig, 234
Mikes, George, 212
Mill, John Stuart, 44
Millay, Edna St Vincent, 58, 89–90
Miller, Duncan, 96
Miller, Gertie, 22
Miller, Lee, 114, 115–6, 121, 126, 132, 133, 134–5, 138, 139, 142, 146, 155, 222
Ministry of Information, 152
Ministry of Transport, 175
Miró, Joan, 114, 117, 118, 120, 148, 183, 223
Mistral, Frédéric, 173
Mitchell, Marion, 219
Mitchison, Naomi, 97
Miyake, Issey, 229–30
Modigliani, Amedeo, 87
Moffat, Curtis, 96
Moholy-Nagy, Laszlo, 145
Monet, Claude, 37
Monro, Harold, 97
Monroe, Marilyn, 222
Monte Carlo, 92
Monte Oliveto, 171
Montevideo (Uruguay), 14
Montmajour, Abbey of, 174
Moore, George, 34
Moore, Henry, 84, 97, 100, 102, 106–7, 115, 122, 130, 146, 147, 150, 157, 189, 194, 216, 219, 223–4
Moore, Irina, 106–7
Moore-Brabazon, Ivon (Lord Brabazon of Tara), 22
More, Sir Thomas, 227
Morgan, Charles, 185
Morley College, 92
Morton, J. B. (Beachcomber & Dr Strabismus), 102–3
Mother England, 81
Mott, Mrs, 152
Mougins, 133–4, 135–43, 216, 220
Mozart, Wolfgang Amadeus, 195
Murry, John Middleton, 92
Museum of Modern Art (New York), 124, 195
Muspratt, Helen, 112
Mussolini, Benito (Il duce), 63, 73
Mussorgsky, Modest, 153
'Sorochinsky Fair': 153

Nairn (Scotland), 21
Nancy University, 212
Naples, 80, 172
Napoleon I, Bonaparte, 93
Nares, Owen, 30
Nash, Margaret, 109, 110–11, 113, 163
Nash, Paul, 1, 28, 30, 84, 106, 109, 110–13, 115, 122, 127, 133–4, 146, 155, 157, 163–4, 223, 235
'Swanage': 112
National Gallery, 158
National Portrait Gallery, 73, 108
National Society of Painters, Sculptors, Engravers and Potters, 102, 109
Nelson, Horatio, 36
Nevinson, C. R. W., 99, 106
New Age, 100
New Art Centre, 218, 219, 220, 224, 226, 228, 229
New Burlington Galleries, 115, 117–20, 121
New English Weekly, 100, 175
'New Movements in Art', 156
Newton, Eric, 170
Newton, Stella, 170
New York, 100, 134, 159, 186
Nice, 22
Nicholson, Ben, 107, 129, 130, 183, 195
Nietzsche, 155
Nietzsche, Friedrich, 64, 100, 206
Nightmare Abbey, 110
Nin, Anaïs, 114
North, Marianne, 227
Northcliffe, Lord, 109–10
Norton, Clifford, 110
Norton, Peter, 110

Obelisk Gallery, 188, 190
Observer, 73, 223
Odyssey, 101
Olinda (Brazil), 14
Oliver, Jock, 224
Oliver, Mary, 143, 224
Omnibus, 228
On Liberty, 44
Oppenheim, Meret, 117
Orage, A. R., 100–1, 106, 151, 175
Orage, Jessie, 106
O'Riordan, Conal, 131
Orwell, George, 41
Oxford, 34, 155, 176

Ozanne sisters, 30–1
Ozannes (finishing school), 30–1, 154
Ozenfant, Amedée, 48

Paalen, Wolfgang, 114
Padua, 171
Paganini, Niccolo, 28
Paget, Dorothy, 151
Pangbourne, 33
Paris, 20, 31, 46, 48, 59, 66, 68, 84–90, 100, 106, 131, 135, 146, 148, 214, 222
Pascoe, Mrs, 192, 194
Patmore, Derek, 170
Patti, Adelina, 69
Pazmany University, 58, 64
Peacock, Thomas Love, 110
Penrose, Becus, 132
Penrose, Roland, 114, 115–17, 122, 123, 124, 126, 127, 132, 133, 134, 135, 139, 140, 142, 146, 147, 155, 166, 197, 207, 221, 222, 227–8
Penrose, Valentine (née Boué), 114, 123, 223
Penzance, 192
Picabia, Francis, 3, 117
Picasso, Pablo, 114, 117, 132, 134, 135–43, 148, 153, 154, 183, 211, 216, 220, 222
 'Guernica': 140
Piero della Francesca, 171
Pilcher, Velona, 98–9
Pisan Cantos, 169
Piscator, Erwin, 193
Pitchforth, Vivian, 219
Ploumanach, 124, 229
Poems and Narrations, 114
Poetry Bookshop, 97
Poets Club, 158, 209
Point Counter Point, 86
Poiret, 22
Ponsonby, Madeleine, 218
Port-Cros, 144
Portofino, 75, 76, 79–80, 81, 82–3, 87
Potter, Stephen, 102
Pound, Dorothy, 79, 89
Pound, Ezra, 58, 75–9, 82–3, 86–7, 169, 176, 185, 194, 207, 209–10
 on Yeats: 76–7, 78
 his parents: 77, 88–9
 on art: 77
 helping Joseph Bard: 78
 on Aldous Huxley: 86
 on Natalie Barney: 87
 on *The Island*: 98
 discourages Joseph Bard: 99
 on Orage: 100
Powys brothers, 175
Poynter, Cherry, 24
Poynter, Sir Edward, 24, 32
Prado, the, 49
Press, John, 203, 215
Proust, Marcel, 2, 59
Provence, 75, 173, 174
Puerto de la Cruz, 178, 182, 216
Pulszky, Augustus, 59
Puppets in the Mirage, 83
'Purism', 48

Quin-Smith, Colonel, 152
Quin-Smith, Dorothy (née Agar), 151, 221, 223, 227

Racine, Jean, 87
Rackham, Arthur, 23
Rapallo, 75–8, 79, 82, 83, 86, 99, 198
Rasputin, Gregori, 33
Ras Tafari, 95
Ray, Man, 114, 121, 134, 135, 139, 140
 'Les Amants': 134
Raymond, Ernest, 166
Read, Herbert, 115, 117, 119, 122, 127–30, 146, 177, 200–1
Read, Ludo, 129–30
Reavey, George, 122
Red Cross, the, 27, 56, 85
Redfern Gallery, 157, 162, 201
Reggio nell'Emilia (Italy), 59
Reid, Norman, 219
Reinach, Salomon, 87
Remy, Michel, 212, 221
Renoir, Pierre Auguste, 27
Renzio, Toni del, 127
Reuters, 60
Revenge, 35, 110
Rhine, 120
Richards, Ceri, 166, 194
Richmond and Gordon, Duke of, 17
Richmond Park, 64, 224
Rijksmuseum (Amsterdam), 231
Rilke, Rainer Maria, 87
Rimbaud, Arthur, 115, 130–1
Rio de Janeiro, 14–15, 95
Roquebrune, 91
Rodin, Auguste, 37
Rohan, Princess Dilkusha de, 154, 155
Romance, 30
Rome, 62, 171
Ronda, 49
Rossetti, D. G., 75
Rossignol, Arthur le (The Bird), 20, 35, 40
Rothenstein, Sir John, 198
Rothschild, 179
Rousseau, Douanier, 227
Royal Academy, 36, 37, 106, 117, 156, 226
Royal College of Art, 164
Royal Institute Galleries, 102
Royal Society of Literature (RSL), 158, 175, 185, 187–8, 190, 194, 195, 203, 206, 208, 209, 214, 216, 222
Rubens, Peter Paul, 166
 'The Rape of the Sabines', 166
Rubinstein, Anthony, 200
Rudge, Olga, 79
Ruiz, Antonio, 183, 185
Russell, Archibald, 110–11
Russell, Janet, 111
Russell, Walter, 43

Sackville-West, Eddie, 104, 105, 116
Sade, marquis de, 118
Sainsbury, Alan, 190, 192
Sainsbury, Babette, 190, 192
St Ives, 192, 194, 196, 225
St Jean-de-Luz, 88
St Mawes, 46, 47, 225
Saint-Rémy, 174
St Tropez, 168
Salisbury, 221, 223
Samuel, Edwin, 166
Samuel, Lord, 166
San Francisco, 226
Sangster, Florence, 109
Santa Cruz, 179, 183
Santa Margherita, 76
Santanna, Christina, 70, 73

Sark, 96–7, 144
Saurat, Professor Denis, 154, 167, 209
Savage Club, 106, 130, 131, 160, 175, 184, 191
Schiaparelli, 120, 155
Schoenberg, Arnold, 60, 90
Scott, Harold, 48
Scottish National Gallery, 223
Seitz, William, 195, 196
Selene, 122
Seltman, Dr Charles, 178
Senat, Conrad, 161
Servaes, Michael, 218
Sesame Club, 209
Seville, 49
Sewell, Mita, 22–3
Shakespear, Olivia, 169
Shakespeare, William, 36, 178
Shaw, G. B., 233
Sheean, Vincent, 199, 200
Sheffield City Art Gallery, 220
Shelley, Percy Bysshe, 179
Sherborne School, 103
Shipwreck in Europe, 68, 82, 83
Siena, 171
Simpson, Henry, 158, 209
Sims, Charles, 36–7
Sitwell, Edith, 209
Sitwell, Osbert, 76, 77, 141
Sketch, 32
Slade School of Art, 29, 36, 37–8, 42, 43–4, 47, 48, 50, 73, 92, 93, 229
Smiley, Lady, 150, 151, 156
Smith, Jessie Aliston, 43
Snowdon, Lord, 229–30
Sorbonne, 59
Sotheby's, 222
Southampton, 26, 109
Southampton Museum and Art Gallery, 220
Spanish Civil War, 122, 123–4
Spanish Institute (Tenerife), 183, 185
Spender, Stephen, 170
Spengler, Oswald, 67
Squire, J. C., 175
Squire, Raglan, 175
Steadman, Ralph, 223
Stendhal, 28
Stockholm, 166, 170
Stockport, 157
Stoke Poges, 29
Stokes, Adrian, 76
Stone Age, 227
Storsch, Baron, 212
Stowe School, 152
Steer, Wilson, 38, 43–4
Strand Magazine, 33
Streatham, 41
Successful Calamity, 193
Sunday Times, 166
Sundrum Castle, 33
Surrealism, 85, 93, 101, Chapter 5, 153, 154, 159, 168, 188–9, 201, 202, 205, 207–8, 212, 221, 222, 223, 227–8, 231, 234
Surrealism, 128
'Surrealism Today', 154
'Surrealist Objects and Poems', 127
Sutherland, Graham, 122
Swanage, 15, 108–12, 235
Swinburne, Algernon Charles, 167–8, 188, 209

Taboris, the, 166
Tacaronte, 183
Talaber, Mr, 58
Talcott, Dud, 48
Tanguy, Yves, 120, 121
Tapies, 114, 197
Tasso, 210
Tate Gallery, 93, 107, 108, 112, 128, 197–8, 201, 219, 228, 235
Tatler, 32
Tchaikovski, Pyotr Ilyich, 84
Teide, 181–2
Teller, Edward, 59, 197
Tenerife, 178–85, 186, 190, 197, 216, 226–7
Tennant family, 31
Tennant, Peggy, 31
Tennyson, Lionel, 29
Tennyson, Lord, 29, 131, 209
'The Adventure of Modern Art', 99
The Aspern Papers, 25
The Beggar's Opera, 160
The Cabinet of Dr Caligari, 41
The Dial, 78
'The Enchanted Domain', 205
The Flower in the Mouth, 48
'The Game of Chess', 190
The Green Hat, 175
The Island, 97–100, 101, 223, 224
The Loom of Youth, 103
The Mind of Europe, 68, 83, 99, 199
The River Line, 185
'The Tale of a Child', 88, 100
The Times, 30, 100
'The Thirties', 223
Thirkell, Angela, 188
Thomas, Sir Brummel, 41
Thomas, Dylan, 100, 107–8, 209
Thomas, Joan, 219, 227
Thomas, Rodney, 38, 41–2, 79, 95, 96, 101, 109, 112, 151, 160, 164, 175–6, 189, 219, 224, 227
Thompson, Dorothy, 55, 56, 62–3, 64, 65, 67, 68–9, 70–2, 77, 80–2, 83, 89, 94, 154, 167, 194, 199–200, 203–4, 235
Thorneycroft, Hamo, 189
Thornley, William, 37, 38
Tiberio, Emperor, 172, 173
Tigré, river, 13–14, 16, 17
Time, 199, 200
Titania, 109, 110
Todd, Ruthven, 122
Tokyo, 157
Toledo, 49
Tolly Cobbold Exhibition, 220
Tolstoy, Leo, 88
Tonks, Professor, 38, 43, 44, 50, 73, 93
Torquay, 150
Toulon, 143, 145, 220
TR, 223
Transition, 100
Travers, Camillus, 151
Travers, H. L., 100, 151, 170
Trevelyan, Julian, 101, 116, 127, 176
Trevelyan, Mary, 176
'Tricorne', 154
Tring, 179
Truro, 46, 132
Truth, 33
Tschiffely, A. F., 160–1
Tudor Hall, Chislehurst, 26–9, 30, 51
Tyrwhitt, Ursula, 182
Tzara, Tristan, 87, 98

Ulysses, 76, 86

Underwood, Jean, 97
Underwood, Leon, 38, 39, 107, 219
'Venus in Kensington Gardens': 38
his school at Brook Green: 38, 41, 42, 43, 54, 89, 95, 97, 219
and *The Island*: 97, 98
Underwood, Mary, 219
United Artists Exhibition, 156
Untermeyer, Louis, 74

Vaduz (Liechtenstein), 67
Valéry, Paul, 115
Vambéry, Rustum, 62
Varengeville, 50, 51–2, 66, 67
Venice, 24, 170, 191
Verdun, 221
Vermont, 193
Victoria and Albert Museum, 101, 223, 224
Vienna, 59, 60, 62, 63, 64, 68, 84, 88, 90, 186, 204
Vienna Opera Chorus, 62
Vile Bodies, 104
Villiers, Catherine de (Katusha), 153, 154–5
Vinton, Warren, 38, 54–5, 68, 72

Wagner, Cosima, 63–4
Wagner, Siegfried, 63–4
Wallace, Edgar, 106
War and Peace, 40
Warren, Dorothy, 84
Warren Gallery, 84
Waterville, 162
Watson, Spencer, 28
Watts-Dunton, Mrs, 167–8
Watts-Dunton, Theodore, 167–8
Waugh, Alec, 12, 91, 100, 103–4, 106, 145, 150, 170, 223
Waugh, Evelyn, 48, 67, 91–2, 95–6, 103, 104–6, 162, 191, 223
Waugh, Joan, 103, 104
Wavell, Lord, 209, 216
Weekley, Barbara, 38, 89
Weekley, Professor, 38, 89
Wells, H. G., 39, 106, 232, 233
Wendover, 179
West Bay, 108
West, Rebecca, 62, 154
Westerdahl, Eduardo, 183
Westerdahl, Maud, 183
Whistler, Rex, 44
Whitechapel Art Gallery, 190
Whyte, Lance, 174
Wigmore Hall, 152
Wigner, Eugene, 60
Wilde, Gerald, 161
Wilde, Oscar, 34, 191, 234
Wildenstein's, 196
Wilkinson, Louis, 175
William II, Kaiser, 30
Wilson, Woodrow, 30
Winchelsea, 106
Witney, Mr and Mrs Jock, 190
Wittersham, 106, 216
Wodehouse, P. G., 191
Woolf, Virginia, 69
Wordsworth, William, 49
Wretham, Isabel, 189–90, 194, 205, 220
Wyatt, Miss, 24, 30
Wyatt, Woodrow, 191

Yeats, W. B., 76, 77, 78, 163, 182
Yolan, 64–5, 185
Youssopov, Prince, 33

Zennor, 194
Zurich, 148
Zwemmer Gallery, 154